# Dramas of Testimony

THE WASHINGTON STRINDBERG
Translations and Introductions by Walter Johnson

*Strindberg and the Historical Drama* by Walter Johnson

# Dramas of Testimony

THE DANCE OF DEATH I AND II,
ADVENT, EASTER,
THERE ARE CRIMES AND CRIMES

By AUGUST STRINDBERG
*Translations and Introductions*
*by Walter Johnson*

University of Washington Press
Seattle and London

Library of Congress Cataloging in Publication Data

Strindberg, August, 1849–1912.
    Dramas of testimony.

    (The Washington Strindberg)
    Includes bibliographical references.
    CONTENTS: The dance of death I and II.—Advent.—
Easter.—There are crimes and crimes.
    I. Title.
PT9811.A3J57   1975        839.7′2′6        75-16218
ISBN 0-295-95433-7

# Preface

IN THE LAST of the three very personal and confessional Damascus plays, the character of The Stranger (*Den okände*) or, if you will, Strindberg promised never again to relate the tale of his own suffering:

> PRIOR: . . . But will you promise me now to forget the story of your own suffering and never relate it again?
> STRANGER: I promise!

He did not promise, however, not to testify about the nature of human life, or the good and evil other human beings do, or the suffering they experience. In the course of testifying about such matters in one work after the other in the post-Inferno period (from 1897 until his death in 1912) Strindberg did manage to keep the promise to some extent, but by no means completely, since he was a man inclined to using his own experiences, real and imagined, in his creative art. In his writing, perhaps unconsciously, he changed what he observed in others as it filtered through his thoughts, his imagination, and his emotions. Other human beings, and certainly other gifted artists, distort what they observe, but it is doubtful if any other artist of Strindberg's stature has done so in quite the same way or with as rewarding results.

The plays in this volume tell the stories of other people though Strindberg himself is ever present. Swedish scholars have long since pointed out in scholarly studies that the companion plays, *The Dance of Death I and II,* are based primarily on Strindberg's interpretation of the marriage of his sister Anna (1855–1937) and Hugo

Philp (1844–1906), and that Kurt is modeled on Strindberg himself. In all the other plays models for various characters and the stories have been pointed out rather convincingly by various scholars, each of whom has been at pains to emphasize that Strindberg himself has never been absent. In a highly complex and psychologically sound sense, such a conclusion can undoubtedly be justified.

But far more important is the fact that every one of these plays will stand up under the close scrutiny of anyone who may not know a single fact about Strindberg and his life. The two *Dance of Death* plays are no more in need of autobiographical interpretation to be accepted as superb works of dramatic art than are, for example, their American offspring, Eugene O'Neill's *A Long Day's Journey into Night* and Edward Albee's *Who's Afraid of Virginia Woolf?* Details in *Advent* and *Easter* may need some explanation for those who are not familiar with the church and its special seasons, but certainly the plays require little or no identification of possibly autobiographical elements. And the idea that the crimes punishable by law are not the only ones committed by human beings can very well be considered in terms of universal experience without reference to Strindberg's own.

The plays do convey testimony about human beings and the lives they lead. The approach is thoroughly Strindbergian in its frank appraisal and presentation of what he believed he saw and sensed. The ultimate implication of his conclusions may be summarized by quoting the refrain from *A Dream Play* (1901), "Human beings are to be pitied." But as that play summarizes what he had to say in his final years about deity, man, and the world, the plays in this volume deal in a manner that is highly effective on the stage with such ever important matters as human relations, the family, women's liberation, irrationality, the individual's conscience, and the possibility of a life after this.

WALTER JOHNSON

# Contents

# Illustrations

*Dramas of Testimony*

# Introduction to
# 'The Dance of Death'
# I and II

WHILE STRINDBERG REMAINED as fascinated as ever by his own time after his Inferno years of 1894 to 1897, he became more intensely interested than ever before in the late Middle Ages as well. That twofold interest helped lead to many developments, among them his creation of new dramatic techniques through (1) the extension of his superb realistic-naturalistic technical practices of the pre-Inferno period, (2) the transformation of medieval dramatic ideas and devices into techniques that became highly Strindbergian, and (3) the addition of modern technical elements that were essentially his own. These three elements, taken together, are frequently and loosely spoken of as expressionistic by some scholars and critics.

Strindberg's intensified post-Inferno interest in the Middle Ages stemmed both from his renewed interest in history and from his so-called conversion. The latter led to increased attention to biblical morality and religious faith and to a concern with the medieval mystery and morality plays throughout the post-Inferno years. It is significant that all the major historical plays except *Master Olof* were written after 1897, and all of them are concerned in more ways than one with morality. It is also significant that all his other post-Inferno plays are in technique or thought or both related in varying degrees to the medieval drama.

The three Damascus plays are, to an appreciable extent, adaptations of the techniques of such morality plays as *Everyman*. *Advent* and *Easter,* to cite two more examples, are highly reminiscent of both the morality and the mystery plays. Parallels to the medieval stress on life as a pilgrimage appear again and again in the post-Inferno plays, both historical and nonhistorical. In all these plays there are, moreover, parallels to the biblically inspired medieval concern with human nature, the relationship between the individual and what Strindberg calls the Eternal One, and the moral problems implicit in both. There is, in addition, Strindberg's amazing psychological insight into the tragic tensions within modern man and his uncanny ability to bring those tensions into tangible expression for the stage.

The companion plays, *The Dance of Death I* and *The Dance of Death II* (1901), received a name that is medieval in its implications, and they contain such elements as an emphasis on death, the vampire motive, and the repetition of the pattern of life generation after generation, which were of decided concern to the Middle Ages. Yet these two plays are as modern as any plays could be. Strindberg had the genius to take what he needed by way of inspiration and detail and transform what he received into something peculiarly his own and always subtly different from anything he had done before. *The Dance of Death* plays illustrates this.

The story Strindberg tells in *The Dance of Death I* is one of a modern marital hell created by a frustrated army captain stationed on an island called Little Hell and his equally frustrated ex-actress wife. *The Dance of Death II* is the story of the same captain, now retired and for the first time really free to go to work as a vampire. What the late Middle Ages held for Strindberg by way of inspiration and detail for the dramatization of these stories can easily be demonstrated.

Medieval Europeans had good reasons to be aware of death as ugly, horrible, and gruesome. Plague, war, disease, disaster, and want provided constant visible evidence that the priests were quite right in insisting that Death was not only taking neighbors, friends, and relatives but might at any moment take the individual himself. Both the morality and the mystery plays were used by the medieval church to warn the people about their frequently frantic attempts to conceal the macabre realities from themselves by escaping into worldly pleasures.

Recorded on thousands of medieval paintings (murals, frescoes, oils, and water colors), engravings, and woodcuts, and in many sculptures, poems, sermons, and plays, was the so-called "dance of death" or *danse macabre*. These works of art stressed such macabre matters as the omnipotence of death, its usually unexpected and un-desired coming to everyone, its disregard for both rank and position, and the ugly and horrifying details of dying. Death, often repre-sented as a skeletonlike personified figure, is presented as ready to lead everyman, everywoman, and everychild into a rough equivalent of the long dance, which ends for each individual in his final col-lapse as he holds the hand of Death. The medieval dances of death that survive emphasize the grotesque and the horrible; they were de-signed to serve as warnings to prepare for the next life by accepting the moral code of the church and trying to live up to it. The church took advantage of the medieval fear of death and of the agony of dying by emphasizing the transitory nature of human life and the terrifying consequences of sin—Judgment Day and eternal punishment in Hell. The priests did not mince words about the frailties of human nature and presented both Purgatory and Hell in vivid, literal detail.

In the last of the Damascus plays, Strindberg promised never again to relate the story of his own suffering as he had been doing from the beginning of his literary career through the Damascus tril-ogy. He did not promise, however, not to direct his attention to other people's suffering or to the evil in other people's lives. In fact, with his newly reacquired faith in the moral nature of the universe, his suspicion that this life may be something like a dream state rather than the *real* life, and his intensified interest in both good and evil, Strindberg naturally enough turned his attention to a family situation well known to him, found in it resemblances to the medi-eval dance of death, and composed in the companion plays two of the most effective dramas the modern theater possesses.

Strindberg's interpretation of the marriage is not primarily an objective case study in dramatic form; it is, instead, a deliberately distorted transformation of the source material to intensify the marital misery so that it will serve, figuratively, as a modern dance of death.

To understand what is at the core of the particular marital hell, one should recall that the plays Strindberg wrote during the last fifteen years of his life deal to a very great degree with the problem of evil, its nature, its origins and causes, and its results. Perhaps no passage in all these plays throws more light on Strindberg's thinking about human nature and its potentials for evil than Indra's daughter's speech in *A Dream Play* (1901): "All these are my children! Each one by himself is good, but they have only to get together to start quarreling and turn into demons."

That both Edgar and Alice in *The Dance of Death* have had potentials for personal and social good, Strindberg suggests in abundant detail, but he makes it clear that they have become demons, whose inherent selfishness and egotism, in an unhappy environment, have never had a real chance to be effectively curbed or controlled. Their whole marriage has been the nominal union of two unremittingly selfish and egotistic human animals. In their struggle for the freedom of their individual egos, they have become a devious aging vampire and a frustrated middle-aged coquette, whose only bond is an animal-like sexual attraction for each other, whose tactics are those of the jungle, and whose lives are, in the words of a Strindbergian disciple, a "long day's journey into night." In that journey, neither one has been willing to accept the smallest degree of personal responsibility: instead they blind themselves through rationalizing. Nor does Strindberg feel that Edgar and Alice are exceptional:

ALICE: Is he human?

KURT: When you asked me that the first time, I said no! Now I think he's the most common kind of human being among those who possess the earth . . . Perhaps we're a little like that, too— using people and favorable opportunities.

Strindberg applies what he says about evil universally and, through what Kurt suggests, provides a remedy—humanity, submission, and resignation, all of them in striking agreement with the implications of the medieval dances of death. For the worldly life that Edgar and Alice lead is, figuratively speaking, a dance that usually turns their thoughts from death and the true sadness of their days. It is significant that so many theater critics down through the years have found Edgar's solo performance of a Hungarian dance to the accompaniment of Alice's playing of Halvorsen's *Entry of the Boyars* one of the high points in the stage productions of the first *Dance of Death*. The lively, enthusiastic dance performed in grotesque contrast to the deadly, boring environment serves as an effective parallel to the medieval dance in which the living try to escape from thoughts of their own mortality. Just as the medieval dance ends in certain death, the captain's dance ends with his own collapse.

In a much broader and figurative sense, the twenty-five years have been a dance of death. The story Strindberg tells as illustration of his major theme in *Dance of Death I* may be said to be a repetition of basic steps which promise to lead to something that will break the ghastly pattern, but each time the promise fails and the pattern begins again. The lives of these two have tended to turn their thoughts from both death and the sad reality of their days.

Yet they never quite succeed in rationalizing away completely either thoughts of death or awareness of the sadness of reality. Against the dismal and symbolic background of their prisonlike home, these two have lived in "the most unreasoning hatred, without cause, without purpose . . . ," seemingly "without end." Except on rare occasions, they have tortured each other so effectively and thoroughly that Kurt can say with well-motivated justification: "But tell me: What are you up to in this house? What's happening here? It smells like poisonous wallpaper, and a person gets sick as soon as he comes in. I'd prefer to leave, but I promised Alice I'd stay. There are dead bodies under these floors; there's so much hate it's hard to breathe."

That the two are undergoing tortures similar to those depicted in a Swedenborgian hell—or, for that matter, any kind of hell—is clear to anyone who reads the play with a little care. That they are aware of the nature of their reality even though they usually try to conceal it from themselves is clear enough. As Edgar says, "But all life is horrible." But only when Edgar has been struck down by his heart attack can he even approach the idea of assuming his partial responsibility for having created this living death: "Life is strange! So difficult, so evil, from childhood on . . . and people are so evil I became evil too . . ." Strindberg's presentation of the reality of one marital hell is a macabre interpretation of tortured human beings, tortured not only by each other and others but by themselves.

In the midst of the nightmare of their life together, they rarely succeed in eliminating thoughts of death. Alice is keenly aware of it, not as something that will strike her personally but as a twofold thing: (1) her own release from the prison of her marriage to Edgar, and (2) a weapon by means of which to torture Edgar. She is, for example, delighted by the signs of Edgar's aging—his failing eyesight, his increasing inability to enjoy his tobacco and whiskey, his illness. Edgar, on the other hand, tries to conceal as long as he can the significance of all these matters by insisting to Alice that he has never been seriously ill, that he will live for twenty years more, and that he will die like an old soldier—suddenly, painlessly. Yet his very insistence and occasional involuntary admissions reveal that he fears death and that he does not really believe that when it is over there is "nothing left but what can be put on a wheelbarrow and spread on the garden beds." Strindberg traces, unobtrusively but with great care, Edgar's concern with death: the outward statements, the inner anguish, the heightened fears when it looks as if he is going to die, his grasping for straws then, and his renewed pretense when he recovers a little. There is, for Edgar, no resignation, no humility, no submission. He has become one of the living dead, figuratively, just as his marriage has been a living death.

But the first *Dance of Death* ends in a fashion parallel to another aspect of the medieval dance of death. Just as the *danse macabre* combines the gruesome and the grotesque with grim humor, Strindberg's first play ends with the grimly humorous scene of the two principals in the marital hell planning the celebration of their silver wedding:

CAPTAIN: . . . Think how dull life is nowadays! In the old days a person struck, now one only shakes a fist!—I'm almost certain we'll celebrate our silver wedding in three months . . . with Kurt giving you away! . . . And the doctor and Gerda present . . . The ordnance officer will make the speech, and the sergeant major lead the cheering. If I know the colonel, he'll invite himself. Yes, go ahead and laugh! Do you remember Adolf's silver wedding? . . . His wife had to wear her wedding ring on her right hand because the groom in a tender moment had chopped off the left ring finger with a knife. (ALICE *holds her handkerchief to her mouth to keep from laughing.*) Are you crying?—No, I think you're laughing! Yes, we weep in part, and laugh in part! Which is more proper . . . don't ask me! . . . I read the other day in a paper that a man who had been divorced seven times, consequently married seven times . . . finally ran away when he was ninety-eight years old to remarry his first wife! That's love! . . . If life is serious or only a joke, I can't tell! When it's a joke, it can be most painful, and when it's serious, it's really pleasantest and calmest . . . But when a person finally tries to be serious, someone comes along to play a joke on him! For example, Kurt! . . . Do you want a silver wedding? (ALICE *silent*) Say yes!— They'll laugh at us, but what difference does that make? We'll laugh, too, or be serious . . . whichever seems best!

ALICE: All right!

CAPTAIN (*seriously*): We'll celebrate our silver wedding, then! . . . (*Gets up*) Cross out, and go on!—So, let's go on!

## II

The companion play takes place in a setting directly opposite to that of the first play. Instead of a home that is a prison, figuratively and literally, the setting is that of the beautiful quarters Kurt has arranged for himself. They are cheerful, beautifully furnished, designed for pleasant living. The man who has provided himself with this home has achieved to a remarkable degree the submission, resignation, and humanity needed for living in a world where other people, too, have their being. It is a promising setting, threatened, however, by the implications of Strindberg's well-motivated reversal of themes.

In the first *Dance of Death,* the dominant theme is that of the marital hell, but one other important theme—Edgar as vampire—is introduced and appreciably developed. A third important theme—the repetition of a pattern of life in one generation after the other—is suggested. In the second *Dance of Death,* the importance of the themes is reversed. The dominant theme is that of Edgar as vampire, the theme of the repetition of patterns in following generations is developed, and the marital hell is reduced to a secondary theme. All three are important, however, and Strindberg again treats them in counterpoint to each other.

It is the vampire theme, however, that in the second *Dance of Death* primarily supplies the macabre elements. In the first play Strindberg makes clear what he means by vampire:

> KURT: . . . for just now when he felt his life slipping away, he clung to mine, began to settle my affairs as if he wanted to creep into me and live my life.
>
> ALICE: That's his vampire nature exactly . . . to seize hold of other people's lives, to suck interest out of other people's lives, to arrange and direct for others, when his own life has become absolutely without interest for him. And remember, Kurt, don't ever let him get hold of your family affairs, don't ever let him meet your friends, for he'll take them away from you and make them his own . . . He's a magician at doing that! . . . If he meets your children, you'd soon see them on intimate terms with him; he'd advise them and bring them up according to his own whims, and above all against your wishes.

The Edgar who in the first play was in constant danger of discharge has now been retired and, on the basis of a pension that cannot be revoked, is free to go to work as his egotism directs. The tragic mortal afraid of both life and death in *The Dance of Death I* has become one of the exceptionally active living dead in *The Dance of Death II*. It is to his activities in the destruction or selfish use and manipulation of the genuinely alive that the second play is primarily devoted. Edgar thrives and flourishes through the theft of ideas, things, and people. The illustrations are many; the point is clear: even those who have resigned themselves to earthly life and have accepted the ideal of humane living are in constant danger of losing in the uneven struggle with the vampires. The implications are macabre indeed.

Note, for example, the development of the secondary theme of the repetition of the pattern of life in a following generation. Edgar's daughter, Judith, is lovely to look at, endowed with potentialities for becoming not only her father's image but also a woman who can love as well as hate. Judith is a major pawn by which Edgar manipulates and uses the whole community—the aging colonel would like to marry her, and Edgar, as the prospective father-in-law of the person in somewhat remote control of Little Hell, can use the colonel's name most conveniently and effectively to gain his ends. It is egotistical Judith, however, who—humanized by love—gives the vampire the death blow. When he is dealt that blow, Edgar in his self-deception says, without ironic intention, "Forgive them for they know not what they do."

In Strindbergian terms, everything repeats itself; even the good repeats itself. In his development of the relationship between Judith and Allan, Strindberg has not only indicated clearly the possibilities for evil, but has shown just as clearly the possibilities for good in human beings in association with each other.

In the second play's continuing but somewhat subdued battle between husband and wife appears the use of a technique mentioned by Strindberg in an unpublished note: "What if all [the characters] should talk in asides? And in so doing blurt out their real thoughts, which they have to conceal in the masquerade of life, have to conceal for the sake of bread and butter and social acceptance, because of wife and children." It is true, of course, that Edgar and Alice usually say what they believe will benefit themselves selfishly, but it is also true that they frequently say exactly what they think about each other, relatives, acquaintances, and neighbors. It is one of the remarkable facts about Strindberg's dialogue that it frequently becomes the blunt expression of inner thought, rather than the measured conventional exchange of primarily controlled ideas or patter.

In spite of the fact that Strindberg supplied unsurpassed psychological motivations for this macabre tragedy, and detailed analysis of character which penetrates even to the unconscious and the subconscious, the major emphasis is placed not on either the dramatic motivation or the construction of plot but on the intensity of the atmosphere of horror and comfortless isolation. Concentrating on one point, symbolized by the dance of death, Strindberg presents a nightmare in which life becomes an evil dream. The plays suggest that actual death may be something great and even majestic in its release from the horror of a living death on Little Hell.

However distressing the companion plays may have been for the easily identified primary models for Edgar, Alice, and Judith at the time the plays first appeared and were presented, they are, dramatically and theatrically, among the very best plays in modern drama. As far as I have been able to discover, the only production that was a complete failure was a mutilated version presented on Broadway in 1948. Two Americans apparently rewrote the plays, condensed them into one, changed the setting to Hawaii and the characters to Americans, and called the result *The Last Dance*. It closed after seven nights. The plays as Strindberg wrote them can hardly fail to grip and to fascinate readers or theater audiences.*

* An earlier version of this Introduction appeared in *Modern Drama* 3 (May 1960):8–15.

# The Dance of Death I

## Characters

EDGAR, *captain in the artillery*
ALICE, *his wife an ex-actress*
KURT, *quarantine master*
*Minor characters:* JENNY, THE OLD WOMAN, THE SENTINEL *(silent)*

# ACT I

## SETTING

*The interior of the round tower of a granite fortress.*

*At the back a large double entrance with glass doors, through which one can see a seashore with batteries and the sea.*

*On either side of the entrance a window with flowers and birds.*

*To the right of the entrance an upright piano; farther downstage a sewing table and two armchairs.*

*To the left, in the center of the stage a desk with a telegraph instrument; farther downstage a whatnot with large photographs. Next to it a chaise longue or sofa. Next to the wall a china cupboard.*

*A ceiling lamp. On the wall by the piano are two large laurel* [1] *wreaths with ribbons, one on either side of a large photograph of a woman in theater costume.*

*By the door a large movable clothes tree with military garb, sabers, and the like. Next to it a chiffonier.*

*To the left of the door hangs a large quicksilver barometer.*

*It is a warm autumn evening. The entrances are open, and one can see a* SENTINEL *on duty on the shore battery; he is wearing a helmet; his saber glitters now and then in the red glow of the setting sun. The sea lies dark and silent.*

*The* CAPTAIN *is sitting in an armchair by the sewing table to the*

15

*left fingering an extinguished cigar. He is dressed in a worn fatigue uniform with riding boots and spurs. Looks tired and bored.*

ALICE *is sitting in an armchair to the right doing nothing. Looks tired and expectant.*

CAPTAIN: Won't you play for me?

ALICE (*indifferently but not unkindly*): What shall I play?

CAPTAIN: Anything you like.

ALICE: You don't like my repertory!

CAPTAIN: And you don't like mine!

ALICE (*avoiding the issue*): Do you want the doors to stand open?

CAPTAIN: If you do.

ALICE: Let them be, then! . . . (*Pause*) Why don't you smoke?

CAPTAIN: I'm getting so I can't quite take strong tobacco.

ALICE (*almost friendly*): Smoke a milder kind, then! It's your only pleasure, you say.

CAPTAIN: Pleasure! What do you mean?

ALICE: Why ask me? I don't know any more than you do! . . . Wouldn't you like your whiskey now?

CAPTAIN: I'll wait a little. . . . What do you have for dinner?

ALICE: How should I know? Ask Kristin.

CAPTAIN: They ought to be getting mackerel in pretty soon. It's fall.

ALICE: Yes, it is fall.

CAPTAIN: Outside and in. But in spite of the cold that comes with fall, outside and in, a broiled mackerel with a slice of lemon and a glass of white Burgundy wouldn't really be too bad.

ALICE: That was really eloquent!

CAPTAIN: Do we have any Burgundy in the wine cellar?

ALICE: As far as I know, we haven't had a wine cellar for five years . . .

CAPTAIN: You never know. All the same we'll have to stock up for our silver wedding . . .

ALICE: Do you really intend to celebrate that?

CAPTAIN: Naturally!

ALICE: It would be more natural for us to conceal our misery, our twenty-five years of misery . . .

CAPTAIN: Alice, dear, it has been miserable, but we've had fun . . . at times. And we'd better use what little time we have left—afterward it will all be over.

ALICE: All over? If it only were!

CAPTAIN: It will all be over! There'll only be enough to haul out in a wheelbarrow to dump in the garden!

ALICE: What a lot of trouble just for a garden!

CAPTAIN: Well, that's how it is. I didn't make the world.

ALICE: What a lot of trouble! (*Pause*) Did you get the mail?

CAPTAIN: Yes.

ALICE: Did the butcher's bill come?

CAPTAIN: Yes.

ALICE: How big is it?

CAPTAIN (*takes the bill from his pocket, puts on his glasses, but puts them away again*): You read it. I can't see any more . . .

ALICE: What's wrong with your eyes?

CAPTAIN: I don't know.

ALICE: You're getting old!

CAPTAIN: Nonsense! Not I!

ALICE: Certainly not I!

CAPTAIN: Hm.

ALICE (*looks at the bill*): Can you pay it?

CAPTAIN: Yes. But not just now!

ALICE: Later, then. In a year when you'll be retired with a little pension, and it's too late. Then, when you get sick again . . .

CAPTAIN: Sick? I've never been sick—I simply didn't feel well that time! I'll live twenty more years!

ALICE: That's not what the doctor said.

CAPTAIN: The doctor!

ALICE: Well, who else would know about sickness?

CAPTAIN: There's nothing wrong with me, and there never has been. And there never will be, for I'll die suddenly, like an old soldier!

ALICE: Talking about the doctor. You know they're giving a dinner
   tonight.

CAPTAIN (*annoyed*): So what? We weren't invited because we don't
   associate with them, and we don't associate with them because we
   don't want to, for I despise the two of them! They're trash!

ALICE: That's what you say about everybody!

CAPTAIN: Because they're all trash!

ALICE: Except you!

CAPTAIN: Yes, because I've behaved decently all the way! That's why
   I'm not trash! (*Pause*)

ALICE: Do you want to play cards?

CAPTAIN: All right.

ALICE (*takes a deck of cards from a drawer in the sewing table and
   begins to shuffle them*): Think of it! The doctor gets the military
   band for a private party!

CAPTAIN (*furious*): That's because he plays up to the colonel in town!
   Play up to—If I only could!

ALICE (*deals*): Gerda and I were friends, but she let me down.

CAPTAIN: They're all false!—What do you have by way of trumps
   over there?

ALICE: Put on your glasses!

CAPTAIN: They don't help. (*Sighs*)

ALICE: Spades are trumps.

CAPTAIN (*dissatisfied*): Spades? . . .

ALICE (*plays*): Yes, you may be right, but they've turned the new
   officers' wives against us at any rate.

CAPTAIN (*plays and takes the trick*): What difference does that
   make? We never give any parties, so we won't notice. I can be
   alone . . . I always have been.

ALICE: I, too. But the children! The children are growing up without
   friends!

CAPTAIN: They'll have to find their own in town . . . I took that
   one! Do you have any trumps left?

ALICE: I have one. That was mine!

CAPTAIN: Six and eight make fifteen . . .

ALICE: Fourteen, fourteen!

CAPTAIN: Six and eight give me fourteen . . . I think I've forgotten how to count, too. And two make sixteen . . . (*Yawns*) You deal.

ALICE: You are tired.

CAPTAIN (*deals*): Not in the least.

ALICE (*listening*): I can hear the music all the way in here. (*Pause*) Do you think they've invited Kurt, too?

CAPTAIN: He got here this morning, so he's had time to get out his tux . . . But he hasn't had time to visit us!

ALICE: Quarantine officer? Is there going to be a quarantine station here?

CAPTAIN: Yes! . . .

ALICE: But he is my cousin, and I once had the same name as he . . .

CAPTAIN: That's nothing to be proud of . . .

ALICE: Listen . . . (*sharply*) leave my family alone, and I'll leave yours alone!

CAPTAIN: There, there. Let's not start that again.

ALICE: Is the quarantine officer a doctor?

CAPTAIN: No. He's only a sort of civil manager or bookkeeper, and Kurt never did get to amount to anything, of course.

ALICE: He was a weakling . . .

CAPTAIN: Who has cost me money . . . And when he deserted his wife and children, he was really dishonorable!

ALICE: Not quite that bad, Edgar!

CAPTAIN: Yes, he was! . . . What he's been up to in America . . . well . . . I can't say I'm anxious to see him. But he was a decent fellow, and I liked to discuss things with him.

ALICE: Because he was so agreeable . . .

CAPTAIN (*pompously*): Agreeable or not, he was a person I could talk with at least . . . There isn't a person on this island who understands what I'm saying . . . It's a community of idiots . . .

ALICE: It's strange Kurt should come just now . . . to our silver wedding . . . Whether we celebrate it or not . . .

CAPTAIN: What's strange about that? . . . I see; yes, he was the one who brought us together, or married you off, as they said . . .

ALICE: Didn't he?

CAPTAIN: Of course! . . . It was his idea . . . You judge the idea!

ALICE: A silly notion . . .

CAPTAIN: That we've had to pay for—not he!

ALICE: Imagine if I had stayed on at the theater! All my friends are stars now!

CAPTAIN (*gets up*): There, there . . . Now I'll have a drink! (*Goes to the cupboard and mixes a drink, which he drinks standing*) There ought to be a railing to put my foot on; then I could imagine I was in the American Bar in Copenhagen!

ALICE: Let's have a railing made so we'll be reminded of Copenhagen. Those were our best moments, all the same!

CAPTAIN (*drinks quickly*): Yes! Do you remember Nimb's *navarin aux pommes?*

ALICE: No, but I remember the concerts at Tivoli.[2]

CAPTAIN: You do have such good taste.

ALICE: You ought to be glad you have a wife with good taste!

CAPTAIN: I am . . .

ALICE: Occasionally, when you need her for your bragging . . .

CAPTAIN (*drinks*): They must be dancing at the doctor's . . . I can hear the three-quarter-time beat of the bass tubas—boom—boom—boom!

ALICE: I can hear the whole melody of the Alcazar waltz.[3] Well, it wasn't yesterday I danced a waltz . . .

CAPTAIN: Do you think you still can?

ALICE: Still?

CAPTAIN: Well-l? You're done with dancing, you as well as I!

ALICE: Why, I'm ten years younger than you!

CAPTAIN: Then we're the same age since they say a wife should be ten years younger!

ALICE: You ought to be ashamed! Why, you're an old man, but I'm in my best years!

CAPTAIN: Oh yes, of course—you can certainly be charming—toward others, when you want to.

ALICE: May we light the lamp?

CAPTAIN: Fine!

ALICE: Ring for her, then!

(CAPTAIN *goes slowly to the desk and rings.*)

(JENNY *enters from the right.*)

CAPTAIN: Would you please light the lamp, Jenny?

ALICE (*sharply*): Light the ceiling lamp!

JENNY: Yes, ma'am. (*Lights the ceiling lamp, while the* CAPTAIN *looks at her*)

ALICE (*curtly*): Have you wiped the glass properly?

JENNY: Yes, a little!

ALICE: Is that the way to answer?

CAPTAIN: Listen . . . Listen . . .

ALICE (*to* JENNY): Get out! I'll light it myself! That's probably best!

JENNY: I think so, too! (*Going*)

ALICE (*gets up*): Go!

JENNY (*tarries*): I wonder what you'd say if I did go? (ALICE *does not answer.* JENNY *exits. The* CAPTAIN *goes up to the lamp and lights it.*)

ALICE (*uneasy*): Do you think she'll leave?

CAPTAIN: I wouldn't be amazed, but then we'd be in . . .

ALICE: It's your fault. You spoil them!

CAPTAIN: Oh no! You know they're always polite to me!

ALICE: Because you toady to them! As far as that goes, you toady to all subordinates because you're by nature a slave and a despot.

CAPTAIN: There, there!

ALICE: Yes, you toady to your men and to the noncommissioned officers, but you can't get along with your equals or superiors.

CAPTAIN: Ah-h!

ALICE: All tyrants do! . . . Do you think she'll leave?

CAPTAIN: Yes, if you don't go out and say a kind word to her.

ALICE: I?

CAPTAIN: If I did, you'd say I was playing up to the maids.

ALICE: Imagine if she does leave! Then I'll have to do all the work as I had to last time, and ruin my hands!

CAPTAIN: That won't be the worst! If Jenny leaves, Kristin will leave, and we'll never get any other servant to come out to this island. The mate on the steamer frightens away all the new ones . . . and if he forgets to, my gunners do.

ALICE: Yes, your gunners that I have to feed in my kitchen, and that you don't dare to show the door . . .

CAPTAIN: No, for they'd leave at the first chance . . . and we'd have to close the gunshop.

ALICE: This will ruin us!

CAPTAIN: For that reason the officers have planned to petition the government for supplementary pay . . .

ALICE: For whom?

CAPTAIN: For the gunners!

ALICE (*laughs*): You're too crazy!

CAPTAIN: Yes, laugh a little for me! I need it.

ALICE: I'll soon have forgotten how to laugh . . .

CAPTAIN (*lights his cigar*): One should never forget that . . . it's all so boring anyway.

ALICE: It certainly isn't fun . . . Do you want to play some more?

CAPTAIN: No, I get tired of it. (*Pause*)

ALICE: You know it annoys me all the same that my cousin, the new quarantine officer, calls on our enemies first.

CAPTAIN: What's the use of talking about that?

ALICE: Did you see in the newspaper that he was listed as a *rentier*? [4] He must have made money!

CAPTAIN: *Rentier!* Well-l. A rich relative. That's certainly the first one in this family.

ALICE: In your family, yes. But there have been many rich ones in mine.

CAPTAIN: If he has made money, I suppose he'll be proud, but I'll put him in his place! And he's certainly not going to get a look at my cards! (*The telegraph clicks.*)

ALICE: Who's that?

CAPTAIN (*remains standing*): Quiet, please!

ALICE: Go over there, then!

CAPTAIN: I can hear what they're saying . . . It's the children! (*Goes up to the apparatus, taps out an answer; there is an answer, and the* CAPTAIN *taps out an answer*)

ALICE: Well-l?

CAPTAIN: Wait! . . . (*Gives the final tap*) The children are in the main office in town. Judith isn't feeling well again and is staying home from school.

ALICE: Again! What else did they say?

CAPTAIN: Money, of course!

ALICE: Why should Judith be in such a hurry? If she took the examinations next year, that would be early enough.

CAPTAIN: Tell her that, and you'll see if it helps.

ALICE: You should tell her!

CAPTAIN: How many times haven't I told her? But you certainly know children do as they want to.

ALICE: In this family at least! . . . (CAPTAIN *yawns.*) Do you have to yawn in your wife's presence?

CAPTAIN: What should I do? . . . Haven't you noticed that we say the same thing every day? Just now when you made the same old reply: "In this house at least," I should have answered with my old one: "It's not only my family." But since I've already given that answer five hundred times, I yawn instead. My yawn can mean I'm too lazy to answer, or that "You're right, my angel," or "Now we'll stop."

ALICE: You're really charming tonight.

CAPTAIN: Aren't we having dinner soon?

ALICE: Did you know the doctors have ordered their dinner from the Grand Hotel in town?

CAPTAIN: No! Then they're having hazel hens! You know those are the finest of birds, but it's pure barbarism to fry them in lard . . .

ALICE: Ugh! To talk about food!

CAPTAIN: About wines, then? I wonder what those barbarians drink with a hazel hen?

ALICE: Shall I play for you?

CAPTAIN (*sits down at the desk*): The last resource! Yes, if only you'd not play your funeral marches and sad songs—they sound as if you were trying to preach. And I always add: "Listen to how unhappy I am! Meow, meow! Listen to what a horrible husband I have! Hum, hum, hum! If only he were dead." The drum of joy, fanfares; finally the Alcazar waltz! Champagne *galop!* Talking about champagne, I think there are two bottles left. Shall we bring them up and pretend we have company?

ALICE: No, we shan't, for they're mine. They were gifts to me!

CAPTAIN: You always know what's yours.

ALICE: And you're always stingy—at least toward your wife.

CAPTAIN: Oh, I don't know. What shall I do?—Shall I dance for you?

ALICE: No, thanks. You're done with dancing, I suspect.

CAPTAIN: You ought to have a woman friend here.

ALICE: Thanks!—You ought to have a man friend here.

CAPTAIN: Thanks! We've tried that, and it didn't work. But as interesting as the experiment was, as soon as an outsider came into this house, we both were very happy . . . at first . . .

ALICE: But afterward!

CAPTAIN: Yes, don't talk about it. (*Someone knocks on the door to the left.*)

ALICE: Who can that be, this late?

CAPTAIN: Jenny usually doesn't knock.

ALICE: Open the door and don't shout, "Come in." That sounds as if you were in a shop.

CAPTAIN (*going toward the left door*): You don't like shops! (*Someone knocks again.*)

ALICE: Open it!

CAPTAIN (*does so and takes a calling card which someone hands him*): It's Kristin.—Has Jenny left? (*Since the answer cannot be heard by the audience, he says to* ALICE) Jenny has left!

ALICE: So I'm to be a maid again!

CAPTAIN: And I'm to be a hired man!

ALICE: Can't you have one of your men help out in the kitchen?

CAPTAIN: Not in times like these.

ALICE: But surely it's not Jenny's card?

CAPTAIN (*looks at the card with his glasses on; then gives it to* ALICE): You read it—I can't.

ALICE (*reads the card*): Kurt! It's Kurt! Go and tell him to come in!

CAPTAIN (*going out to the left*): Kurt! Well, this is nice. (*Pause.* ALICE *arranges her hair and seems to come alive.*)

CAPTAIN (*enters, with* KURT, *from the left*): Here he is, the traitor! Welcome, old boy!

ALICE (*to* KURT): Welcome to my house, Kurt!

KURT: Thank you . . . It's a long time since we saw each other.

CAPTAIN: How long has it been? Fifteen years! And we've got old . . .

ALICE: Oh, I don't know. Kurt certainly hasn't changed.

CAPTAIN: Sit down, sit down—First of all, your schedule. Have you been invited out tonight?

KURT: Yes, to the doctor's. But I didn't promise I'd come.

ALICE: Than you'll stay with your relatives?

KURT: That seems the natural thing, but the doctor is my superior in a way, and there may be repercussions later.

CAPTAIN: Nonsense! I've never been afraid of my superiors . . .

KURT: Afraid or not, there'll be repercussions.

CAPTAIN: I'm the master on this island! Stay behind me, and no one will dare touch you.

ALICE: Quiet, Edgar! (*Takes Kurt's hand*) Don't bother about masters and superiors; you stay with us. That's fitting and proper.

KURT: All right.—Especially since I feel welcome here.

CAPTAIN: Why shouldn't you feel welcome . . . We haven't any bones to pick . . .

(KURT *cannot conceal a certain dejection.*)

CAPTAIN: What would that be? You were a little careless when you were young, but I've forgotten that. I don't carry a grudge.

ALICE (*pained. All are now sitting by the sewing table*): So you've been all over the world?

KURT: Yes, and now come to you . . .

CAPTAIN: Whose marriage you arranged twenty-five years ago.

KURT: That's not how it was, but that doesn't matter. It's nice to see you've stayed together for twenty-five years . . .

CAPTAIN: Yes, we've put up with each other; sometimes it has been only so-so, but we've managed to stay with each other. And Alice hasn't had anything to complain about; we've had everything we've needed, and money has flowed in. You probably don't know that I'm a famous writer, a writer of textbooks . . .

KURT: Yes, I remember when I saw you last, you had just had a textbook on firearms published, and it was selling well! Are they still using it in the military schools?

CAPTAIN: It's still in print, and it's holding its own as number one, though they've tried to replace it with a poor one . . . that one's being used, of course, but it's absolutely valueless! (*Painful silence*)

KURT: You've been abroad, I've heard.

ALICE: Yes, we've been in Copenhagen five times.

CAPTAIN: Yes, indeed. You see when I took Alice from the theater . . .

ALICE: Did you?

CAPTAIN: Yes, I took you as a wife should be taken . . .

ALICE: How brave you've become.

CAPTAIN: But as I've had to swallow that I robbed her of a brilliant career since . . . hm . . . I've had to make up for it by promising to take her to Copenhagen . . . and I've kept that promise—faithfully! We've been there five times! Five (*holds up the five fingers of his left hand*) . . . Have you been in Copenhagen?

KURT (*smiles*): No, I've been mostly in America . . .

CAPTAIN: America? That's really a rough country, isn't it?

KURT (*dejected*): Well, it isn't Copenhagen!

ALICE: Have you . . . heard anything . . . from your children?

KURT: No.

ALICE: Forgive me, Kurt, but it was certainly thoughtless to desert them like that . . .

KURT: I didn't desert them—the court awarded them to their mother . . .

CAPTAIN: We shouldn't talk about that now. I think you were lucky to get out of that mess.

KURT (*to* ALICE): How are your children?

ALICE: Fine, thanks. They're going to school in town . . . they're almost grown up!

CAPTAIN: Yes, they're fine children, and the boy's brilliant! Brilliant! He's going to train as a general staff officer . . .

ALICE: If they'll take him.

CAPTAIN: Him? He has the makings of a minister of war!

KURT: From one thing to another . . . There's going to be a quarantine station here . . . the cholera and all that. The doctor's going to be my superior as you know . . . What sort of man is he?

CAPTAIN: Man? He's no man! He's a stupid rascal!

KURT (*to* ALICE): That's extremely unpleasant for me.

ALICE: Oh, it isn't as bad as Edgar says, but I can't deny I don't like him . . .

CAPTAIN: He's a rascal! And so are the others . . . the customs collector, the postmaster, the woman in charge of the telephone, the druggist, the pilot . . . and, what's he called—the guildmaster—they're rascals the lot of them. That's why I won't associate with them.

KURT: Are you on bad terms with all of them?

CAPTAIN: All of them!

ALICE: Yes, it's true one can't associate with these people.

CAPTAIN: It's as if all the tyrants in the country had been imprisoned on this island.

ALICE (*ironically*): Yes, that's true.

CAPTAIN (*good-naturedly*): Hm. Was that a hit at me? I'm not a tyrant, at least not in my house.

ALICE: Watch out!

CAPTAIN (*to* KURT): Don't believe what she says! I'm a very decent married man, and the old girl is the best wife in the whole world.

ALICE: Would you like something to drink, Kurt?

KURT: Thank you, not just now.

CAPTAIN: Have you become . . .

KURT: Moderately, only.

CAPTAIN: American?

KURT: Yes.

CAPTAIN: I like a lot; otherwise I'd just as soon not have any! A man should be able to take his liquor.

KURT: Coming back to the neighbors on the island. My position will bring me into contact with all of them . . . and I suppose it'll be hard going, for even if one doesn't want to get involved, one alway is.

ALICE: You go to them—you'll always come back to us, for we're your real friends.

KURT: Isn't it terrible to be isolated among enemies as you are?

ALICE: It isn't fun.

CAPTAIN: It isn't terrible at all. I've had only enemies all my life, and they've helped me rather than hurt me. When I die, I'll be able to say I don't owe anyone anything and I've never got anything from anyone. Everything I have, I've had to fight for.

ALICE: Yes, Edgar's path hasn't been strewn with roses . . .

CAPTAIN: With thorns and stones, hard stones . . . but one's own strength! Do you know that?

KURT (*simply*): Yes, I learned how inadequate it was—ten years ago!

CAPTAIN: You are a miserable creature!

ALICE (*to the* CAPTAIN): Edgar!

CAPTAIN: Well, he is a miserable creature if he doesn't have strength of his own. It's true, of course, when one's body gives out, there's only a wheelbarrowful to put in the garden, but as long as the body lasts, one has to kick and strike with hands and feet, as long as one can. That's my philosophy.

KURT (*smiles*): You're amusing to listen to . . .

CAPTAIN: But you don't believe I'm right?

KURT: No, I don't.

CAPTAIN: But I am all the same! (*The wind has been increasing, and now one of the outer doors at the back slams shut.*)

CAPTAIN (*gets up*): It's beginning to storm. I could feel it. (*Goes and shuts the doors and taps the barometer*)

ALICE (*to* KURT): You'll stay for dinner?

KURT: Yes, thank you.

ALICE: But it will be very simple, for our maid has left.

KURT: That will be fine.

ALICE: You don't demand much, Kurt.

CAPTAIN (*by the barometer*): If you could only see how the barometer is falling! I could feel it!

ALICE (*aside to* KURT): He's nervous.

CAPTAIN: We should have dinner soon.

ALICE (*gets up*): I was just going out to arrange it. You sit and talk things over (*aside to* KURT) but don't contradict him or he'll lose his temper. And don't ask him why he didn't get to be a major!

(KURT *nods in agreement.* ALICE *goes to the right.*)

CAPTAIN (*sits down at the sewing table by* KURT): See to it we get something good, old girl.

ALICE: Give me some money, and I will.

CAPTAIN: Always money! (ALICE *exits.*) Money, money, money! All day I go with my pocketbook so I finally imagine I'm a pocketbook! Do you know what I mean?

KURT: Oh, yes! But with this difference: I thought I was a billfold!

CAPTAIN (*laughs*): So you've known that, too! Women! (*Laughs*) And *you* got the right kind!

KURT (*patiently*): Let that be dead and buried, now.

CAPTAIN: She was a real jewel! . . . But I have in any case—in spite of everything—had a fine woman; for she's all right, in spite of everything.

KURT (*smiles good-naturedly*): In spite of everything!

CAPTAIN: Don't laugh!

KURT (*as before*): In spite of everything!

CAPTAIN: Yes, she has been a faithful wife . . . an excellent mother, exceptionally so . . . but (*glances toward the door to the right*) she has a diabolic temperament. You know, there are times I curse you for palming her off on me!

KURT (*good-naturedly*): But I didn't! Listen, man . . .

CAPTAIN: Ta, ta, ta, you talk nonsense and forget things that aren't pleasant to remember. Don't mind me—I'm used to commanding and barking, but you know me and won't get angry.

KURT: Not at all! But I didn't get you a wife. Quite the opposite!

CAPTAIN (*without letting himself be disturbed in his volubility*): Don't you think life is strange all the same?

KURT: Yes, it certainly is.

CAPTAIN: And growing old! It isn't pleasant, but it is interesting. Well, I'm not old, but I'm beginning to feel it. All one's acquaintances die, and one gets very lonely.

KURT: Lucky the man who has a wife to grow old beside him!

CAPTAIN: Lucky? Yes, it is fortunate for one's children desert a person, too. You shouldn't have deserted yours!

KURT: No, but I didn't! They were taken away from me . . .

CAPTAIN: Don't get angry when I tell you . . .

KURT: But it wasn't so . . .

CAPTAIN: However it was, I've forgotten it in any case, but you are alone.

KURT: But one gets used to everything.

CAPTAIN: Can one . . . can one get used to . . . being absolutely alone, too?

KURT: Look at me!

CAPTAIN: What have you been doing these fifteen years?

KURT: What a question! These fifteen years!

CAPTAIN: They say you've made a lot of money.

KURT: I'm not exactly rich . . .

CAPTAIN: I'm not thinking of borrowing . . .

KURT: If you were, I'd be only too glad . . .

CAPTAIN: Thank you, but I have my own accounts. You see (*looking at the door to the right*), nothing may be lacking in this house; and the day I don't have any money . . . she'll leave me!

KURT: Oh, no!

CAPTAIN: No? I know, I do know!—Can you imagine—she always manages just for the fun of it when I don't have any money—to prove to me that I'm not supporting my family—

KURT: But you have a large income, you said.

CAPTAIN: Of course, I have a large income . . . but it's not enough.

KURT: Then it's not large, according to the general way of looking at it . . .

CAPTAIN: Life is strange, and so are we! (*The telegraph starts clicking.*)

KURT: What's that?

CAPTAIN: It's only a time signal.

KURT: Don't you have a telephone?

CAPTAIN: Yes, in the kitchen, but we use the telegraph since the operators tell everything we say.

KURT: Life must be terrible out here by the sea!

CAPTAIN: Yes, it's simply terrible! All of life is terrible! And you who believe in a life after this, do you believe we'll get peace then?

KURT: I suppose there'll be struggles and storms there, too.

CAPTAIN: There, too—if there is a there! Rather, then, absolute nothing.

KURT: Do you know if you'll get that without pain?

CAPTAIN: I'm going to die suddenly, without pain.

KURT: Well, you know that?

CAPTAIN: Yes, I know that!

KURT: You don't seem to be satisfied with your life?

CAPTAIN (*sighs*): Satisfied? The day I die, I'll be satisfied.

KURT (*gets up*): You don't know that! . . . But tell me: what are you up to in this house? What's happening here? It smells like poisonous wallpaper, and a person gets sick as soon as he comes in. I'd prefer to leave, but I promised Alice I'd stay. There are dead bodies under these floors; there's so much hate it's hard to breathe.

(CAPTAIN *collapses and stares straight ahead.*)

KURT: What's the matter? Edgar!

(CAPTAIN *does not move.*)

KURT (*takes the* CAPTAIN *by the shoulder*): Edgar!

CAPTAIN (*comes to*): Did you say something? (*Looks about*) I thought it was . . . Alice! . . . Oh, it's you! . . . Listen . . . (*Again becomes listless, unaware of everything*)

KURT: This is terrible! (*Goes to the door at the right and opens it*) Alice! (*Pause*)

ALICE (*enters wearing an apron*): What is it?

KURT: I don't know! Look at him!

ALICE (*calmly*): He gets listless like that now and then . . . I'll play . . . then he'll wake up!

KURT: No, don't! Don't! . . . Wait! . . . Can he hear? Can he see?

ALICE: Just now he can neither hear nor see!

KURT: And you say that calmly! . . . Alice, what are you up to in this house?

ALICE: Ask that fellow!

KURT: Fellow? . . . Why, he's your husband!

ALICE: A stranger to me, as much of a stranger as he was twenty-five years ago! I don't know anything about that man . . . except . . .

KURT: Sh-h! He can hear you!

ALICE: He doesn't hear a thing now! (*A trumpet signal outside*)

CAPTAIN (*leaps up, takes his saber and his officer's cap*): Excuse me! I'm only going to inspect the sentries! (*Exits through the doors at the back*)

KURT: Is he sick?

ALICE: I don't know!

KURT: Has he lost his mind?

ALICE: I don't know!

KURT: Does he drink?

ALICE: Far less than he says!

KURT: Sit down—tell me, but calmly and truthfully.

ALICE (*sits down*): What shall I say? . . . That I've been a prisoner in this tower for a generation, locked up and watched by a man I've always hated . . . I hate him so much that the day he dies I'll laugh for joy!

KURT: Why haven't you left each other?

ALICE: You tell me! We broke our engagement twice; we've tried to separate every day since then . . . but we're bound together and can never escape from each other! Once we lived apart—within this house—for five years! Only death can separate us. We know that, so we wait for death as our deliverer.

KURT: Why are you so isolated?

ALICE: Because he isolates me! First, he rooted out all my brothers and sisters from the house—he calls it "rooting out"—then my women friends and the others . . .

KURT: But *his* relatives? Did *you* get rid of them?

ALICE: Yes, they were almost the death of me once they had taken away my honor and reputation . . . Finally I had to keep in touch with the world and people by means of that telegraph—the telephone operators listened to evertyhing . . . I've taught myself to telegraph, but he doesn't know that. You mustn't tell him . . . he'd kill me!

KURT: Terrible! Terrible! . . . But why does he blame me for your marriage? Let me tell you how it was . . . He was my friend. When he saw you for the first time, he fell in love with you! He asked me to speak for him. I told him, "No"! And I knew how tyrannical and cruel you can be, Alice! I warned him . . . When he became insistent, I told him to ask your brother.

ALICE: I believe you, but he has lied to himself all these years, so you'll never be able to change his mind now.

KURT: Well, let him blame me if that can help him.

ALICE: That's too much, though . . .

KURT: I'm so used to that . . . but what does hurt me is his unjust accusation that I deserted my children . . .

ALICE: He's like that; he says what he pleases, and then he believes it. But he seems to like you, mostly because you don't contradict him . . . Try not to get too weary of us . . . I think you came at a most fortunate time . . . for us; it's like a sign of . . . Kurt! You mustn't get weary of us, for I think we're the most unfortunate people in the whole world! (*Weeps*)

KURT: I've seen one marriage at close range . . . and that was horrible! But this is almost worse!

ALICE: Really?

KURT: Yes!

ALICE: Whose fault is it?

KURT: Alice! The minute you stop asking whose fault it is, you'll feel a measure of relief. Try to accept it as a fact, a trial, which you must bear . . .

ALICE: I can't! That's too much! (*Gets up*) There's nothing that can be done about it.

KURT: Poor people! . . . Do you know why you hate each other?

ALICE: No. It's the most unreasonable hatred, without cause, without purpose, and without end. And why do you think he's afraid of dying? He's afraid I'll remarry.

KURT: Then he loves you!

ALICE: Most likely. But that doesn't prevent him from hating me!

KURT (*as if to himself*): They call that love-hate, and it comes from hell! . . . Does he like to have you play for him?

ALICE: Yes, but only ugly melodies . . . for example, that ghastly "Entrance of the Boyards." [5] When he hears that, he becomes possessed and wants to dance.

KURT: Dance!

ALICE: Yes, he's amusing now and then.

KURT: One question . . . forgive me for asking. Where are the children?

ALICE: Didn't you know two of them are dead?

KURT: So you've had to bear that, too!

ALICE: What haven't I had to bear?

KURT: But the two others?

ALICE: They're in town. They couldn't stay at home! Because he turned them against me . . .

KURT: And you turned them against him.

ALICE: Naturally. And then they took sides, had to be bribed . . . so as not to ruin the children we sent them away! The very ones who should have been the bond became the source of division . . . What should have been the blessing in our home became its curse . . . Yes, sometimes I think we belong to the damned!

KURT: After the fall from grace . . . Yes, that's how it is.

ALICE (*with a "poisonous" look and a sharp voice*): What fall?

KURT: Adam and Eve's!

ALICE: Oh! I thought you meant something else! (*Embarrassed silence; with folded hands*) Kurt! You're my relative. You used to be my friend. I haven't always behaved toward you as I should have. But I've been punished, and you have your revenge.

KURT: Not revenge! This is not revenge! Don't say that!

ALICE: Do you remember a Sunday when you were engaged? I had invited the two of you to dinner.

KURT: Don't speak of it!

ALICE: I must speak; be kind! . . . When you came to dinner, we weren't at home.

KURT: You had been invited out yourselves. What's the point of talking about that now?

ALICE: Kurt! When I asked you to stay for dinner today, I thought there was something left in the pantry (*Covers her face with her hands*) There isn't anything, not even a slice of bread! . . . (*Weeps*)

KURT: Poor, poor Alice.

ALICE: But when he comes back and wants his dinner and there isn't anything to eat . . . he'll be furious. You've never seen him when he's furious! . . . Oh, God, how humiliating this is!

KURT: Mayn't I go out and buy something?

ALICE: You can't get anything on this island.

KURT: Not for my sake, but for his and yours, let me think of something . . . something . . . we'll have to make a joke of it when he comes back . . . I'll suggest that we take a drink . . . I'll think of something in the meanwhile . . . Get him in a good humor; play for him anything at all he likes . . . Sit down at the piano; be ready!

ALICE: Look at my hands! I've had to polish the brass and wipe glasses, make fires, and straighten up . . .

KURT: But you have two servants.

ALICE: That's what we have to say, because he's an officer . . . but servants always leave us very quickly . . . sometimes we don't have any . . . usually not . . . How will I solve this . . . this matter of dinner? If only the house caught on fire . . .

KURT: Hush, Alice!

ALICE: If only the sea would rise and sweep us away!

KURT: No, no, no, I can't listen to you!

ALICE: What will he say? What will he say? Don't go, Kurt; don't leave me!

KURT: No, Alice . . . I won't go!

ALICE: Yes, but when you have gone . . .

KURT: Has he ever beaten you?

ALICE: Me? Oh no, he knows I'd leave him! One has to have some pride!

(*Outside two people cry: "Halt! Who goes there?" "A friend!"*)

KURT (*rises*): Is it he?

ALICE (*frightened*): Yes, it's he! (*Pause*)

KURT: What in the world are we going to do?

ALICE: I don't know, I don't know!

CAPTAIN (*enters from the back; very cheerful*): There! Now I'm off duty . . . Well, now she's had time to complain! Isn't she unfortunate . . . eh? . . .

KURT: What's the weather like out there?

CAPTAIN: It's pretty stormy! . . . (*Jokingly, opens one of the outer doors a little*) Bluebeard with the young lady in the tower; and out there the sentry marches with drawn saber and keeps an eye on the beautiful lady . . . and then the brothers come, but the sentry's there! Look at him! One, two! He's a good sentry! Look at him! . . . Shall I dance the sword dance? Kurt ought to see me do that!

KURT: No, do "The Entrance of the Boyards" instead!

CAPTAIN: Do you know that one? You? . . . Alice in the apron, come and play! Come, I said!

(ALICE *goes unwillingly to the piano.*)

CAPTAIN (*pinches her arm*): Now you've lied about me!

ALICE: I?

(KURT *turns away.*)

(ALICE *plays "The Entrance of the Boyards."*)

(CAPTAIN *does a sort of Hungarian dance* [6] *behind the desk and jangles his spurs. Then he collapses on the floor without being noticed by* KURT *and* ALICE. ALICE *plays the number to its end.*)

ALICE (*without turning*): Shall I play it again? (*Silence*)

ALICE (*turns; catches sight of the* CAPTAIN *who is lying unconscious, concealed from the audience by the desk*): Good heavens! (*She stands, her arms crossed, sighs as if in thankfulness and relief.*)

KURT (*turns; hurries up to the* CAPTAIN): What is it? What's wrong?

ALICE (*intensely*): Is he dead?

KURT: I don't know! Help me!

ALICE (*does not move*): I can't bear to touch him . . . Is he dead?

KURT: No! He's alive!

(ALICE *sighs.* KURT *helps the* CAPTAIN, *who has come to, to get up and sit down on a chair.*)

CAPTAIN: What was that? (*Silence*) What was it?

KURT: You fell down.

CAPTAIN: What?

KURT: You fell to the floor! How do you feel?

CAPTAIN: I? I don't feel anything! Why are you two standing there staring at me?

KURT: You're sick!

CAPTAIN: That's nonsense! Go ahead, play, Alice . . . Ah! It's back again! (*Puts his hands to his head*)

ALICE: You see—you're sick!

CAPTAIN: Don't scream! I only feel faint!

KURT: We must get a doctor! . . . I'll telephone . . .

CAPTAIN: I don't want any doctor!

KURT: You must! We must call him for our sake; otherwise we'll be blamed!

CAPTAIN: I'll kick him out if he comes! . . . I'll shoot him! . . . Ah! it's back again! (*Puts his hands to his head*)

KURT (*going to the door at the right*): I'm going to telephone! (*Exits*)

   (ALICE *takes off her apron.*)

CAPTAIN: Would you give me a glass of water?

ALICE: I suppose I have to! (*Give him a glass of water*)

CAPTAIN: How sweet you are!

ALICE: Are you sick?

CAPTAIN: Forgive me for not being well.

ALICE: Will you take care of yourself then?

CAPTAIN: You're not likely to look after me!

ALICE: You can be sure of that!

CAPTAIN: The time you've waited for so long has come.

ALICE: Yes, the time you thought would never come!

CAPTAIN: Don't be angry with me!

KURT (*enters from the right*): It's disgraceful . . .

ALICE: What did he say?

KURT: He hung up without answering!

ALICE (*to the* CAPTAIN): That's what you get for your boundless arrogance!

CAPTAIN: I think I'm getting worse! . . . Try to get a doctor from town!

ALICE (*goes to the telegraph*): I'll have to telegraph, then.

CAPTAIN (*half rises; amazed*): Can . . . you . . . telegraph?

ALICE (*does so*): Yes, I can.

CAPTAIN: So-o? . . . Well, go ahead . . . How deceitful you are! (*To* KURT) Come and sit down by me.

    (KURT *sits down beside the* CAPTAIN.)

CAPTAIN: Take hold of my hand. I can't sit up. Can you imagine! Something's done for. It is strange!

KURT: Have you had attacks like this before?

CAPTAIN: Never! . . .

KURT: While you're waiting for an answer from town, I'll go to the doctor and talk with him. Has he ever had you under his care?

CAPTAIN: Yes, he has.

KURT: Then he knows your constitution . . . (*Going to the left*)

ALICE: I'll get an answer in a little while. This is kind of you, Kurt. Hurry back!

KURT: As fast as I can! (*Exits; pause*)

CAPTAIN: Kurt is kind. And how he has changed!

ALICE: Yes, for the better. I pity him, though, for having stumbled into our troubles just now.

CAPTAIN: And wishing us well! . . . I wonder how things really are for him. Did you notice he didn't want to talk about himself?

ALICE: Yes, but I don't think we asked him, either.

CAPTAIN: Imagine . . . his life! . . . And ours! I wonder if all people's lives are like that?

ALICE: Probably, though they don't talk about it as we do.

CAPTAIN: Sometimes I've believed misery attracts misery, and that fortunate people avoid misfortune. That may be why we never see anything but misery.

ALICE: Have you ever known any fortunate people?

CAPTAIN: Let me think . . . No! . . . Yes . . . The Ekmarks!

ALICE: Are you crazy? She had an operation last year . . .

CAPTAIN: That's true. Well, then, I don't know . . . yes, the von Kraffts.

ALICE: Yes, that family had an idyllic life—they had money, prestige, fine children, good marriages . . . until they were fifty. Then a cousin of theirs committed a crime and was sent to prison; that was the end of their idyll. The newspapers blackened their family name . . . The von Krafft murder made it impossible for any of them to appear in public; the children had to be taken out of school . . . God in heaven!

CAPTAIN: I wonder what's wrong with me!

ALICE: What do you think?

CAPTAIN: My heart or my head. It's as if my soul wanted to escape and dissolve in a cloud of smoke.

ALICE: Do you have any appetite?

CAPTAIN: Yes. How's dinner coming?

ALICE (*walks uneasily across the floor*): I'll ask Jenny.

CAPTAIN: Why, she has left!

ALICE: Yes, yes, yes!

CAPTAIN: Ring for Kristin, so I can have some fresh water.

ALICE (*rings*): Imagine if . . . (*Rings again*) She doesn't hear!

CAPTAIN: Go and see . . . Imagine if she has left, too!

ALICE (*goes to the door at the left and opens it*): What's this? Her trunk has been packed . . . it's here in the hall!

CAPTAIN: Then she has left!

ALICE: This is hell! (*Begins to weep, throws herself to her knees, puts her head on a chair, sobs*)

CAPTAIN: And everything at once! . . . And then Kurt had to come and see our mess! If there is a single humiliation left, let it come now, right now!

ALICE: You know, I have a feeling Kurt will never come back.

CAPTAIN: I can believe that of him.

ALICE: Yes, we're under a curse . . .

CAPTAIN: What's that?

ALICE: Don't you see how everyone avoids us?

CAPTAIN: I don't give a damn about that! (*The telegraph sounds.*) There's the answer! Quiet, so I can hear it! . . . No one has time! Excuses! . . . That crowd!

ALICE: That's what you get for despising your doctors . . . and for not paying their bills . . .

CAPTAIN: That's not true . . .

ALICE: Even when you could pay them, you didn't want to, because you despised their work! as you've belittled mine . . . and everybody else's work! . . . They don't want to come. And they've disconnected the telephone because you didn't consider that worth having. Nothing's worth mentioning but your guns and cannons!

CAPTAIN: Don't stand there chattering . . .

ALICE: Everything comes back!

CAPTAIN: That's pure superstition . . . That's what old women say!

ALICE: You'll see, I suspect . . . Do you know we owe Kristin six months' wages.

CAPTAIN: Well, she has stolen that much!

ALICE: And I've had to borrow from her, too!

CAPTAIN: I can believe that of you!

ALICE: How ungrateful you are! You know I borrowed for the children's tickets to town!

CAPTAIN: Well, Kurt certainly came back. A rascal, that fellow, too. And a coward! He didn't dare to say he had had enough, and that it would be more fun at the doctor's dance. Expected a poor dinner here, I suppose . . . That rascal is just what he always was!

KURT (*rushes in from the left*): This is how it is . . . The doctor knows your heart thoroughly . . .

CAPTAIN: My heart?

KURT: Yes, you've had arteriosclerosis for a long time . . .

CAPTAIN: Arteriosclerosis?

KURT: And . . .

CAPTAIN: Is that dangerous?

KURT: Yes, that is . . . to say . . .

CAPTAIN: It is dangerous!

KURT: Yes!

CAPTAIN: I'm going to die?

KURT: You have to be very careful. First: no more cigars. (*The* CAPTAIN *throws away his cigar.*) And then: No more whiskey . . . Then, to bed!

CAPTAIN (*frightened*): No, I don't want to! Not bed! Then it's all over! I'll never get up again! I'll sleep on the sofa tonight. What else did he say?

KURT: He was very friendly and will come right away if you call him.

CAPTAIN: Was he friendly? That hypocrite? I don't want to see him! . . . May I have anything to eat?

KURT: Not tonight. And only milk the next few days.

CAPTAIN: Milk! Why, I can't stand milk!

KURT: You'll have to learn.

CAPTAIN: No, I'm too old to learn! (*Puts his hands to his head*) Ah! There it is again! (*He sits staring.*)

ALICE (*to* KURT): What did the doctor say?

KURT: That he may die!

ALICE: Thank God!

KURT: Careful, Alice! Careful! . . . Go in and get a pillow and a blanket—I'll put him to bed here on the sofa. Then I'll sit up with him all night.

ALICE: And I?

KURT: You go to bed. Your presence seems to make him worse.

ALICE: Tell me what to do. I'll do it, for you mean well by us both. (*Going to the left*)

KURT: *Both of you!* Don't forget that. I'm not taking sides! (ALICE *exits.* KURT *takes the water pitcher and goes out to the right. The wind can be heard blowing outside; then the outer doors at the back blow open and an* OLD WOMAN *who looks poor and most un-pleasant peeks in.*)

CAPTAIN (*comes to, rises, looks about*): So! They've left me, the rascals! (*Catches sight of the* OLD WOMAN *and becomes frightened*) . . . Who are you? What do you want?

WOMAN: I just wanted to shut the doors, sir.

CAPTAIN: Why? Why?

WOMAN: Because they blew open just as I went by.

CAPTAIN: You meant to steal something!

WOMAN: There isn't much to steal, Kristin says.

CAPTAIN: Kristin!

WOMAN: Good night, sir; sleep well. (*Shuts the doors and goes*)
  (ALICE *enters from the left with pillows and blanket.*)

CAPTAIN: Who was that at the door? Was there anyone?

ALICE: Yes, it was old Mary from the poorhouse who went by.

CAPTAIN: Are you sure?

ALICE: Are you afraid?

CAPTAIN: I, afraid? Oh, no!

ALICE: Since you don't want to go to bed, lie down here.

CAPTAIN (*goes over to the sofa and lies down*): Yes, I'll lie here. (*Wants to take* ALICE'S *hand, but she pulls it away.* KURT *enters with a water carafe.*) Kurt, don't leave me!

KURT: I'll stay with you all night. Alice is going to bed.

CAPTAIN: Good night, Alice.

ALICE (*to* KURT): Good night.

KURT: Good night. (*Pause. Then* KURT *takes a chair and sits down by the* CAPTAIN'S *bed.*) Don't you want to take off your boots?

CAPTAIN: No! A soldier must always be ready!

KURT: What are you expecting? A battle?

CAPTAIN: Perhaps! . . . (*Raises himself*) Kurt, you're the only person to whom I've ever revealed myself. Listen to one thing . . . If I should die tonight . . . think of my children!

KURT: I will!

CAPTAIN: Thank you, I rely on you!

KURT: Can you explain why you rely on me?

CAPTAIN: We haven't been friends, for I don't believe in friendship, and our two families were born enemies and have always been fighting . . .

KURT: Yet you rely on me?

CAPTAIN: Yes! And I don't know why (*Silence*) Do you think I'm going to die?

KURT: Like everyone else. You won't be an exception.

CAPTAIN: Are you bitter?

KURT: Yes! . . . Are you afraid to die? The wheelbarrow and the garden!

CAPTAIN: Imagine, if death weren't the end!

KURT: Many think that it isn't.

CAPTAIN: What could follow?

KURT: Pure surprises, I suspect.

CAPTAIN: But no one knows for certain.

KURT: No, that's just it. That's why one must be ready for everything.

CAPTAIN: Surely you're not childish enough to believe in hell?

KURT: Don't you believe in it, you who are in the very midst of it?

CAPTAIN: That's only a figure of speech!

KURT: Your realistic description of your private hell eliminates every thought of figures of speech! (*Silence*)

CAPTAIN: If you only knew what agony I'm suffering!

KURT: Physical agony?

CAPTAIN: No, not physical!

KURT: Then it's spiritual—there isn't a third possibility! (*Pause*)

CAPTAIN (*raises himself*): I don't want to die!

KURT: Just now you wanted annihilation!

CAPTAIN: Yes, if it were painless!

KURT: But it isn't!

CAPTAIN: Is this annihilation?

KURT: Only the beginning of it! (*Pause*)
CAPTAIN: Good night!
KURT: Good night!

[CURTAIN]

# ACT II

*The same setting. The lamp is about to go out. Through the windows and the panes of the doors at the back can be seen a cloudy morning. The waves are beating on the shore. The* SENTINEL *as before. The* CAPTAIN *is lying on the sofa sleeping;* KURT— *pale and exhausted—is sitting on a chair next to him.*

ALICE (*enters from the left*): Is he asleep?
KURT: He's been sleeping since the sun should have come up.
ALICE: How was the night?
KURT: He has dozed off occasionally, but he has talked a lot.
ALICE: About what?
KURT: He has been talking about religion like a schoolboy but claims he has solved the mysteries of the universe! Finally, towards morning, he discovered the immortality of the soul.
ALICE: In his honor!
KURT: Exactly! . . . He's really the most arrogant person I've ever met. "I am, therefore God is."
ALICE: So you understand . . . Look at those boots! He would have trampled the world underfoot if he had had the chance! With them he has trampled on everyone and everything possible . . . he has trampled on other people's feet and on my head! . . . [*Facing the* CAPTAIN] You beast, now you've been hit!

KURT: He'd be comic if he weren't tragic, and there are elements of greatness in all his littleness! Can't you say one good word about him?

ALICE (*sits down*): Yes, if he can't hear me. For if anyone says one encouraging word to him, he's beside himself with pride.

KURT: He can't hear anything—he's been given morphine.

ALICE: Well . . . he was born in a poverty-stricken home with many brothers and sisters. When he was very young, he had to start tutoring others so he could support the family—his father was undependable or worse. It's hard, I suppose, for a youngster to have to give up all the pleasures of youth to slave for a crowd of ungrateful children he didn't bring into the world. I was a little girl when I saw him as a very young man—without an overcoat in winter when it was twenty-five degrees below freezing . . . His little sisters had winter coats . . . that was nice, and I admired him, but I was horrified by his ugliness. Isn't he extremely ugly?

KURT: Yes, and there may be something evil in his ugliness! I used to notice that particularly when we happened not to be on good terms. When he wasn't present, my image of him grew, took on terrifying proportions and forms, and he literally haunted me!

ALICE: Imagine what it has been for me! . . . Still, his early days as an officer must have been martyrdom. But he did get help from wealthy people occasionally. He never admits that—everything he has ever received, he considers a tribute that he has had coming and that he doesn't need to thank anyone for!

KURT: We should speak well of him.

ALICE: Since he's dead! Oh, well . . . I don't remember anything else.

KURT: Have you found him mean?

ALICE: Yes—yet he could be both good and tender!—As an enemy he is absolutely terrible!

KURT: Why wasn't he promoted to major?

ALICE: You ought to understand that! They certainly didn't want anyone as their superior when he was a tyrant as their subordinate! But don't ever mention the matter to him! He says he didn't want to become a major . . . Did he say anything about the children?

KURT: Yes, he was longing for Judith.[7]

ALICE: I imagine! Do you know who Judith is? She's his image that he has set up against me! My daughter, my own daughter . . . has actually struck me!

KURT: No, that's too much!

ALICE: Sh-h! He's moving! . . . Imagine if he heard us! . . . He's sly, too!

KURT: He's really waking up!

ALICE: Doesn't he look like a troll? I'm afraid of him! (*Silence*)

CAPTAIN (*moves, awakens, raises himself, looks about*): It's morning! Finally!

KURT: How do you feel?

CAPTAIN: Not too good.

KURT: Do you want a doctor?

CAPTAIN: No, I want to see Judith. My child!

KURT: Wouldn't it be wise to set your house in order before . . . or . . . if something should happen?

CAPTAIN: What do you mean? What would happen?

KURT: What happens to everyone!

CAPTAIN: Nonsense! I won't die that quickly, you know. Don't rejoice ahead of time, Alice.

KURT: Think of your children! Make your will so that your wife at least keeps the furniture!

CAPTAIN: Is she to inherit while I'm alive?

KURT: No. But if something happens, she shouldn't be thrown out in the street. The one who has cleaned, dusted, and polished this furniture for twenty-five years has the right to keep it. Shall I call a lawyer?

CAPTAIN: No!

KURT: You are cruel, far more than I had thought!

CAPTAIN (*collapses*): Now there it is again! (*Becomes unconscious*)

ALICE (*going to the right*): There are people in the kitchen! I must go!

KURT: Go ahead. There's not much to be done here. (ALICE *exits. Pause*)

CAPTAIN (*awakens*): Well, Kurt, how do you plan to arrange your position here?

KURT: That will be easy enough.

CAPTAIN: No, I'm the commandant on this island, and you'll have to deal with me. Don't forget that!

KURT: Have you ever seen a quarantine station?

CAPTAIN: Have I? Yes, before you were born! And I'll give you a bit of advice: don't put the disinfecting ovens too close to the shore.

KURT: I think they ought to be as close to the water as possible . . .

CAPTAIN: Now I know how well you understand your business. Why, water's the element for germs—their very life element!

KURT: But the salt sea water is necessary for washing away the impurities.

CAPTAIN: Idiot! . . . Well, when you get a place to live, you ought to take your children in to live with you.

KURT: Do you think they'd be willing?

CAPTAIN: Of course, if you're anything of a man. It would make a good impression on this whole community if you showed you had a sense of duty even in that way . . .

KURT: I've always done my duty in that way!

CAPTAIN (*raises his voice*): . . . on that point, which is your weakest!

KURT: Haven't I told you . . .

CAPTAIN (*continues as if* KURT *had not said anything*): . . . for a man doesn't desert his children like that . . .

KURT: Go on!

CAPTAIN: As your relative, your older relative, I feel I have a certain right to tell you the truth even if it's bitter . . . and you mustn't misunderstand . . .

KURT: Are you hungry?

CAPTAIN: Yes, I am . . .

KURT: Do you want something light?

CAPTAIN: No, I want something substantial.

KURT: That will finish you!

CAPTAIN: Isn't it enough to be sick? Does one have to starve, too?

KURT: That's how it is.

CAPTAIN: And I mustn't drink . . . nor smoke. Then life isn't worth much.

KURT: Death demands sacrifice; otherwise, he comes right away.

ALICE (*enters with some bouquets of flowers, some telegrams, and letters*): These are for you. (*Throws the flowers on the desk*)

CAPTAIN (*flattered*): For me! . . . May I have them? . . .

ALICE: Oh, they're only from the noncommissioned officers, the members of the band, and the policemen.

CAPTAIN: You're envious!

ALICE: Oh, no! If it were laurel wreaths . . . that would be different, but you'll never get any of those!

CAPTAIN: Well! . . . Here's a telegram from the colonel . . . You read it, Kurt. The colonel's at any rate a gentleman . . . though he is something of an idiot! . . . Here . . . from . . . What does it say! It's from Judith! . . . Please wire her to come home with the next boat! . . . Here . . . yes!—I'm not without friends in any case, and it's nice that they think about a sick person, who's deserving beyond his station, and who's without fear and blame.

ALICE: I don't understand. Are they congratulating you on being sick?

CAPTAIN: Hyena!

ALICE (*to* KURT): Well, we had a doctor who was so hated that when he left the island, they had a banquet—after his departure, not *for* him.

CAPTAIN: Put the flowers in vases . . . I'm certainly not easily deceived, and people are riffraff, but these simple expressions of appreciation are sincere, by God . . . they can't be anything but sincere!

ALICE: Fool!

KURT (*looking at a telegram*): Judith says she can't come—the steamboat's delayed because of the storm!

CAPTAIN: Is that all she says?

KURT: No-o!—There's something else.

CAPTAIN: Out with it!

KURT: Well, she asks you not to drink so much!

CAPTAIN: Shameless! . . . That's one's children! That's my only daughter . . . my beloved Judith! My idol!

ALICE: And image!

CAPTAIN: This is life! And its greatest joy! To hell with it!

ALICE: You're reaping what you sowed! You turned her against her mother; now she's turning against you! Don't tell me there isn't a God!

CAPTAIN (*to* KURT): What does the colonel say?

KURT: He grants you sick leave . . . as of now, immediately!

CAPTAIN: Sick leave? I haven't asked for any.

ALICE: No, but I have!

CAPTAIN: I won't accept it!

ALICE: The orders have already been signed!

CAPTAIN: That doesn't concern me!

ALICE: You see, Kurt, for this man there are no laws, no regulations that affect him, no set human pattern . . . He's above everything and everyone; the universe was created for his special use; the sun and moon follow their courses simply to carry his praises to the stars! That's what my husband is like! The insignificant captain who couldn't even get promoted to major, at whose self-importance everyone laughs while he thinks they're afraid of him; this beast who's afraid of the dark and believes in barometers and all this about and ending in: a wheelbarrowful of manure that isn't even first-rate in quality!

CAPTAIN (*fans himself with a bouquet of flowers, with self-satisfaction, without listening to* ALICE): Have you given Kurt breakfast?

ALICE: No.

CAPTAIN: Cook two, two excellent steaks right away.

ALICE: Two?

CAPTAIN: I'm going to have one, too!

ALICE: But there are three of us!

CAPTAIN: Oh, are you going to have one, too? Well, three, then!

ALICE: Where shall I get them? Last night you invited Kurt to dinner, and there wasn't a slice of bread in the house. Kurt has had to keep watch all night and hasn't had a thing to eat . . . he hasn't had any coffee, because there isn't any, and we don't have any credit any more!

CAPTAIN: She's angry because I didn't die last night!

ALICE: No, but because you didn't die twenty-five years ago, because you didn't die before I was born!

CAPTAIN (*to* KURT): Listen to her! . . . That's how it is when one gets married, Kurt. It's certain this marriage wasn't made in heaven!

(ALICE AND KURT *exchange meaningful glances.*)

CAPTAIN (*gets up and goes toward the door*): However! Say what you will. Now I'm going back on duty! (*Puts on an old-fashioned artillery helmet, the saber at his side, and his coat*) If anyone wants me, I'll be at the battery. (ALICE *and* KURT *try to stop him in vain.*) Out of the way! (*Exits*)

ALICE: Well, go ahead! You always go—turn your back when the going gets tough and let your wife cover your retreat, you hero in your liquor, you braggart, you liar! (*Hisses with contempt and disgust*)

KURT: There isn't any end to this!

ALICE: Well, you don't know all yet!

KURT: Is there still more?

ALICE: Yes, but I'm ashamed to . . .

KURT: Where is he going now? Where does he get the energy?

ALICE: That's a good question! Well, he's going to the noncommissioned officers to thank them for the flowers, and then he'll eat and drink with them. And he'll slander the rest of the officers . . .

If you knew how many times he has been threatened with discharge! Only sympathy for his family has kept him in the service. And he imagines it's out of fear because of his superiority! And the poor officers' wives who've gone out of their way to help us, he hates and slanders!

KURT: I have to confess that I came out here to find a peaceful refuge . . . I didn't know anything about your circumstances . . .

ALICE: Poor Kurt! . . . How are you going to get anything to eat?

KURT: Oh, I'll go to the doctor's. But how about you? Let me arrange this for you.

ALICE: Just so he doesn't find out . . . then he'd kill me!

KURT (*looking out of the window*): Look, there he stands on the rampart right in the wind!

ALICE: He's to be pitied . . . for being what he is!

KURT: You're both to be pitied! . . . What can be done?

ALICE: I don't know! . . . Some bills came, too, that he didn't notice . . .

KURT: It can be good not to notice bills occasionally!

ALICE (*at the window*): He has opened his coat and exposed his chest to the wind! Now he wants to die!

KURT: I don't think he wants to, for just now when he felt his life slipping away, he clung to mine, began to settle my affairs as if he wanted to creep into me and live my life.

ALICE: That's his vampire nature exactly . . . to seize hold of other people's lives, to suck interest out of other people's lives, to arrange and direct for others, when his own life has become absolutely without interest for him. And remember, Kurt, don't ever let him get hold of your family affairs, don't ever let him meet your friends, for he'll take them away from you and make them his own . . . He's a magician at doing that! . . . If he meets your children, you'd soon see them on intimate terms with him; he'd advise them and bring them up according to his own whims, and above all against your wishes.

KURT: Alice, wasn't he the one who took my children away from me when I was divorced?

ALICE: Since it's all in the past: yes, it was he!

KURT: I've suspected that, but I haven't been sure. It was he!

ALICE: When you sent my husband—with full confidence in him—to come to terms with your wife, he began to make up to her and taught her the trick by which she would get the children.

KURT: Good God! . . . God in heaven!

ALICE: There you have another side of him! (*Silence*)

KURT: You know, last night . . . when he thought he was dying . . . he made me promise . . . I'd look after his children!

ALICE: But you surely don't want to get your revenge through my children?

KURT: By keeping my promise! Yes! I'll look after your children!

ALICE: That's really the worst revenge you could take, for there's nothing he despises as much as generosity of mind!

KURT: Then I'll consider myself as revenged. Without taking revenge!

ALICE: I love vengeance as I love justice; it delights me to see evil get its punishment!

KURT: You're still at that point!

ALICE: I'll always be at that point. The day I'd forgive or love an enemy, I'd be a hypocrite!

KURT: Alice, it may be one's duty not to say everything, not to see everything. That's called mercy, and we all need that.

ALICE: Not I! My life is open and aboveboard, and I've always played with honest cards.

KURT: That is saying a lot!

ALICE: No, it says too little! For what I've had to suffer innocently because of this man, whom I've never loved . . .

KURT: Why did you marry him?

ALICE: Who knows? . . . Because he took me! Deceived me! I don't know! And then I wanted the social prestige . . .

KURT: And deserted your art!

ALICE: Which was despised!—But, you know, he deceived me! He promised me a good life, a beautiful home . . . and all there was, was debt upon debt . . . the only gold was on his uniform, and even that wasn't gold! He deceived me!

KURT: Wait a minute! When a young man falls in love, he's very optimistic about the future . . . That his hopes aren't always realized must be forgiven him. I have the same sort of deception on my conscience without feeling guilty. . . . Why are you looking at the rampart?

ALICE: I'm looking to see if he has fallen.

KURT: Has he?

ALICE: No, unfortunately! He always fools me!

KURT: Then I'll go to the doctor and the authorities.

ALICE (*sits down by the window*): Go ahead, Kurt dear. I'll sit here waiting. I have learned to wait!

[CURTAIN]

# ACT III

*The same setting as before. The* SENTRY *on the battery as before.* ALICE *is sitting on the armchair to the right; her hair is gray.*

KURT (*enters from the left after he has knocked*): Good morning, Alice!

ALICE: Good morning. Sit down, Kurt.

KURT (*sits down in the armchair to the left*): The steamer's just coming in.

ALICE: Then I know what will happen if he is aboard!

KURT: He's aboard! I saw his helmet flashing . . . What has he been doing in town?

ALICE: I can figure that out. Since he put on his dress uniform, he went to the colonel, and, since he put on his white gloves, he has been paying calls.

KURT: Did you notice how quiet he was yesterday? Since he has given up drinking and keeps on a sensible diet, he's like a different person: calm, reserved, considerate . . .

ALICE: I know. And if that man had always been sober, he would have been a danger to humanity. Perhaps it's fortunate for humanity that he has made himself ridiculous and harmless through his whiskey!

KURT: The spirit in the bottle has disciplined him! . . . But have you noticed that, since death has marked him for its own, he has a dignity that elevates him? Perhaps his new faith in immortality has given him a new concept of life.

ALICE: You're wrong! He's up to some evil! Don't believe what he says, for he's a master of the big lie, and he knows every trick of intrigue better than anyone else . . .

KURT (*observes* ALICE): Alice! What's this? You've become gray-haired in these two nights!

ALICE: No, my hair's been gray a long time, but I haven't bothered to touch it up since my husband's dying. Twenty-five years in a fort . . . Did you know this building used to be a prison?

KURT: A prison! The walls look like it!

ALICE: And my complexion. Even the children got pale and gray like prisoners here.

KURT: I can't imagine little children playing happily within these walls.

ALICE: They rarely did play. And the two who died, died from want of light!

KURT: What's going to happen?

ALICE: The final blow against the two of us! I recognized the old familiar glint in his eyes when you read the telegram from Judith. It should have hit her, of course, but he can't hit her, so the hatred was aimed at you!

KURT: What does he intend to do to me?

ALICE: That's hard to tell, but he has an amazing talent or luck for searching out other people's secrets . . . you noticed how he was sort of living in your quarantine station yesterday, how he sucked an interest in life out of your existence, ate your children alive . . . He's a cannibal, you see . . . I know him. His own life is going or has gone . . .

KURT: I had the impression, too, that he had already passed over to the other side. His face sort of glows as if he were dissolving . . . and his eyes flame like lights above graves or swamps . . . He's coming! Have you thought of the possibility that he may be jealous?

ALICE: No, he's too conceited for that! . . . "Show me the man I'd need to be jealous of!" Those are his words!

KURT: All the better: even his flaws have their merits! . . . Shall I get up and go to meet him?

ALICE: Be impolite, or he'll think you're a hypocrite! When he begins to lie, pretend you believe him. I can translate his lies; it's as if I can get at the truth through my own dictionary! . . . I expect something terrible . . . but, Kurt, don't lose your self-control! . . . My only advantage in our long struggle has been always being sober and keeping my presence of mind . . . Whiskey always was his downfall in that struggle! . . . Now, we'll see!

CAPTAIN (*enters from the left in dress uniform, helmet, cape, white gloves. Calm, dignified, but pale and hollow-eyed. Goes stumbling to a chair at the right far from* KURT *and* ALICE; *sits down. Holds the saber between his knees during the following conversation*): Good morning!—Excuse me for sitting down here, but I'm a little tired.

ALICE AND KURT: Good morning.

ALICE: How do you feel?

CAPTAIN: Fine! Just a little tired . . .

ALICE: Any news from town?

CAPTAIN: A little. Good news! Among other things, I saw a doctor, and he said there was nothing wrong with me and that I could live for twenty years if I take care of myself!

ALICE (*softly to* KURT): Now he's lying! (*To the* CAPTAIN) That's good, dear.

CAPTAIN: Yes, it is! (*Silence, during which the* CAPTAIN *stares at* ALICE *and* KURT *as if he wanted them to talk*)

ALICE (*aside to* KURT): Don't say anything—let him talk first, and he'll reveal what he's up to!

CAPTAIN (*to* ALICE): Did you say something?

ALICE: No, I didn't.

CAPTAIN (*slowly*): Listen, Kurt.

ALICE (*aside to* KURT): Now it's coming!

CAPTAIN: I . . . I was in town, as you know! (KURT *nods*) and . . . and I met, among others, a young volunteer (*very slowly*) artilleryman (*pause, during which* KURT *shows he is uneasy*) who . . . we haven't enough volunteers out here so I arranged with the colonel that the young fellow should come out here . . . That ought to please you, especially you, when I tell you that . . . it . . . he's . . . your own son!

ALICE (*aside to* KURT): The vampire! You see!

KURT: Under ordinary circumstances that would please a father, but in my circumstances it can be only painful!

CAPTAIN: I don't see why.

KURT: You don't need to; it's enough that I don't want him to come here.

CAPTAIN: Really! . . . Then you ought to know that the young man already has his orders to report to me here, and that from now on he's under my command!

KURT: Then I'll force him to try to get into another regiment!

CAPTAIN: You can't—you haven't anything to say about your son!

KURT: I haven't?

CAPTAIN: No, the court awarded all parental rights to his mother!

KURT: Then I'll get in touch with his mother!

CAPTAIN: You don't need to!

KURT: Don't need to!

CAPTAIN: No, because I already have!

(KURT *rises, but sinks down again on the chair.*)

ALICE (*aside to* KURT): Now he must die!

KURT: He *is* a cannibal! (*Pause*)

CAPTAIN: That's *that!* (*Directly to them*) Did you say something?

ALICE: No. Have you lost your hearing?

CAPTAIN: Yes, a little . . . But if you come over here, Alice, I'll tell you something that's just for us two.

ALICE: That's unnecessary. And it might be good for both of us to have a witness.

CAPTAIN: You're right about that! Witnesses are always good! . . . First of all, is my will in order?

ALICE (*hands him a document*): The lawyer drew it up himself.

CAPTAIN: In your favor! . . . Fine! (*Scans the document and then tears it carefully to pieces, which he throws on the floor*) That's that! Ta!

ALICE (*aside to* KURT): Have you ever seen a human being like that?

KURT: He's not a human being! (*Pause*)

CAPTAIN: Well, I want to tell you this, Alice! . . .

ALICE (*uneasily*): Go ahead.

CAPTAIN (*calmly as before*): On the basis of your long expressed wish to bring an end to this miserable life in an unhappy marriage, and on the basis of the lack of love with which you have dealt with both your husband and children, and on the basis of the lack of care which you have demonstrated in the economy of this home, I have—during my visit to town—presented in the proper court my petition for divorce!

ALICE: So-o? And on what grounds?

CAPTAIN: Aside from those I've already mentioned, I have purely personal ones. Namely, since it has been determined I may live for twenty more years, I've considered exchanging this unhappy marital union for one more suitable to me. I intend to unite my future with that of a woman who besides affection for her husband can bring into my home youth and—let us say—a little beauty!

ALICE (*takes off her ring and tosses it at the* CAPTAIN): There you are!

CAPTAIN (*picks up the ring and puts it in his vest pocket*): She threw away the ring! Will the witness please note that?

ALICE (*gets up; excited*): And you intend to throw me out and put another woman in my house?

CAPTAIN: Ta!

ALICE: Then we'll talk bluntly! . . . Kurt, my cousin, this man has tried to murder his wife!

KURT: Murder!

ALICE: Yes, he pushed me into the sea!

CAPTAIN: Without witnesses!

ALICE: He's lying! Judith saw it!

CAPTAIN: What difference does that make?

ALICE: She can testify!

CAPTAIN: No, she can't! She says she didn't see anything!

ALICE: You've taught the child to lie!

CAPTAIN: I didn't need to! You had already taught her!

ALICE: Did you see Judith?

CAPTAIN: Ta!

ALICE: My God, my God! (*Pause*)

CAPTAIN: The fortress has been surrendered! The enemy is granted free departure on ten minutes' notice! (*Puts his watch on the table*) Ten minutes! The watch is on the table! (*Standing; puts his hand to his heart*)

ALICE (*comes up to the* CAPTAIN *and takes him by the arm*): What's wrong?

CAPTAIN: I don't know!

ALICE: Do you want something? Something to drink?

CAPTAIN: Whiskey? No, I don't want to die! You! (*Straightens himself*) Don't touch me! . . . Ten minutes or the garrison will be cut down! (*Draws his saber*) Ten minutes! (*Goes out at the back. Pause*)

KURT: Who is that man?

ALICE: He's no man! He's a devil!

KURT: What does he want of my son?

ALICE: He wants him as a hostage so he can control you; he wants to isolate you from the authorities on the island . . . Did you know the people out here call this island "Little Hell?"

KURT: I didn't know! . . . Alice, you're the first woman who has ever aroused my sympathy! All the other have seemed to deserve what they got!

ALICE: Don't desert me now! Don't leave . . . he'll be at me . . . He has beaten me for twenty-five years . . . and in the presence of the children . . . he pushed me into the sea . . .

KURT: That does it! I'm absolutely against him! I came out here without malice, without thinking about his humiliating behavior and slanderous talk in the old days! I forgave him even when you told me he was the one who separated my children from me . . . because he was sick and dying . . . but now when he wants to take my son, he must die—he or I.

ALICE: Good! Don't give up the fort! But blow it and him sky high even if we have to go along! I'll take charge of the powder!

KURT: I wasn't angry when I came, and I thought of leaving when I felt how your hatred infected me, but I feel an irresistible call to hate this man as I've hated evil! . . . What can be done?

ALICE: He has taught me the technique! Call together his enemies and get allies!

KURT: Imagine it! He could find my wife! Why didn't those two meet a generation ago? Then there would have been fighting that would have shaken the world!

ALICE: But now those congenial souls have met . . . and they must

be separated! I suspect I know what his vulnerable spot is . . .
I've suspected it for a long time . . .

KURT: Who is his most faithful enemy on the island?

ALICE: The ordnance officer!

KURT: Is he an honorable man?

ALICE: Yes, he is! . . . And he knows what I . . . I know it, too!
. . . He knows what the sergeant major and the captain have been
up to!

KURT: What they've been up to? . . . Do you mean?

ALICE: Embezzling!

KURT: That's appalling! No, I don't want to stir in that!

ALICE (*laughs*): You'll never defeat an enemy!

KURT: I have in the past, but I can't any more!

ALICE: Why not?

KURT: Because I've discovered . . . that justice is meted out anyway!

ALICE: Are you going to wait for that? He'll have taken your son
away from you! Look at my gray hair . . . yes, feel how thick it
is, for that matter! . . . He intends to get married again . . .
then I'm free to do the same.—I am free! And in ten minutes
they'll have locked him up down there (*stamps on the floor*)
down there . . . and I'll dance on his head; I'll dance "The Entry of the Boyards"! . . . (*Puts her hands to her sides and dances
a few steps; laughs*) And I'll play the piano so he can hear it!
(*Hammers on the piano*) Oh, the tower will open its doors and
the sentinel with his drawn saber will keep watch over him, not
over me . . . (*Hums*) He'll watch him, him, him!

KURT (*has watched her with excited glances*): Alice, are you a devil,
too?

ALICE (*jumps up on a chair and takes down the laurel wreaths*): I'll
take these along on my departure . . . my laurels of triumph!
And waving ribbons! A little dusty, but eternally green and fresh!
—As my youth!—Surely I'm not old, Kurt!

KURT (*with glowing eyes*): You are a devil!

ALICE: In Little Hell! . . . Listen, now I'll get ready . . . (*Loosens her hair*) I'll dress in two minutes . . . go to the ordnance officer in two minutes . . . and then the fort goes up in the air!

KURT (*as before*): You are a devil!

ALICE: That's what you always said when we were children, too! Do you remember when we were children, and got engaged? (*Laughs*) You were bashful, of course . . .

KURT (*very serious*): Alice!

ALICE: Yes, you were! And it was becoming. You see there are coarse women who like bashful men, and there . . . probably are bashful men who like coarse women! . . . At least you liked me a little in those days! . . . Didn't you?

KURT: I'm bewildered . . . Where am I?

ALICE: With an actress who is rather free in her ways but who otherwise is an excellent woman. Yes, indeed! But now I'm free, free, free! . . . Turn around . . . I'm going to change my blouse! (*She unbuttons her blouse.* KURT *rushes up to her, takes her in his arms, lifts her high in the air, and bites her throat so that she screams. Then he throws her on the sofa and hurries out to the left.*)

[CURTAIN]

# ACT IV

*The same setting as in the evening. The* SENTRY *on the battery can still be seen through the windows at the back. The laurel wreaths are draped over the arm of a chair. The ceiling lamp is lighted. The* CAPTAIN, *pale and hollow-eyed, his hair shot through*

*with gray, dressed in a worn fatigue uniform with riding boots, is
sitting at the desk playing solitaire. He is wearing glasses.*

*The between-acts music continues after the curtain goes up until
a second person makes his entrance.*

*Now and then the* CAPTAIN *gives a start, looks up, and listens
anxiously.*

*His game does not seem to turn out successfully; he becomes
impatient and heaps up the cards. He goes to the window at the
left, opens it, and throws the cards out. The window remains
open, but rattles on its hooks.*

*He goes up to the cupboard, becomes frightened by the noise
the window is making so that he turns around to see what it is.
He then takes out three dark, square whiskey bottles, looks at
them carefully, and then throws them out through the open
window. He then takes out cigar boxes, smells in one, and throws
them out.*

*Then he takes off his glasses, wipes them, and tests how he sees
with them. Then he throws them out of the window, stumbles
among the pieces of furniture as if he did not see well, and lights
a candelabra with six candles on the chiffonier. He sees the laurel
wreaths, takes them and goes up to the window, but turns back.
He takes the large scarf on the piano, wraps the scarf carefully
about the wreaths, takes pins from the desk and fastens the corners and puts it all on a chair. He goes up to the piano, strikes
the keys with his fists, shuts the piano, locks it, and throws the
key out of the window. Then he lights the candles on the piano.
Goes up to the wall, takes* ALICE's *picture down, looks at it, then
tears it to pieces, and throws the pieces on the floor. The window
rattles, and he becomes frightened again.*

*When he has become calm again, he takes the picture of his son
and his daughter, kisses them quickly, and stuffs them into the
pocket of his coat. He knocks down the rest of the pictures with
his elbows and heaps them in a pile with his boot.*

*Then he sits down, weary, at the desk and puts his hand to his heart. Lights the candles in a holder and sighs, stares straight ahead as if he were seeing unpleasant visions . . . Gets up and goes to the chiffonier, opens the escritoire and takes out a bundle of letters tied with blue silk ribbons, and throws them into the tiled stove. He shuts the chiffonier. The telegraph sounds once only. The* CAPTAIN *collapses as if in the agony of death and stands with his hand to his heart, listening. But when the telegraph remains silent, he listens to the door at the left. He goes over to it, opens it, takes a step through it and comes out with a cat on his arm which he strokes on the back. Then he goes out to the right. The music ends as* ALICE *enters from the back. She is dressed for walking. Her hair is black; she is wearing both hat and gloves; she looks coquettishly about with amazement at all the lighted candles.* KURT *enters from the left. He is nervous.*

ALICE: This looks like Christmas eve!

KURT: Well-l!

ALICE (*gives him her hand to kiss*): Say "Thank you"! (KURT *kisses her hand unwillingly.*) Six witnesses, four of them absolutely reliable. The accusation has been made, and the answer will come through that telegraph—here, right in his fort!

KURT: Oh!

ALICE: Say "Thank you" instead of "Oh"!

KURT: Why has he lighted so many candles?

ALICE: He's afraid of the dark, of course! . . . Look at the telegraph! Doesn't it look like the handle of a coffee mill—I grind, I grind, and the beans crunch as when one pulls out teeth!

KURT: What has he been doing?

ALICE: It looks as if he intended to move. Yes, he's going to move down there! (*Points at the floor; apparently the basement is used for the detention of prisoners*)

KURT: Alice, don't! I think all of it's depressing . . . He was my friend when I was young . . . he was kind to me many times when the going was hard . . . He's to be pitied!

ALICE: What about me? I haven't done anything wrong, and I've had to sacrifice my career for that monster!

KURT: What is the truth about that career? Was it so brilliant?

ALICE (*beside herself with fury*): What's that? Do you know who I am? Who I have been?

KURT: There, there!

ALICE: Are you, too, starting . . . already?

KURT: Already?

ALICE (*puts her arms about* KURT's *neck and kisses him.* KURT *takes hold of her arms and bites her throat so that she screams*): You're biting me!

KURT (*beside himself*): Yes, I'll bite your throat and suck your blood like a lynx! You've aroused the animal in me! For years I've tried to kill it by self-denial and self-discipline. I thought I was a little better than you two, but now I'm the worst one! Since I saw you in all your terrifying nakedness, since my passion blinded me, I feel the whole strength of evil; ugliness became beauty, goodness became ugliness and weakness! . . . Come here and I'll choke you . . . with a kiss! (*He embraces her.*)

ALICE (*shows him her left hand*): See the mark of the chains you unbound. I was a slave and have been set free! . . .

KURT: But I will bind you . . .

ALICE: You?

KURT: I!

ALICE: For a minute I thought you were . . .

KURT: A pietist?

ALICE: Yes, you chattered about the fall from grace . . .

KURT: Did I?

ALICE: And I thought you came to preach . . .

KURT: Did you? . . . In an hour we'll be in town! Then you'll see who I am . . .

ALICE: We'll go to the theater tonight so people see us! It will be his disgrace if I leave him, you see!

KURT: Yes, I'm beginning to . . . It isn't enough with prison . . .

ALICE: No, it isn't! There has to be disgrace, too!

KURT: A strange world! You commit the disgraceful act, and he gets the disgrace!

ALICE: When the world is that stupid!

KURT: It's as if these prison walls had absorbed all the evil from all the criminals and as if one had only to breathe here to get it, too! You were thinking about the theater and dinner, I suspect! I was thinking about my son!

ALICE (*strikes him across the mouth with her glove*): You old fogey!
    (KURT *raises his hand as if he were going to strike her.*)

ALICE (*shrinks back*): Nice!

KURT: Forgive me!

ALICE: If you get down on your knees! (*He does*). On your face! (*He puts his forehead against the floor.*) Kiss my foot! (*He does.*) And don't ever do that again! . . . Get up!

KURT (*stands up*): Where have I come? Where am I?

ALICE: That you know!

KURT (*looks about with horror*): I believe I almost . . .

CAPTAIN (*enters from the right. Miserable. He supports himself on a cane*): May I speak with Kurt? Alone!

ALICE: About our free departure?

CAPTAIN (*sits down by the sewing table*): Would you sit down by me for a while, Kurt? And, Alice, would you grant us a moment's . . . peace?

ALICE: What now? . . . New signals!—(*To* KURT) Please sit down. (KURT *sits down unwillingly.*) And listen to the words of old age and wisdom . . . If a telegram comes . . . call me! (*Exits to the left*)

CAPTAIN (*with dignity after a pause*): Can you understand a life like mine? Like ours?

KURT: No, as little as I understand my own!

CAPTAIN: What is the meaning of this whole mess?

KURT: In my better moments I've believed that the meaning was just that we shouldn't learn the meaning and yet bow down in surrender . . .

CAPTAIN: Bow down! Without a definite point of reference outside myself, I can't bow down.

KURT: Exactly, but as a mathematician you should be able to look for the unknown when you have several knowns . . .

CAPTAIN: I have looked for it, and—I haven't found it!

KURT: You haven't calculated properly! Try again!

CAPTAIN: I will! . . . Tell me: where did you get your resignation?

KURT: I haven't any left. Don't overestimate me!

CAPTAIN: As you've probably noticed, I've thought the art of living was this: eliminate! That is, cross it out and go on. Long ago I made a sack for myself—I've stuffed every humiliation into it, and when it was filled, I threw it into the sea!—I believe no other person has ever suffered so many humiliations as I. But when I crossed them out and went on, they didn't exist any longer!

KURT: I have noticed how you have the gift of believing your own lies about your life and your environment!

CAPTAIN: How could I have lived otherwise? How could I have stood it? (*Puts his hand to his heart*)

KURT: How do you feel?

CAPTAIN: Sick! (*Pause*) There comes a time when the gift of believing one's own lies about one's life, as you say, ends. Then reality appears in all its nakedness! . . . That is terrible! (*He is now talking with an old man's tear-choked voice, with his lower jaw hanging.*) You see, my friend . . . (*Controls himself and speaks with his usual voice*) Forgive me! . . . When I was in town, I saw the doctor. (*On the verge of tears*) He said it was all up with me . . . (*usual voice*) and that I couldn't live long.

KURT: Did he say that?

CAPTAIN (*tears in his voice*): Yes, he did.

KURT: So you didn't tell us the truth?

CAPTAIN: What's that? Oh . . . no, that wasn't true.

KURT: The rest wasn't true either?

CAPTAIN: What do you mean?

KURT: That my son has orders to report here?

CAPTAIN: I've never heard a word about that.

KURT: You know, your power to cross out your own misdeeds is boundless!

CAPTAIN: I don't understand what you mean, Kurt.

KURT: Then you're done for!

CAPTAIN: Yes, there isn't much left.

KURT: Listen! Perhaps you haven't insulted your wife by applying for a divorce?

CAPTAIN: Divorce! No, I haven't heard anything about that.

KURT (*gets up*): Do you admit you've lied?

CAPTAIN: You use such strong words! We all need forbearance!

KURT: You've learned that?

CAPTAIN (*firmly in a clear voice*): Yes I have learned that! . . . So forgive me, Kurt! Forgive me for everything!

KURT: That was a manly word!—But I haven't anything to forgive you. And I'm not the man you think I am . . . not any more. Least of all the man who is worthy of receiving your confessions.

CAPTAIN (*in a clear voice*): Life is strange! So difficult, so evil, from childhood on . . . and people are so evil I became evil, too . . .

(KURT, *uneasy, crosses the floor, looks at the telegraph.*)

CAPTAIN: What are you looking at?

KURT: Can I shut off a telegraph?

CAPTAIN: No, not easily!

KURT (*with increasing uneasiness*): Who is Sergeant Major Östberg?

CAPTAIN: He's an honorable man—a bit of a businessman, of course.

KURT: And the ordnance officer?

CAPTAIN: He's my enemy, of course, but I haven't anything to say against him.

KURT (*looks out of the window where a lantern can be seen moving about*): What are they doing with the lantern out on the battery?

CAPTAIN: Is there a lantern?

KURT: Yes, and people are moving about!

CAPTAIN: I suppose it's a helping hand, as we say.

KURT: What do you mean?

CAPTAIN: A few men and a military policeman! I suppose it's some poor devil who's to be locked up!

KURT: Oh! (*Pause*)

CAPTAIN: Now that you've got to know Alice again, what do you think of her?

KURT: I don't know . . . I don't understand people at all! She's as hard to understand as you are . . . and as I am! I'm getting to the age when I admit I know nothing, understand nothing!—But when I see an act on somebody's part, I'd like to understand why it was committed . . . Why did you push her into the sea?

CAPTAIN: I don't know! It just seemed natural when she was standing on the dock that I should push her in.

KURT: Haven't you ever regretted it?

CAPTAIN: Never!

KURT: That's strange!

CAPTAIN: Yes, of course it is! So strange I don't believe I was the one who did it!

KURT: Haven't you thought she'd try to get revenge?

CAPTAIN: She certainly has . . . quite sufficiently, and I think that's natural enough!

KURT: How did you come so quickly to this cynical resignation?

CAPTAIN: Since I looked death in the face, life has seemed quite different . . . If you were going to judge between Alice and me, which would you acquit?

KURT: Neither of you! But boundless sympathy for you both—probably a little more for you!

CAPTAIN: Give me your hand, Kurt!

KURT (*extends one hand and puts the other on the* CAPTAIN'S *shoulder*): Old friend!

ALICE (*enters from the left, carrying an umbrella*): Well, how friendly! Huh, that friendship! . . . Hasn't the telegram come?

KURT (*coldly*): No.

ALICE: The delay makes me impatient, and when I get impatient, I speed up the situation! . . . Look here, Kurt, now I'll let him have the last shot! And he'll be finished! . . . First, I'll load—oh, I know the firearms text, the famous textbook about firearms that didn't sell five thousand copies . . . then I'll aim! (*She aims with the umbrella.*)—How's your new wife? That beautiful, young unknown woman! You don't know! But I know how my lover is! (*She puts her arms about* KURT'S *neck and kisses him, but he pushes her away.*) He feels fine, but he's still bashful! . . . You scoundrel, whom I've never loved, you who were too conceited to be jealous, you could never see how I deceived you!

(CAPTAIN *draws his saber and rushes toward her, trying to cut her down, but he hits only pieces of furniture.*)

ALICE: Help! (KURT *stands immovable.*)

CAPTAIN (*falls with his saber in his hand*): Judith! Avenge me!

ALICE: Hurrah! He's dead! (KURT *goes toward the door at the back.*)

CAPTAIN (*gets up*): Not yet! (*Sheaths his saber, sits down in the armchair by the sewing table*) Judith! Judith!

ALICE (*goes toward* KURT): Now I'm going—with you, Kurt!

KURT (*pushes her away from him so violently she falls to her knees*): Go to the hell from which you came! Farewell forever! (*Going*)

CAPTAIN: Don't leave me, Kurt; she'll kill me!

ALICE: Kurt, don't desert me; don't desert us!

KURT: Goodbye! (*Exits*)

ALICE (*changes her attitude*): What a rascal! There's a friend for you!

CAPTAIN (*gently*): Forgive me, Alice, and come here! Come quickly!

ALICE (*to the* CAPTAIN): He's the biggest rascal and hypocrite I've ever met!—You know, you are a man at any rate!

CAPTAIN: Alice, listen . . . I can't live much longer!

ALICE: Oh-h!

CAPTAIN: The doctor said so!

ALICE: The rest was lies, too?

CAPTAIN: Yes!

ALICE (*beside herself*): What have I done?

CAPTAIN: Everything can be set straight!

ALICE: No! This is hopeless!

CAPTAIN: You can do something about anything if you only cross it out and go on!

ALICE: But the telegram! The telegram!

CAPTAIN: What telegram?

ALICE (*on her knees beside the* CAPTAIN): Are we damned? Was this to happen? I've blown myself, us, high in the air! Why did you have to fool me? And why did that man come here to tempt me? . . . We are lost! Everything would be helped, everything would be forgiven with your highmindedness!

CAPTAIN: What is it that can't be forgiven? What haven't I forgiven you?

ALICE: You're right . . . but nothing can be done about this!

CAPTAIN: I can't guess, though I know your gift for concocting evil . . .

ALICE: If I could only get out of this! If I got out of this, I'd take care of you . . . Edgar, I'd love you!

CAPTAIN: Listen to that! What am I to believe?

ALICE: Can anyone help us? . . . No, no human being can help us!

CAPTAIN: Who, then?

ALICE (*looks straight at the* CAPTAIN): I don't know! . . . Imagine! What will become of our children when our name has been disgraced?

CAPTAIN: Have you disgraced our name?

ALICE: Not I! Not I! . . . And they'll have to leave school! And when they get out in life, they'll be as isolated as we are, and just as evil as we are!—So you didn't meet Judith either?

CAPTAIN: No! But cross it out! (*The telegraph starts. Alice jumps up.*)

ALICE (*shouts*): Now disaster is upon us! (*To the* CAPTAIN) Don't listen to it!

CAPTAIN (*calmly*): I shan't listen to it, dear; just calm yourself!

ALICE (*standing beside the telegraph, raises herself on her toes so she can look out of the window*): Don't listen! Don't listen!

CAPTAIN (*covers his ears with his hands*): I've covered my ears, Lisa, my dear!

ALICE (*kneeling, with her hands extended*): God, help us! . . . The men on duty are coming . . . (*Sobbing*) God in heaven! (*She seems to move her lips in silent prayer. The telegraph continues for a while, and a long strip of paper creeps out. Then silence.* ALICE *gets up, tears off the paper, and reads it silently. Then she looks up, goes over to the* CAPTAIN, *and kisses him on the forehead.*) It is done!—It was nothing! (*Sits down in the other chair and weeps violently into her handkerchief*)

CAPTAIN: What secret was that?

ALICE: Don't ask! It's over now!

CAPTAIN: As you wish, my dear.

ALICE: You wouldn't have said that three days ago. Why?

CAPTAIN: Well! When I collapsed the first time, I passed over a little to the other side of the grave. I've forgotten what I saw, but I still have the general feeling.

ALICE: And that was?

CAPTAIN: Hope—for something better!

ALICE: Something better?

CAPTAIN: Yes. I've never really believed that this life should be the real thing . . . This is death! Or something still worse . . .

ALICE: And we . . .

CAPTAIN: . . . have apparently the assignment of torturing each other . . .

ALICE: Have we tortured each other enough?

CAPTAIN: Yes, I think so! And raised havoc since! (*Looks about*) . . . Shall we straighten up? And clean up?

ALICE (*gets up*): Yes, if that's possible.

CAPTAIN (*looks about*): It'll take more than one day. Yes, indeed!

ALICE: Two, then. Many days!

CAPTAIN: Let's hope so! . . . (*Pause. Then the* CAPTAIN *sits down again.*) So you didn't escape this time! But you didn't get me locked up either! (ALICE *amazed*) Yes, I knew you wanted me in prison, but I'll cross that out! . . . You've done worse things than that, I imagine . . . (ALICE *without an answer*) And I'm not guilty of embezzling!

ALICE: And now I'm to be your nurse?

CAPTAIN: If you want to.

ALICE: What else can I do?

CAPTAIN: I don't know.

ALICE (*sits down, apathetic, in despair*): Why, this is the eternal agony! Isn't there any end?

CAPTAIN: Yes, if we're patient. Perhaps when death comes, life will begin.

ALICE: If that only were so! (*Pause*)

CAPTAIN: You think Kurt was a hypocrite?

ALICE: Of course I do!

CAPTAIN: I don't think so! But everyone who comes near us turns evil and leaves us . . . Kurt was weak, and evil is strong! (*Pause*) Think how dull life is nowadays! In the old days a person struck, now one only shakes a fist!—I'm almost certain we'll celebrate our silver wedding in three months . . . with Kurt giving you away! . . . And the doctor and Gerda present . . . The ordnance officer will make the speech, and the sergeant major lead the cheering. If I know the colonel, he'll invite himself. Yes, go ahead and laugh! Do you remember Adolf's silver wedding? . . . His wife had to wear her wedding ring on her right hand because the groom in a tender moment had chopped off the left ring finger with a knife. (ALICE *holds her handkerchief to her mouth to keep from laughing.*) Are you crying?—No, I think you're laughing! Yes, we weep in part, and laugh in part! Which is more proper . . . don't ask me! . . . I read the other day in a paper that a man who had been divorced seven times, consequently married seven times . . . finally ran away when he was ninety-eight years old to remarry his first wife! That's love! . . . If life is serious or only a joke, I can't tell! When it's a joke, it can be most painful, and when it's serious, it's really pleasantest and calmest . . . But when a person finally tries to be serious, someone comes along to play a joke on one! For example, Kurt! . . . Do you want a silver wedding? (ALICE *silent*) Say yes!—They'll laugh at us, but what difference does that make? We'll laugh, too, or be serious . . . whichever seems best!

ALICE: All right!

CAPTAIN (*seriously*): We'll celebrate our silver wedding, then! . . . (*Gets up*) Cross out, and go on!—So, let's go on!

[CURTAIN]

# Notes on
# 'The Dance of Death I'

1. The laurel wreath has been used as a symbol of achievement in Sweden and still is in Swedish universities. Edgar apparently had thought for more than twenty-five years that Alice's wreaths had been given to her as tokens of outstanding performances on the stage.

2. Tivoli, the internationally famous park created in 1843 by G. Carstensen in Copenhagen, provides a great variety of entertainment, including concerts, ballet and other dance performances, vaudeville, and other theatrical fare as well as open-air and indoor restaurants. *Navarin aux pommes* is a mutton stew with vegetables and apples; Nimb's was apparently a restaurant in Copenhagen.

3. *Alcazar* is a Spanish word for "fortress," and Alice's home used to be a fortress and a prison.

4. A *rentier* is an individual who lives on an income from rented properties and other investments.

5. "The Entrance of the Boyards," a march by the Norwegian composer Johan Halvorsen (1864–1935), is available in various recordings, including one by the Boston Pops Orchestra. The Boyards or Boyars were aristocratic Russians who by right of birth were members of a military-civil force which was theoretically supposed to protect the emperor. Peter I abolished the institution in the early eighteenth century. Halvorsen received much of his training in Stockholm and, among other works, composed music for several dramas.

6. The captain's dance is usually performed as a sort of Cossack dance.

7. See the apocryphal Book of Judith for a fascinating account of the Hebrew heroine who defeated her people's enemies by beheading Holofernes, commander of the invading Assyrians. The name of Edgar's daughter Judith has important symbolic significance in the companion plays.

75

# The Dance of Death II

## Characters

EDGAR
ALICE
KURT
ALLAN, *Kurt's son*
JUDITH, *Edgar's daughter*
THE LIEUTENANT

# ACT I

## SETTING

*An oval living room in white and gold. The back wall has several glass doors, which are standing open so that one can see a garden terrace outside with a balustrade of stone columns and soft blue faience pots with petunias and scarlet geraniums. The terrace is a public walk. At the back can be seen the shore battery with a* SENTRY *on duty; in the distance the open sea.*

*To the left in the living room is a yellow sofa with matching chairs and a table. To the right are a grand piano, a desk, and a portable stove.*

*In the foreground an American easy chair.*

*By the desk a copper floor lamp with an attached shelf.*

*On the walls various older oil paintings.*

*As the curtain goes up,* ALLAN *is sitting by the desk working at his mathematics lesson.* JUDITH *enters from the back. She is wearing a short summer dress; has braids down her back, a hat in one hand, a tennis racket in the other. She stops in the doorway.* ALLAN *gets up, serious and respectful.*

JUDITH (*in a serious but friendly fashion*): Why don't you come and play tennis?

ALLAN (*shy; tries to control his feelings*): I'm very busy . . .

JUDITH: Didn't you see I had placed the bicycle *toward* the oak and not *away* from it?

79

ALLAN: Yes, I did.

JUDITH: Well, what does that mean?

ALLAN: It means . . . you want me to come and play tennis . . . but my duties . . . I have to solve several problems . . . and your father's a pretty strict teacher . . .

JUDITH: Do you like him?

ALLAN: Yes, I do! He's interested in all his pupils . . .

JUDITH: He's interested in everyone and everything—Do you want to come?

ALLAN: You know I do—but I shouldn't!

JUDITH: I'll ask Father for permission.

ALLAN: Don't! Then there'll just be talk!

JUDITH: Don't you think I can manage him? He wants what I want!

ALLAN: I suppose that's why you're so . . . hard!

JUDITH: That's what you should be, too!

ALLAN: I don't belong to the family of wolves!

JUDITH: Then you're a sheep!

ALLAN: Rather that!

JUDITH: Tell me why you don't want to play tennis with me!

ALLAN: Don't you know?

JUDITH: Tell me anyway! . . . The lieutenant . . .

ALLAN: Yes, you don't care a bit about me, but you don't have any fun playing with the lieutenant if I'm not there so you can see me suffer!

JUDITH: Am I that cruel? I didn't know!

ALLAN: You do now!

JUDITH: Then I'll change . . . I don't want to be cruel . . . I don't want to seem bad . . . in your eyes.

ALLAN: You say that just to get me in your power! I'm your slave already, but you're not satisfied with that—the slave has to be tortured and thrown to the lions, too! . . . You already have the lieutenant in your claws . . . What do you want of me? Let me go my way, and you go yours!

JUDITH: Are you trying to get rid of me? (ALLAN *does not answer.*)

All right, I'll go—As distant relatives we'll have to meet now and then, but I shan't bother you!

(ALLAN *sits down at the desk and goes to work on his mathematics again.*)

JUDITH (*instead of going, approaches him, and finally is right next to the desk*): Don't be afraid, I'm going soon . . . I just want to see what your home's like . . . (*Looks about*) White and gold!—A grand piano, a Bechstein![1] Ah-h!—We're still in our old prison tower since Father was retired with a pension . . . the tower in which Mother has been for twenty-five years . . . and we're there out of grace, too! You are rich, you . . .

ALLAN (*calmly*): We are not rich!

JUDITH: That's what you say, you who always have such nice clothes. —As far as that goes anything you put on is becoming to you! . . . Are you listening to me? (*Comes closer to him*)

ALLAN (*submissively*): I'm listening.

JUDITH: How can you, when you sit there counting or whatever it is you're doing?

ALLAN: I don't hear with my eyes!

JUDITH: Your eyes, yes! . . . Have you ever looked at them in a mirror? . . .

ALLAN: Why don't you go?

JUDITH: You despise me! . . .

ALLAN: I'm not thinking about you at all!

JUDITH (*comes still closer*): Archimedes[2] was sitting calculating when the soldier came and cut him down! (*Stirs in his papers with her racket*)

ALLAN: Don't touch my papers!

JUDITH: That's what Archimedes said, too! . . . Don't imagine anything, though! You think I can't live without you . . .

ALLAN: Why can't you leave me alone?

JUDITH: Be polite, and I'll help you in your exams . . .

ALLAN: You?

JUDITH: Yes . . . I know the examiners . . .

ALLAN (*sternly*): So?

JUDITH: Don't you know you ought to have your teachers on your side?

ALLAN: You mean your father and the lieutenant?

JUDITH: And the colonel!

ALLAN: So you mean I'd get out of doing my work if I have your protection?

JUDITH: You're a poor translator . . .

ALLAN: Of a poor original . . .

JUDITH: Aren't you ashamed?

ALLAN: Yes, on your account, and my own!—I'm ashamed for having listened to you! . . . Why don't you go?

JUDITH: Because I know you like my company.—Yes, you can always find your way to my window! You always have some errand to go to town on the same boat I take; you can't go sailing unless I'm along to man the foresail!

ALLAN (*shyly*): A young girl doesn't say things like that!

JUDITH: You mean I'm a mere child?

ALLAN: Sometimes you're a good child, sometimes you're a nasty woman. You seem to have chosen *me* for your sheep.

JUDITH: You are a sheep—that's why I'm going to look after you!

ALLAN (*gets up*): A wolf's a pretty poor shepherd, I suspect! . . . You want to devour me . . . that's the secret, most likely you want to trade your lovely eyes to get my head.

JUDITH: So you have looked at my eyes! I didn't think you had the courage!

ALLAN (*gathers his papers in order to go out to the right.* JUDITH *places herself in the doorway*): Out of my way, or . . .

JUDITH: Or?

ALLAN: If only you were a boy! But you're a girl!

JUDITH: So what?

ALLAN: If you had a shred of pride, you would have gone when I as good as threw you out!

JUDITH: I'll get even with you for that!

ALLAN: I don't doubt it!

JUDITH (*furious, going toward the back*): I'll—get—even—with—
you—for that! (*Exits*)

KURT (*enters from the left*): Where are you going, Allan?

ALLAN: Oh, it's you, Father.

KURT: Who was it that left so suddenly . . . that even the shrubs
trembled?

ALLAN: That was Judith!

KURT: She is a little violent, but she's a fine girl!

ALLAN: When a girl is mean and coarse, they always say she's a fine
girl!

KURT: Don't be so strict, Allan! . . . Don't you like your new relatives?

ALLAN: I like Uncle Edgar . . .

KURT: Yes, he has many good qualities . . . What about your other
teachers? The lieutenant, for example?

ALLAN: I can't understand him! Sometimes he seems to have a grudge
against me.

KURT: Oh no! . . . You think about people too much. Don't think
about them, but do your work right and let the rest do theirs.

ALLAN: I do, but . . . they won't leave me alone! They pull me in
just like the cuttlefish down by the dock . . . they don't bite, but
stir up a whirlpool that pulls me in . . .

KURT (*in a friendly fashion*): You're inclined to take things too
seriously, I think. Don't you like living with me? Is there anything
I've neglected?

ALLAN: I've never had it better, but . . . there's something here that
stifles me!

KURT: Here by the sea? Don't you like the sea?

ALLAN: Yes, the open sea! But along the shore there are weeds,
cuttlefish, jellyfish, sea nettles, or whatever they're called.

KURT: You shouldn't be inside so much. Go out and play tennis!

ALLAN: That's no fun!

KURT: You're angry with Judith, I see.

ALLAN: Judith?

KURT: You ask too much of people—you mustn't; if you do, you'll be
isolated.

ALLAN: I don't ask too much, but . . . but I feel as if I were at the
bottom of a woodpile . . . and had to wait my turn to take part
in life . . . it's as if everything above me were bringing pressure
on me . . .

KURT: Wait until your turn comes! The woodpile will get smaller . . .

ALLAN: Yes, but so very slowly, so very slowly! . . . I'll get moldy
while I'm waiting!

KURT: It isn't fun to be young. Yet older people envy the young!

ALLAN: Do they? Would you trade?

KURT: No, thank you!

ALLAN: Do you know what the worst is? To sit silent when older
people talk nonsense . . . I know I know more about some things
than they do . . . yet I have to keep still! Forgive me, Father, I
don't count you among the old!

KURT: Why not?

ALLAN: Perhaps because we really haven't got acquainted until
lately . . .

KURT: And because . . . you had had a different opinion of me!

ALLAN: Yes!

KURT: I suspect you haven't always had friendly feelings for me all
these years?

ALLAN: No!

KURT: Had you ever seen a picture of me?

ALLAN: Only one, and that wasn't flattering!

KURT: An old picture?

ALLAN: Yes!

KURT: Ten years ago my hair turned gray in one night . . . The
color has come back . . . But let's talk about something else . . .
There comes your aunt. My cousin. What do you think of her?

ALLAN: I'd rather not say.

KURT: Then I won't ask.

ALICE (*enters; is wearing a very light summer walking dress and carrying an umbrella*): Good morning, Kurt! (*Gives a look signifying that* ALLAN *should leave*)

KURT (*to* ALLAN): Would you go, Allan? (ALLAN *exits to the right.*)

ALICE (*sits down on the sofa to the left.* KURT *sits down on a chair next to it.* ALICE *is embarrassed as she says*): He's coming right away so you don't need to be embarrassed.

KURT: Why should I be?

ALICE: With your strict principles . . .

KURT: About myself, yes!

ALICE: Yes! . . . I forgot myself one time when I saw my liberator in you, but you kept your common sense . . . so we have a right to forget what has never been.

KURT: Forget it, then!

ALICE: But . . . I don't think he has forgotten . . .

KURT: You mean the night he had a heart attack . . . and you rejoiced too soon, believing he was dead?

ALICE: Yes! . . . Since then he has recovered, but when he gave up drinking, he learned how to keep still, and now he's terrifying. He's up to something . . . I can't understand what it is . . .

KURT: Alice, your husband is a pleasant fool, who's really very friendly toward me . . .

ALICE: Watch out for his friendliness! I know it all too well!

KURT: There, there.

ALICE: So he's blinded you, too, completely! . . . Don't you see the danger? Don't you see the traps?

KURT: No!

ALICE: Then you're doomed to be ruined!

KURT: Nonsense!

ALICE: Imagine: I can sit here seeing misfortune stealing upon you like a cat . . . I point it out to you, but you can't see it!

KURT: With his clear insight, Allan can't see it either! As far as that goes, he sees only Judith, and that's always proof of good relations.

ALICE: Do you know Judith?

KURT: A very young coquettish girl with braids down her back and skirts that are too short . . .

ALICE: Exactly! But I saw her dressed up the other day in long skirts . . . and then she was a young lady . . . not too young, anyway, when her hair had been put up . . .

KURT: She's a little precocious, I admit.

ALICE: And she's playing with Allan.

KURT: That's all right so long as it is playing.

ALICE: Oh, so it's all right! . . . Edgar will soon be here; he'll sit down in that easy chair—he likes it so much he could steal it!

KURT: I'll give it to him!

ALICE: Let him sit there, and we'll stay here. When he talks—he talks a lot in the morning—when he speaks about innocuous matters, I'll translate for you! . . .

KURT: Aren't you too wise, Alice? Too wise? What should I be afraid of as long as I do my work as quarantine master efficiently and behave properly?

ALICE: You believe in justice and honor and all that sort of thing!

KURT: Yes, experience has taught me that. There was a time when I believed the very opposite . . . I had to pay a lot for that lesson!

ALICE: Now he is coming! . . .

KURT: I've never seen you afraid before!

ALICE: I haven't understood how dangerous he can be!

KURT: Dangerous! . . . You'll frighten me soon!

ALICE: If I only could! . . . There he is!

(CAPTAIN *enters from in back, in civilian dress: a black-buttoned frock coat, uniform cap, a cane with a silver crook. He nods to them and goes over to the easy chair and sits down.*)

ALICE (*aside to* KURT): Let him talk first!

CAPTAIN: What a superb chair you have, Kurt! Absolutely superb!

KURT: You may have it if you wish.

CAPTAIN: That wasn't what I meant . . .

KURT: But I do! How much have you not given me?

CAPTAIN (*volubly*): Nonsense! . . . And when I sit here, I can see

the whole island, all the public walks, all the people on their ve-
randas, all the ships going out to sea and coming into harbor . . .
You've certainly managed to get the best bit of this island, which
isn't the island of the blessed at least. Don't you think so, Alice?
. . . Yes, they call it Little Hell, and Kurt has built a paradise for
himself on it . . . without Eve, of course, for when she came that
finished paradise! Right! Did you know this used to be a royal
hunting lodge?

KURT: Yes, I had heard that.

CAPTAIN: You live royally, and it's a shame to say it, but you have to
thank me for that!

ALICE (*aside to* KURT): Now he wants to steal you!

KURT: I have a lot to thank you for.

CAPTAIN: Nonsense!—Did you get your cases of wine?

KURT: Yes.

CAPTAIN: Are you satisfied with them?

KURT: Very much so. Will you thank your wine merchant for them?

CAPTAIN: His wares are always excellent . . .

ALICE (*aside to* KURT): For higher prices, and you have to pay the
difference . . .

CAPTAIN: What did you say, Alice?

ALICE: I? Nothing!

CAPTAIN: Well! When the position of quarantine master was created, I had thought of applying for it . . . to that end I studied
the whole quarantine system.

ALICE (*aside to* KURT): That's a lie!

CAPTAIN (*boastfully*): The old-fashioned ideas about the disinfecting
system the board approved of, I didn't accept! You see, I was on
the Neptunists'[3] side—we called them that since they support the
water method . . .

KURT: Excuse me! I certainly remember I was the one who advo-
cated water, and you, fire . . . at that time.

CAPTAIN: I? Nonsense!

ALICE (*aloud*): Yes, I remember that, too.

CAPTAIN: You? . . .

KURT: I remember it all the more . . .

CAPTAIN (*interrupting sharply*): Maybe, but that makes no difference! (*Raises his voice*) However . . . we've come to the point that a new set of circumstances (*to* KURT *who wants to interrupt him*) . . . Silence! . . . has come up . . . and the whole system of quarantine is about to take a gigantic step forward.

KURT: Talking about that: do you know who wrote those stupid articles in the journal?

CAPTAIN (*blushes*): I don't know! But why do you call them stupid?

ALICE (*aside to* KURT): Careful! He wrote them!

KURT (*to* ALICE): He? . . . (*To the* CAPTAIN) Less reasonable, should we say?

CAPTAIN: You're no judge of that!

ALICE: Do you intend to quarrel?

KURT: Oh, no!

CAPTAIN: It's hard to keep peace on the island, but we ought to set a good example . . .

KURT: Yes, but can you explain this? When I got here, I was soon on friendly terms with all the authorities, and the judge and I particularly became good friends—as close friends as people can be at our age. Then after a while—right after you got better—one after the other turned cool toward me. Yesterday the judge went out of his way not to meet me. I can't tell you how much that hurt me. (*The* CAPTAIN *is silent. Slight pause*) Have you noticed the antagonism toward me, too?

CAPTAIN: No, quite the opposite.

ALICE (*aside to* KURT): Don't you understand he has stolen your friends?

KURT (*to* CAPTAIN): I've wondered if it's because I refused to sign up for shares.

CAPTAIN: No, no! But why didn't you sign up?

KURT: Because I had already invested my small savings in a soda factory. Also, because a new subscription means the old shares aren't very sound.

CAPTAIN (*absentmindedly*): That's a superb lamp you have! Where did you get it?

KURT: In town, of course.

ALICE (*aside to* KURT): Keep an eye on your lamp!

KURT (*to the* CAPTAIN): Don't think I'm ungrateful or suspicious, Edgar!

CAPTAIN: No, but your wanting to get out of a business you helped start doesn't show any confidence.

KURT: But ordinary common sense tells me to save what's mine in time!

CAPTAIN: Save? Is there any danger? Is anyone trying to rob you?

KURT: Why such hard words?

CAPTAIN: Weren't you satisfied when I helped you invest your capital at six per cent?

KURT: Yes, I was even grateful!

CAPTAIN: You aren't grateful—it isn't in your nature, but you can't be blamed for that!

ALICE (*aside to* KURT): Listen to him!

KURT: My nature's undoubtedly very imperfect, and my struggle against it is relatively a failure, but I admit my obligations . . .

CAPTAIN: Show it, then! (*Extends his hand and picks up a newspaper*) What's this? . . . An announcement! (*Reading*) The medical councilor is dead!

ALICE (*aside to* KURT): He's already speculating with the corpse.

CAPTAIN (*as if to himself*): This will mean certain . . . changes . . .

KURT: In what way?

CAPTAIN (*gets up*): We'll get to see, I suspect.

ALICE (*to* CAPTAIN): Where are you going?

CAPTAIN: I think I'll have to go into town! . . . (*Catches sight of a letter on the desk, picks it up as if absentmindedly, reads the return address, and puts it back*) Excuse me! I'm absentminded!

KURT: Doesn't matter.

CAPTAIN: There's Allan's compass box. Where is he?

KURT: He's out playing with the girls.

CAPTAIN: That big boy? I don't like that! And Judith may not run about like that! . . . Keep an eye on your young man, and I'll see to my young lady! (*Goes past the piano, strikes a few chords*) Superb tone in that instrument! A Steinbeck, eh?

KURT: Bechstein!

CAPTAIN: Yes, you do have it good! Thanks to me who got you your position here!

ALICE (*aside to* KURT): That's a lie—he tried to keep you from getting it!

CAPTAIN: So long. I'll take the next boat. (*As he goes, he scrutinizes the paintings on the walls.*)

ALICE: Well-l?

KURT: Well-l?

ALICE: I still don't understand what he's planning. But—tell me one thing. That envelope he looked at . . . From whom is that letter?

KURT: That was my only secret!

ALICE: And he has already found it out! You see, he can do magic, as I've told you before! . . . Is anything printed on the envelope?

KURT: Yes, "League of Voters."

ALICE: Then he has guessed your secret. You want to become a member of parliament, I take it. Now, you'll see, he'll become one instead of you!

KURT: Has he ever thought of it?

ALICE: No, but he's thinking about it now. I could tell by his face when he was reading the return address.

KURT: So that's why he's going into town?

ALICE: No, he decided that when he saw the death announcement.

KURT: What does he hope to gain by the death of the medical councilor?

ALICE: Who knows? . . . Perhaps he was an enemy who stood in his way.

KURT: If he's as terrible as you say, I really have cause to fear him!

ALICE: Didn't you hear how he wanted to capture you, bind your hands by reminding you of debts of gratitude that don't exist? For example: he never got you your position; he tried to keep you from getting it! He steals people—he's an insect, a termite who'll eat you up from within so that one day you'll find yourself hollow as a rotten evergreen . . . He hates you, though he's bound to you by his memories of your friendship in the old days . . .

KURT: How sharp you get when you hate!

ALICE: And stupid when one loves! Blind and stupid!

KURT: Oh, no! Don't say that!

ALICE: Do you know what a vampire is? . . . They say it's the soul of a dead man that seeks a human body to live in as a parasite. Edgar is dead, has been ever since he collapsed that time. Why, he doesn't have any interests of his own, no personality, no initiative. But if he can only take hold of a human being, he attaches himself, forces his tentacle roots into him, and begins to grow and bloom. Now he has attached himself to you!

KURT: If he gets too close, I'll shake him off!

ALICE: Try shaking off a burr! . . . Do you know why he doesn't want Judith and Allan to play together?

KURT: I suppose he's afraid of their feelings.

ALICE: Not in the least! . . . He wants to marry off Judith to . . . the colonel!

KURT (disturbed): That old widower?

ALICE: Yes!

KURT: That's horrible! . . . What about Judith?

ALICE: If she could get the general, who's eighty years old, she'd take him to humiliate the colonel, who's sixty. Humiliating others is her goal in life, you see. Trampling and humiliating other people—those are the keys to that family!

KURT: Is Judith like that? That beautiful, proud, splendid girl!

ALICE: Yes! I know her! . . . May I sit here and write a letter?

KURT (straightens up on the desk): Yes, go ahead.

ALICE (*takes off her gloves and sits down at the desk*): Now I'll try the art of war. I failed once when I tried to slay my dragon. But I've learned the technique since then!

KURT: Do you know you should load before you shoot?

ALICE: Yes, with cartridges! (KURT *exits at the right.* ALICE *thinks and then writes.*)

(ALLAN *rushes in without noticing* ALICE *and throws himself headlong on the sofa, sobbing into a lace handkerchief.*)

ALICE (*first observes him for a moment, then gets up and goes over to him. With a gentle voice*): Allan! (ALLAN *sits up, embarrassed, and hides the handkerchief behind his back.* ALICE *speaks gently, in womanly fashion, witih genuine sympathy*) You mustn't be afraid of me, Allan; I'm not dangerous to you . . . What's wrong? Are you sick?

ALLAN: Yes!

ALICE: In what way?

ALLAN: I don't know!

ALICE: Do you have a headache?

ALLAN: No-o!

ALICE: Is something wrong with your heart? Pangs?

ALLAN: Ye-s!

ALICE: Pangs as if your heart would break!

ALLAN: How did you know?

ALICE: And you wish you were dying, that you were dead, and everything looks hopelessly dark. And you can think of only one thing, of only one person . . . but if two persons were thinking about the same one, it would be heavy for the one . . . (ALLAN *forgets himself and looks at the handkerchief.*) That's the sickness no one can cure . . . one doesn't want to eat . . . or drink . . . one wants only to cry, and one does cry bitterly . . . preferably out in the forest where no one can see one . . . for people laugh at that sickness . . . Cruel people! . . . What do you want of her? Nothing! You don't want to kiss her mouth, for you think you'd die then. You feel as if death were coming when you think

of her! And it is death, child, the death that brings life! But you
don't understand that yet!

There's a fragrance of violets! Hers! (*Takes the handkerchief
gently from* ALLAN) It is she! She's everywhere! Only she! (*Sighs.*
ALLAN *sees no other way out but to conceal his face in* ALICE's
*arms.*) Poor boy! Poor boy! It does hurt! It does hurt! (*She dries
his tears with the handkerchief.*) There, there! Go ahead, weep
. . . like that! It will help! . . . But now, get up, Allan, and be a
man! Otherwise, she won't look at you! That cruel girl who isn't
cruel!

Has she tortured you?—Through the lieutenant? Listen, my
boy! Become the lieutenant's friend, so you can talk about her
together! That generally helps . . . a little!

ALLAN: I don't want to look at the lieutenant!

ALICE: My boy, it won't be long before the lieutenant looks you up
so he can talk with you about her! For . . . (ALLAN *looks up with
a gleam of hope.*) Well, shall I say it? (ALLAN *inclines his head.*)
He's just as unhappy as you!

ALLAN (*happy*): No?

ALICE: Yes, that's certain, and he'll need someone to confide in when
Judith hurts him! That seems to delight you!

ALLAN: Doesn't she want the lieutenant?

ALICE: She doesn't want you either—she wants the colonel! (ALLAN
*becomes sad again.*) Raining again?—Well, you mayn't have the
handkerchief, for Judith's careful about her belongings and wants
her dozen complete! (ALLAN *looks disappointed.*) Yes, Allan, that's
what Judith is like! . . . Sit down while I write another letter,
then you can run an errand for me! (*Goes to the desk, sits down,
and writes*)

LIEUTENANT (*enters from the back; he looks depressed but not ridic-
ulous. Does not notice* ALICE *but walks directly up to* ALLAN):
Private! (ALLAN *gets up; stands at attention*) Please sit down!
   (ALICE *observes them.*)
   (LIEUTENANT *sits down next to* ALLAN. *Takes out a handkerchief*

*exactly like the one* ALLAN *had. Wipes his forehead.* ALLAN *looks at the handkerchief enviously. The* LIEUTENANT *looks at* ALLAN *sadly.* ALICE *coughs. The* LIEUTENANT *jumps up and comes to attention.*)

ALICE: Do sit down!

LIEUTENANT: I beg your pardon, ma'am!

ALICE: That's all right! . . . Please sit down and keep the private company. He feels a little lonely here on the island. (*Writes*)

LIEUTENANT (*talks to* ALLAN *softly, with embarrassment*): It's terribly hot!

ALLAN: Yes!

LIEUTENANT: Have you finished the sixth book yet?

ALLAN: I'm just on the last proposition.

LIEUTENANT: That is a hard one. (*Silence*) Have you . . . (*searching for words*) played tennis today?

ALLAN: No, it was too hot in the sun.

LIEUTENANT (*in anguish but without becoming ridiculous*): Yes, it's terribly hot today!

ALLAN (*whispers*): Yes, it's very warm! (*Silence*)

LIEUTENANT: Have you . . . been out sailing today?

ALLAN: No, I couldn't get anyone to man the foresail.

LIEUTENANT: Would you . . . let me take care of the foresail?

ALLAN (*respectfully as before*): That would be too great an honor for me, sir!

LIEUTENANT: Not at all, not at all . . . Do you think . . . the wind will be right today, about noon . . . that's the only time I'm free.

ALLAN (*slyly*): It will be dying down then . . . and . . . Miss Judith has a lesson then . . .

LIEUTENANT (*distressed*): Oh, does she? Hm!—Do you think that . . .

ALICE: Would either of you two young men deliver a letter for me? (*The* BOYS *look suspiciously at each other.*) . . . to Miss Judith? (ALLAN *and the* LIEUTENANT *jump up, go up to* ALICE *with a certain dignity to conceal their feelings.*)

ALICE: Both of you! Then it certainly will be delivered! (*Gives the* LIEUTENANT *the letter*) . . . Lieutenant, may I have that handkerchief? My daughter's very careful about her laundry! She's a little petty by nature . . . Give me the handkerchief! . . . I don't want to laugh at you, but you mustn't make yourselves ridiculous unnecessarily. And the colonel wouldn't like to be Othello! (*Takes the handkerchief*) Now go, young men, and try to conceal your feelings as well as you can! (*The* LIEUTENANT *bows and goes, followed immediately by* ALLAN. *Just as he is about to exit,* ALICE *calls.*) Allan!

ALLAN (*stops, extremely unwillingly, in the doorway*): Yes, Aunt Alice?

ALICE: Stay here if you don't want to hurt yourself more than you can bear!

ALLAN: But he's going!

ALICE: Let him hurt himself! Take care of yourself!

ALLAN: I don't want to!

ALICE: Then you'll cry afterward! And I'll have the trouble of comforting you!

ALLAN: I want to go!

ALICE: Go ahead! But when you come back I'll have the right to laugh at you!

(ALLAN *runs.* ALICE *resumes her writing.*)

KURT (*in*): Alice, I've just got an anonymous letter that upsets me very much.

ALICE: Have you noticed that since he put away his uniform Edgar's a different person? I never thought a coat could make that much difference.

KURT: You didn't answer my question!

ALICE: That wasn't a question! It was a bit of information! What are you afraid of?

KURT: Everything!

ALICE: He went to town. Every one of his trips to town always has terrible consequences.

KURT: But I can't do anything! I don't know just where the attack will start!

ALICE (*seals her letter*): I wonder if I've guessed!

KURT: Will you help me?

ALICE: Yes! . . . as far as my interests permit! Mine . . . that's to say, my children's!

KURT: I can appreciate that . . . Can you hear how silent everything is, outside, on the sea, everywhere?

ALICE: I hear voices behind the silence . . . murmurs, screams.

KURT: Sh-h. I hear something, too . . . No, it was only the gulls!

ALICE: I hear something else! . . . Now I'll go to the post office with this letter!

[CURTAIN]


# ACT II

(*The same setting.* ALLAN *is sitting by the desk studying;* JUDITH *is standing in the doorway; she is wearing a tennis hat and has bicycle handlebars in her hand.*

JUDITH: May I borrow your key?

ALLAN (*without looking up*): No, you mayn't!

JUDITH: You're impolite the minute I run after you!

ALLAN (*not sarcastically*): I'm not anything at all . . . All I ask is to be left in peace!

JUDITH (*rushes forward*): Allan!

ALLAN: Yes, what is it?

JUDITH: Don't be angry with me!

ALLAN: I'm not!

JUDITH: Shake hands on that.

ALLAN: I won't, but I am not angry with you . . . What do you want of me, really?

JUDITH: You're stupid!

ALLAN: I suppose I am!

JUDITH: You think I'm only mean!

ALLAN: No . . . I know you can be kind, too! You can be kind!

JUDITH: Well, it's not my fault . . . that . . . you and the lieutenant are always crying. Why do you? (ALLAN *embarrassed*) Tell me . . . I never cry. And why are you such good friends? . . . What do you talk about on your walks? (ALLAN *without an answer*) Allan! You'll soon see who I am, and that I can do something for people I like! . . . And I'll give you a bit of advice . . . though I don't want to gossip! . . . Be prepared!

ALLAN: For what?

JUDITH: For unpleasantness!

ALLAN: From what direction?

JUDITH: From the direction you'd least expect it!

ALLAN: I'm pretty used to trouble, and I haven't had much fun in life . . . What's up now?

JUDITH (*thoughtful*): You poor boy! . . . Give me your hand! (*He takes her hand.*) Look at me! . . . Don't you dare to? (ALLAN *hurries out to the left to conceal his feelings.*)

LIEUTENANT (*enters from in back*): Excuse me! I thought the private . . .

JUDITH: Lieutenant, will you be my friend and confidant . . .

LIEUTENANT: I'd be honored . . .

JUDITH: Yes! . . . Just a word! . . . Don't desert Allan when misfortune strikes him!

LIEUTENANT: What misfortune?

JUDITH: You'll soon see! Probably today! . . . Do you like Allan?

LIEUTENANT: That young man is my best pupil, and I respect him personally for his strength of character . . . There are times when a person *needs* (*emphatically*) the strength to bear, to put up with, to suffer, in a word.

JUDITH: That was more than one word! . . . But you do like Allan?

LIEUTENANT: Yes!

JUDITH: Find him and keep him company . . .

LIEUTENANT: That's why I'm here . . . *that* and nothing else! I didn't have any other reason for coming!

JUDITH: I hadn't any suspicion of—what you mean! . . . Allan went that way. (*Points to the left*)

LIEUTENANT (*goes slowly to the left*): Yes . . . I'll do that.

JUDITH: That's really kind of you. (*He exits.*)

ALICE (*enters from in back*): What are you doing here?

JUDITH: I was going to borrow a key.

ALICE: Will you listen to me for a minute?

JUDITH: Certainly. (ALICE *sits down on the sofa.* JUDITH *remains standing.*) But say it quickly. I don't like long lectures.

ALICE: Lectures? . . . Well, then: put up your hair and put on a longer dress.

JUDITH: Why?

ALICE: Because you're no longer a child! And you're too young to pretend you're younger!

JUDITH: What does all that mean?

ALICE: That you're old enough to get married! And that the way you dress is scandalous!

JUDITH: I'll change, then!

ALICE: You do understand?

JUDITH: Oh, yes!

ALICE: And we're agreed?

JUDITH: Absolutely!

ALICE: On all points!

JUDITH: Even the touchiest!

ALICE: At the same time will you stop playing—with Allan?

JUDITH: This is serious, then?

ALICE: Yes!

JUDITH: Then we'll begin right now. (*She puts away the handlebar, lets down her cycling skirt, and puts up her braids, takes a hairpin out of her mother's hair and fastens her braids.*)

ALICE: It isn't proper to do that sort of thing here!

JUDITH: Will I do? . . . Then I'm ready! Let him come who dares!

ALICE: You look at least decent! . . . And leave Allan in peace!

JUDITH: What do you mean by that?

ALICE: Don't you see he's suffering . . .

JUDITH: Yes, I think I've noticed that, but I don't know why. I'm not suffering!

ALICE: That's your strength! But there will come a day . . . when you will suffer! . . . Now go home, and don't forget to wear a decently long dress!

JUDITH: Am I to walk differently, too?

ALICE: Try to!

JUDITH (*tries to walk like a lady*): Oh, it's as if I had chains about my feet; I'm a prisoner and can't run any more!

ALICE: Yes, child, the journey's beginning, the slow journey toward the unknown that one knows all the same but has to pretend to ignore! . . . Shorter steps and much, much slower ones! The child's shoes are gone, and you have heels, Judith! . . . You don't remember when you put away your baby shoes and put on girl's shoes, but I do!

JUDITH: I'll never be able to bear this!

ALICE: But you have to all the same! Have to!

JUDITH (*comes up to her mother, kisses her lightly on the cheek, and walks offstage with the dignity of a lady, but forgets the handlebar*): 'Bye, then!

KURT (*enters from the right*): So you're already here?

ALICE: Yes!

KURT: Has he returned?

ALICE: Yes!

KURT: How did he come?

ALICE: As if on parade!—So he's seen the colonel. Two orders on his chest!

KURT: Two! . . . I knew he was going to get the Order of the Sword [4] when he retired. What was the other one?

ALICE: I don't know, but it had a white cross within a red one.

KURT: A Portuguese order, [5] then . . . Let me think . . . Didn't his articles in the journal deal with quarantine stations in Portuguese harbors?

ALICE: Yes. So far as I can remember.

KURT: And he has never been in Portugal?

ALICE: Never.

KURT: But I've been there!

ALICE: Why did you tell him so much? He's a good listener and has an exceptional memory!

KURT: Don't you think it's because of Judith he got that honor?

ALICE: Well, really! . . . There are limits . . . (*gets up*) and you've gone beyond them!

KURT: Are we going to be enemies?

ALICE: That depends on you! Don't touch my interests!

KURT: When they conflict with mine, I have to touch them! if only with a careful hand . . . There *he* comes!

ALICE: Now it's going to happen!

KURT: What's—going to happen?

ALICE: We'll see.

KURT: May it be an open attack, for this state of siege makes me nervous. I haven't one friend on the island any more.

ALICE: Just wait! . . . Sit down here . . . he'll sit down in the easy chair, I think . . . then I can prompt you!

CAPTAIN (*enters from in back; dressed in his dress uniform and wearing the Order of the Sword and the Portuguese Order of Christ*): Good day!—So this is the meeting place!

ALICE: You are tired. Sit down. (*Unexpectedly, the* CAPTAIN *sits down at her left on the sofa.*) Make yourself comfortable!

CAPTAIN: This is a really nice place!—You're too kind! (*The latter to* ALICE)

ALICE (*aside to* KURT): Careful!—he's suspicious of us!

CAPTAIN (*furiously*): What's that you said?

ALICE (*aside to* KURT): He's been drinking, I think!

CAPTAIN (*coarsely*): Nah, he hasn't! (*Silence*) Well-l? . . . What have you two been doing?

ALICE: What about you?

CAPTAIN: Are you looking at my orders?

ALICE: No-o!

CAPTAIN: I imagine not—you're envious.—Otherwise, it's proper to congratulate a man on his receiving honors.

ALICE: Congratulations!

CAPTAIN: We get some like these instead of the laurel wreaths actresses get.

ALICE: You mean the wreaths from the wall at home in the tower . . .

CAPTAIN: That you got from your brother . . .

ALICE: Oh, keep still!

CAPTAIN: And that I've had to bow down before for twenty-five years! . . . and that I've needed twenty-five years to expose!

ALICE: You've seen my brother?

CAPTAIN: Yes! (ALICE *crushed. Silence*) Well, Kurt! You're not saying anything!

KURT: I'm waiting.

CAPTAIN: Listen to this! You know the latest news, I suppose!

KURT: No.

CAPTAIN: Well, it isn't any pleasure for me to have to tell you . . .

KURT: Just tell me!

CAPTAIN: The soda factory has failed!

KURT: That's really bad news!—How are you hit?

CAPTAIN: Not badly—I sold out in time!

KURT: You did the right thing!

CAPTAIN: But how is this going to hit you?

KURT: Badly!

CAPTAIN: It's your own fault! You should have sold in time or signed up for new shares.

KURT: Then I would have lost them, too!

CAPTAIN: Oh, no! Then the company could have been saved.

KURT: Not the company, but the directors! I looked at the new issue as a collection for the benefit of the directors.

CAPTAIN: Can your way of looking at it save you? That's the question.

KURT: No, I'll lose everything.

CAPTAIN: Everything?

KURT: Even the house and the furniture.

CAPTAIN: Why, that's terrible!

KURT: Worse has happened to me. (*Silence*)

CAPTAIN: That's what happens when amateurs start dabbling.

KURT: You amaze me, for you know if I hadn't invested I'd have been ostracized . . . Livelihood for the people along the coast, the laborers at sea, limitless capital, limitless as the ocean . . . philanthropy and national gain . . . That's how you people wrote and had it put into print! . . . And now you call it dabbling!

CAPTAIN (*unaffected by this*): What will you do now?

KURT: I suppose I'll have to sell everything.

CAPTAIN: That's the right thing to do!

KURT: What do you mean?

CAPTAIN: What I said! . . . There (*slowly*) will be certain changes here, you see . . .

KURT: Here on the island?

CAPTAIN: Yes! . . . For example . . . your apartment will be exchanged for a simpler one.

KURT: Really!

CAPTAIN: Yes, the quarantine station is to be built on the other side of the island, by the water!

KURT: My original idea!

CAPTAIN: Was it? . . . I don't know your ideas about that matter! . . . Still—it would be a good thing to get rid of your furniture now: then there won't be such an open—scandal!

KURT: *What?*

CAPTAIN: Scandal! (*Gets irritated*) For it is a scandal to come to a new place and get into a mess that's most unpleasant for your relatives . . . most of all for your relatives!

KURT: It'll be most unpleasant for me, I suspect.

CAPTAIN: I'll tell you one thing, Kurt; if you hadn't had me on your side in this matter, you'd have lost your position!

KURT: That, too!

CAPTAIN: It's a little hard for you to be proper! . . . There have been complaints about your work!

KURT: Justified complaints?

CAPTAIN: Ta! for you are—along with your otherwise admirable qualities—a careless person!—Don't interrupt me!—You are a very careless person!

KURT: That's strange!

CAPTAIN: However! The change I mentioned will be made rather soon. And I'd advise you to have an auction or try to sell privately.

KURT: Privately? Where would I find a buyer here?

CAPTAIN: You certainly don't mean I should settle down with your furniture? That would be a nice story!—(*abruptly*) hm! especially when a person thinks about what happened—that time . . .

KURT: What's that?—Do you mean what did *not* happen?

CAPTAIN (*changing his manner*): Alice is very quiet. What's wrong, old girl? You're not talking as usual.

ALICE: I'm thinking.

CAPTAIN: Good heavens! Are *you* thinking? But think quickly, correctly, and sharply if it's going to help!—Think away! One, two, three!—(*Laughs*) Can't you? . . . Well, then I'll . . . Where's Judith?

ALICE: Somewhere about.

CAPTAIN: Where's Allan? (ALICE *is silent.*) Where's the lieutenant?

(ALICE *remains silent.*) Listen, Kurt!—What are you going to do with Allan now?

KURT: Do with him?

CAPTAIN: Yes, you certainly can't afford to keep him in the artillery now.

KURT: Probably not.

CAPTAIN: You'll have to try to get him into some inexpensive infantry regiment up in Norrland or some other place.

KURT: In Norrland?

CAPTAIN: Yes. Or maybe you should get him into some practical work.—If I were you, I'd put him into an office. . . . Why not? (KURT *silent*) In these enlightened times. Ta! . . . Alice is so *unusually* quiet! . . . Yes, my children, this is the seesaw of life: now you're up and look bravely about, then you're way down, and then you get up again! And so on and on! Well, that's that! (*To* ALICE) Did you say something?

(ALICE *shakes her head*)

CAPTAIN: We can expect company in a few days.

ALICE: Are you saying that to me?

CAPTAIN: We can expect company in a few days. Important company!

ALICE: Who?

CAPTAIN: See? You *are* interested! . . . So you can sit back and guess who's coming, and, while you're guessing, you might read this letter once more! (*Gives her an opened letter*)

ALICE: My letter? Opened? Back from the post office?

CAPTAIN (*gets up*): Yes, as head of the family I have the duty of protecting the most sacred interests of the family and will ruthlessly cut off every attempt to dissolve the family ties by criminal correspondence! Ta!

(ALICE *winces.*)

CAPTAIN: I am not dead, you see, but don't get angry just now when I intend to lift all of us out of an undeserved setback—undeserved at least as far as I am concerned!

ALICE: Judith! Judith!

CAPTAIN: And Holofernes! [6]—Is that what I'm supposed to be? Bah!
  (*Exits at the back*)

KURT: Who is that man?

ALICE: I certainly don't know!

KURT: We're defeated!

ALICE: Yes! . . . No doubt of it!

KURT: He has gnawed me out, but so cleverly that I can't accuse
  him of anything.

ALICE: That? On the contrary, you owe him a debt of gratitude.

KURT: Does he know what he's doing?

ALICE: No, I don't think so. He follows his nature and his instincts,
  and now he seems to be in favor wherever fortune and misfortune
  are meted out!

KURT: I suppose it's the colonel who's coming.

ALICE: Most likely. That's why Allan must go.

KURT: You think that's as it should be?

ALICE: Yes!

KURT: Then our ways part!

ALICE (*ready to go*): A little . . . But they'll join again!

KURT: Presumably?

ALICE: Do you know where?

KURT: Here!

ALICE: You know that?

KURT: That's plain. He'll take the house and buy the furniture.

ALICE: I think so, too. But don't desert me!

KURT: Not for so little!

ALICE: Good-bye! (*Going*)

KURT: Good-bye!

[CURTAIN]

# ACT III

*The same setting, but it is cloudy, and it is raining outside.* ALICE *and* KURT *enter from in back carrying umbrellas and raincoats.*

ALICE: So I managed to get you to come! . . . I can't be so cruel, Kurt, as to bid you be welcome in your own home . . .

KURT: Why not? I've lived through three forced sales . . . more than that . . . It doesn't matter to me!

ALICE: Did he summon you?

KURT: Yes, it was a formal summons, but I don't understand on what basis.

ALICE: He isn't your superior, is he?

KURT: No, but he's established himself as the king on this island! And if anyone opposes him, he mentions the colonel's name, and then he gets his way in everything!—Is the colonel coming today?

ALICE: They're expecting him—but I'm not sure!—Do sit down!

KURT (*sits down*): Nothing has been changed here.

ALICE: Don't think about it!—Don't hurt yourself by thinking about it!

KURT: Hurt? I only think it's a little strange. As strange as that man!—You know when I met him as a young man, I tried to get away from him . . . But he wouldn't let me. He flattered me, offered to do me favors, and bound me . . . I tried to escape from him time and again . . . but I couldn't . . . Now I'm his slave!

ALICE: Yes, but why? He's indebted to you, but you're the debtor!

KURT: Since I lost all my money, he has offered to help Allan until he has passed his examinations . . .

ALICE: That will prove expensive—for you! Are you still a candidate for parliament?

KURT: Yes, as far as I can see, there's nothing to hinder that. (*Silence*)

ALICE: Is Allan really leaving today?

KURT: Yes, if I can't prevent it.

ALICE: That was a short pleasure.

KURT: Short, like everything else except life itself, which is terribly long!

ALICE: Yes, it is! . . . Won't you come into the sitting room? If you don't mind, I do mind . . . this setting.

KURT: If you wish.

ALICE: I'm ashamed, so ashamed I'd like to die . . . but I can't do anything about it.

KURT: Let's go in, then. As you wish.

ALICE: Besides, someone's coming! (*They exit to the left.*)

(*The* CAPTAIN *and* ALLAN *enter from in back; both are in military uniforms and capes.*)

CAPTAIN: Sit down here, my boy, so I can talk with you! (*Sits down in the easy chair;* ALLAN *sits down on the chair to the* CAPTAIN'S *left.*) It's raining today; otherwise, I'd just sit here and look at the sea. (*Silence*) Well-l?—You don't want to go, do you?

ALLAN: I don't like to leave Father.

CAPTAIN: Yes, your father! He is a very unfortunate man! (*Silence*) And parents rarely know what's best for their children. That's to say—there are exceptions. Hm. Listen, Allan. Do you have any contact with your mother?

ALLAN: Yes, she writes occasionally.

CAPTAIN: Do you know she's your guardian?

ALLAN: Yes-s.

CAPTAIN: Listen, Allan! You know that your mother has given me power of attorney to act in her stead.

ALLAN: I didn't know that!

CAPTAIN: You know it now in any case. And on that basis the discussion of your career is finished . . . So you'll go to Norrland!

ALLAN: But I don't have the means.

CAPTAIN: I've procured them.

ALLAN: In that case I can only say, "Thank you, sir"!

CAPTAIN: You *are* grateful.—It isn't everyone who is! Hm . . . (*Raises his voice*) The colonel . . . Do you know the colonel?

ALLAN (*embarrassed*): No, I don't.

CAPTAIN: The colonel (*emphasizing*) is my special friend—(*speeds up*) as you probably know. Hm. The colonel has interested himself in my family, my wife's family included. Through his efforts the colonel has succeeded in procuring the means which were required for the completion of your course.—Now you know your debt and your father's debt—to the colonel. . . . Have I spoken plainly enough? (ALLAN *bows.*) So go and pack your things. The money will be given you at the dock. And so, good-bye, my boy! (*Extends one finger*) Good-bye! (*The* CAPTAIN *gets up and exits at the right.*)

(ALLAN, *alone, stands bewildered, looking about the room.*)

JUDITH (*enters from in back wearing a hood and carrying an umbrella. She is wearing a long attractive dress, and her hair is pinned up*): Is that you, Allan?

ALLAN (*turns, observes* JUDITH *carefully*): Is that you, Judith?

JUDITH: Don't you recognize me? But where have you been so long? . . . What are you looking at?—My long dress . . . and my hair . . . You haven't seen me like this before! . . .

ALLAN: No!

JUDITH: Do I look grown-up?

(ALLAN *turns away from her.*)

JUDITH (*seriously*): What are you doing here?

ALLAN: I've just said good-bye!

JUDITH: What? Are you—leaving?

ALLAN: I'm being transferred to Norrland.

JUDITH (*crushed*): To Norrland?—When are you leaving?

ALLAN: Today!

JUDITH: Whose idea was that?

ALLAN: Your father's!

JUDITH: I can believe it! (*Takes a few steps; stamps her foot*) I wish you had stayed until tomorrow!

ALLAN: So I could meet the colonel!

JUDITH: What do you know about the colonel? . . . Do you have to go?

ALLAN: I haven't any choice. Besides, I want to go . . . now. (*Silence*)

JUDITH: Why?

ALLAN: I want to get away from here! Away, out into the world!

JUDITH: It's too depressing here. I understand you, Allan; it's unbearable here!—They speculate—in soda and in people! (*Silence. Then she says with genuine emotion*) Allan . . . as you know, I've been fortunate enough to be unable to suffer—but—I'm beginning to!

ALLAN: You?

JUDITH: Yes!—I'm beginning to now! (*She presses both her hands to her heart.*) Now I'm really suffering!

ALLAN: What's wrong?

JUDITH: I don't know!—I'm choking! I think I'm dying!

ALLAN: Judith?

JUDITH (*screams*): So that's how it feels! Is that how it is . . . poor boys!

ALLAN: I'd smile if I were as cruel as you!

JUDITH: I'm not cruel, but I didn't know any better . . . you mustn't leave!

ALLAN: I have to!

JUDITH: Leave, then! . . . But give me something to remember!

ALLAN: What do I have to give you?

JUDITH (*with profound seriousness and anguish*): You! . . . No, I'll never live through this! (*Screams with her hands to her heart*) I'm suffering agony . . . What have you done to me? . . . I don't want to live any more!—Allan, don't go, not alone! We'll leave together; we'll take the little sloop, the little white sloop—and we'll sail out but with firm sails—the wind's really blowing . . . and we'll go down—far, far out in the sea where there aren't any weeds or any jellyfish—shall we?—But we should have washed the sails yesterday—they should be pure white [7]—I want to see white in that hour—and then you'll swim with me on your arm until you tire . . . and then we'll go down . . . (*Turns*) That would really be something, a lot better than going about here feeling sad and smuggling letters that Father would open and make fun of! Allan! (*She takes him by the arms and shakes him.*) Are you listening?

ALLAN (*who has watched her with glowing eyes*): Judith! Judith! Why weren't you like this before?

JUDITH: I didn't know! How could I say what I didn't know?

ALLAN: And now I have to leave you! . . . But most likely that's the best and only thing to do! . . . I can't compete with a man . . . who . . .

JUDITH: Don't talk about the colonel!

ALLAN: Isn't it true?

JUDITH: It is true—and it isn't true!

ALLAN: Can it become absolutely false?

JUDITH: Yes, it's going to become false! In an hour!

ALLAN: Will you keep your word? I can wait, I can be patient, I can work! . . . Judith!

JUDITH: Don't go yet!—How long do I have to wait?

ALLAN: A year.

JUDITH (*jubilant*): A year! I'd wait a thousand years, and if you didn't come then, I'd turn the vault of heaven around so the sun would rise in the west . . . Sh-h, someone's coming!—You have to go, Allan . . . Sh-h!—Take me in your arms! (*They embrace.*) But you mayn't kiss me! (*Turns her head away*)—There, go now!—Go!

ALLAN (*goes to the back and puts on his cape. Then they rush into each other's arms again so that* JUDITH *disappears under the cape. They kiss quickly.* ALLAN *rushes out.* JUDITH *throws herself headlong on the sofa and sobs.* ALLAN *re-enters and falls to his knees beside the sofa.*): No, I can't go! I can't leave you . . . now!

JUDITH (*raises herself*): If you only knew how beautiful you are now! If you only could see yourself!

ALLAN: Hush—a man can't be beautiful! But you, Judith! You—you —when you're kind, you're another Judith . . . you're my Judith! . . . But if you fail me now, I'll die!

JUDITH: I think I'll die anyway! . . . If I only could die now when I'm happy! . . .

ALLAN: Someone's coming!

JUDITH: Let them come! I'm not afraid of anything in the whole world now! But I wish you'd take me under your cape (*she pretends to hide herself under his cape*) and fly away with me to Norrland. What are we going to do up there? Go into a rifle regiment . . . be one of those with a plume on your hat . . . that's nice and would become you very much. (*Plays with his hair*)

    (ALLAN *kisses the tips of her fingers, one after the other; then he kisses her shoe.*)

JUDITH: What are you doing? Crazy! Your mouth will be black! (*Gets up violently*) . . . And then I can't kiss you when you go! . . . Come; I'll go with you!

ALLAN: No, then I'll be arrested!

JUDITH: I'll go to prison with you!

ALLAN: They won't let you! . . . Now we must part!

JUDITH: I'll swim after the steamer . . . and you'll jump in and save me . . . and they'll write it up in the newspaper, and then we can get engaged! Shall we do it that way?

ALLAN: Can *you* still joke?

JUDITH: There'll be time enough for weeping! . . . Say good-bye now! (*They rush into each other's arms; then* ALLAN *exits through the door at the back, which remains open. They embrace outside in the rain.*)

ALLAN: It's raining on you, Judith!

JUDITH: I don't care! (*They tear themselves apart.* ALLAN *goes.* JUDITH *remains standing in the rain and the wind, which dis-*

*arranges her hair and clothes while she waves her handkerchief.* JUDITH *then rushes in, throws herself on the sofa with her face in her hands.*)

ALICE (*enters; goes up to* JUDITH): What's this? . . . Are you sick? —Get up, so I can look at you!

(JUDITH *gets up.*)

ALICE (*observes her carefully*): You aren't sick! . . . But I won't comfort *you!* (*Exits to the right*)

(LIEUTENANT *appears in the doorway at the back.*)

JUDITH (*gets up; puts on her hooded cape*): Would you go with me to the telegraph station, Lieutenant?

LIEUTENANT: I'd like to . . . but I don't think it would be proper!

JUDITH: So much the better! That's the idea, that you're to compromise me—without any illusions! . . . You go first! (*They exit at the back.*)

(CAPTAIN *and* ALICE *enter from the right; he is wearing a fatigue uniform.*)

CAPTAIN (*sits down in the easy chair*): Let him come in!

(ALICE *goes to the left and opens the door; then she sits down on the sofa.*)

KURT (*enters from the left*): You wanted to talk with me?

CAPTAIN (*friendly but somewhat condescending*): Yes, I have a number of important things to say to you.—Sit down.

KURT (*sits down on the chair to the left*): I'm all ears!

CAPTAIN: Well, then . . . (*Oratorically*) You know that our quarantine system has been in a state of decay for almost a century . . . hm!

ALICE (*aside to* KURT): That's the candidate for parliament talking!

CAPTAIN: . . . But—with our times' unprecedented development in . . .

ALICE (*aside to* KURT): Communications, of course!

CAPTAIN: . . . All possible respects, the government has been considering an extension. Toward that goal the medical authorities have appointed inspectors—and!

ALICE (*aside to* KURT): He's making it up . . .

CAPTAIN: . . . You may as well know it now as later. I have been appointed quarantine inspector! (*Silence*)

KURT: Congratulations!

CAPTAIN: Our personal relationship will because of close family ties remain unchanged. However, to talk about something else!—At my request your son Allan has been transferred to an infantry regiment in Norrland!

KURT: But I don't want that!

CAPTAIN: In this case his mother's wishes are the ones that count . . . and since she has given me the power of attorney to make the decision, I have made the aforementioned decision!

KURT: I admire you!

CAPTAIN: Is that all you feel at the moment you are being separated from your son? Haven't you any other—purely human feelings?

KURT: You mean I should be suffering?

CAPTAIN: Yes!

KURT: That would please you! You want me to be able to suffer, do you?

CAPTAIN: Can *you* suffer? . . . There was a time when I got ill—you were present . . . and I can remember only that your face expressed unconcealed pleasure!

ALICE: That isn't true! Kurt sat by your side all night and comforted you when your pangs of conscience got too heavy to bear . . . but when you recovered, you became ungrateful . . .

CAPTAIN (*pretending not to hear* ALICE): Consequently Allan is going to leave us!

KURT: Who's going to supply the means?

CAPTAIN: I already have; that's to say, we, a group of us, have taken an interest in the young man's future.

KURT: A group!

CAPTAIN: Yes!—And so that you will know that it has been properly arranged, you may see these lists. (*Hands* KURT *some papers*)

KURT: Lists? (*Reads*) Why, they're donation lists!

CAPTAIN: Call 'em that.

KURT: So you've been begging for my son?

CAPTAIN: Are you ungrateful again?—An ungrateful person is the heaviest burden this earth bears!

KURT: So I'm socially dead! . . . And I can't run for parliament! . . .

CAPTAIN: Were *you* going to?

KURT: Yes!

CAPTAIN: Surely you've never dreamed of that! . . . So much the less as you ought to have sensed that I who have been here longer intended to volunteer my services . . . I whom you seem to have underestimated!

KURT: Well! So that, too, is finished!

CAPTAIN: It doesn't seem to affect you at all!

KURT: Now you've taken everything! Do you want still more?

CAPTAIN: Do you have anything more? And do you have anything to blame me for? Think it over carefully—to see if you have anything to blame me for. (*Silence*)

KURT: Strictly speaking, no! Everything has been done correctly and legally as between respectable people in daily life! . . .

CAPTAIN: You say that with a resignation I'd call cynical. But you are inclined to be cynical by nature, Kurt, and there are times when I'm tempted to share Alice's impression of you, and think you're a hypocrite, a hypocrite of the worst kind!

KURT (*calmly*): Is that what you think, Alice?

ALICE (*to* KURT): I thought so at one time. But not any more—for what you've taken requires genuine courage, or—something else!

CAPTAIN: This discussion can be considered finished now, I think. Kurt, go and say good-bye to Allan. He's leaving on the next boat.

KURT (*gets up*): That soon? . . . Well, I've been in on worse!

CAPTAIN: You say that so often I've begun to wonder what you were up to in America.

KURT: Up to? I had bad luck over there. And every person has the undeniable right to run into bad luck.

CAPTAIN (*sharply*): There are forms of bad luck you bring on your-self. Were yours like that?

KURT: Is that a matter of conscience?

CAPTAIN (*curtly*): Do *you* have a conscience?

KURT: There are wolves and there are sheep. It's not a human honor to be the sheep. But I'd rather be that than a wolf!

CAPTAIN: You don't know the old saying that everyone creates his own misfortune?

KURT: Is that a truth?

CAPTAIN: And you don't know that one's own strength . . .

KURT: Yes, I know that since that night when your own strength failed you and you collapsed on the floor!

CAPTAIN (*raises his voice*): A deserving man like me—yes, look at me—I have fought for fifty years—against a world, but I have finally won the game through perseverance, faithfulness to duty, energy, and—integrity!

ALICE: You ought to let others say things like that!

CAPTAIN: Others won't, because they're envious! However!—Company is coming! My daughter Judith is going to meet her future today . . . Where is Judith?

ALICE: She's out.

CAPTAIN: In the rain? . . . Have her called!

KURT: May I leave now?

CAPTAIN: No, stay! . . . Is Judith dressed? Properly?

ALICE: Yes, pretty much . . . Do you have the colonel's word he's coming?

CAPTAIN (*gets up*): Yes . . . that's to say, he wants to come and surprise us, as they say . . . And I'm expecting his telegram—at any moment! (*Going to the right*) It will come very soon! (*Exits*)

ALICE: There you have him! Is he human?

KURT: When you asked me that the first time, I said no! Now I think he's the most common kind of human being among those who possess the earth . . . Perhaps we're a little like that, too? Using people and favorable opportunities!

ALICE: He has consumed you and yours alive . . . and you defend him?

KURT: I have been in on worse . . . But that cannibal has not touched my soul—he couldn't swallow that!

ALICE: What "worse" have you been in on?

KURT: *You* ask that? . . .

ALICE: Are you being impolite?

KURT: No, I don't want to be, so . . . don't ask me again!

CAPTAIN (*enters from the right*): Here was the telegram, however!— Please read it, Alice—I don't see very well . . . (*Sits down pompously in the easy chair*) . . . Go ahead, read it!—Kurt doesn't need to go!

(ALICE *reads it first hastily and silently; looks amazed.*)

CAPTAIN: Well-l? Don't you like it?

(ALICE *says nothing but stares at the* CAPTAIN.)

CAPTAIN (*ironically*): Who is it from?

ALICE: It's from the colonel!

CAPTAIN (*with satisfaction*): I thought so! . . . What does he say?

ALICE: He says this: "Because of Miss Judith's impertinent telephone call I consider our relations broken—forever!" (*Stares at the* CAPTAIN)

CAPTAIN: Once more! If you will!

ALICE (*reads rapidly*): "Because of Miss Judith's impertinent telephone call I consider our relations broken—forever!"

CAPTAIN (*becomes pale*): That's Judith!

ALICE: And you're Holofernes!

CAPTAIN: What does that make you? . . .

ALICE: You'll soon see!

CAPTAIN: You did this!

ALICE: No!

CAPTAIN (*beside himself with fury*): You did this!

ALICE: No!

(CAPTAIN *tries to rise and draw his saber, but collapses with a stroke.*)

ALICE: There! You got what you had coming!

CAPTAIN (*with the tear-choked voice of an old man*): Don't be angry with me! I'm so sick!

ALICE: Are you? I'm glad to hear it!

KURT: Let's get him to bed!

ALICE: No, I don't want to touch him! (*Rings*)

CAPTAIN (*as before*): You mustn't be angry with me! (*To* KURT) Look after my children!

KURT: This is sublime! I'm to look after his children, and he has stolen mine!

ALICE: This self-deception!

CAPTAIN: Look after my children! (*Continues stammering sounds that cannot be understood*)

ALICE: That tongue has stopped at last!—Can't brag any more, can't lie any more, can't wound any more! Kurt, you who believe in God, thank Him on my behalf! Thank Him for setting me free from the tower, from the wolf, from the vampire!

KURT: Don't, Alice!

ALICE (*with her face close to the* CAPTAIN'*s*): Where's your own strength now? Eh? And your own energy?

(CAPTAIN *speechless; spits in her face.*)

ALICE: If you can, vomit poison still, you rattlesnake, I'll tear your tongue out at its roots! (*Slaps the* CAPTAIN) The head's off, but you can still blush! . . . Oh, Judith, splendid girl, whom I've carried like vengeance under my heart. You, you, have freed us all!—Do you have more heads, you hydra? We'll take those, too! (*Pulls the* CAPTAIN'*s beard*) To think there is justice on earth! I used to dream there was, but I never believed it! Kurt, ask God to forgive me for not knowing Him as He is! Oh, there is justice! Then I want to be a sheep, too! Tell Him that, Kurt! A little success makes us better; it's only our reverses that make us wolves!

(LIEUTENANT *enters from the back.*)

ALICE: The captain has had a stroke! Please roll out his chair!

LIEUTENANT: Ma'am! . . .

ALICE: What is it?

LIEUTENANT: Well, Miss Judith . . .

ALICE: Help us with this first. Then you can tell us about her afterward.

(LIEUTENANT *rolls out the chair to the right.*)

ALICE: Out with the cadaver! Out with it, and open the doors wide! Let the fresh air come in! (*Opens the doors at the back wide; it has become clear outside. Says with disgust*) Ugh . . .

KURT: Are you going to desert him?

ALICE: Men leave a shipwreck, and the crew save their own lives! . . . I don't need to wind the shroud about a rotten animal! Garbage collectors or medical porters may have him! A garden would be too fine for a barrowful of dirt like this! . . . Now I'll wash and bathe away all this filth, if I can ever be clean again!

(JUDITH *appears outside by the balustrade, bareheaded, waving her handkerchief toward the sea.*)

KURT (*going to the back*): Who's there? Judith! (*Calls*) Judith!

JUDITH (*enters, screams*): He has gone!

KURT: Who?

JUDITH: Allan has gone!

KURT: Without saying good-bye?

JUDITH: We said good-bye, and he asked me to say good-bye to you, sir!

ALICE: Was that it?

JUDITH (*throws herself into* KURT's *arms*): Allan has gone!

KURT: He'll come back, Judith.

ALICE: Or we'll go, too!

KURT (*makes a gesture toward the door at the right*): Leave him?— What would people . . .

ALICE: People! Puh! . . . Judith, let me embrace you!

(JUDITH *approaches* ALICE, *who kisses her forehead.*)

ALICE: Do you want to go, too?

JUDITH: Can you doubt it?

ALICE: But Father is sick!

JUDITH: What do I care about that?

ALICE: That's Judith!—Oh, I love you, Judith!

JUDITH: Besides, Father isn't petty . . . and he doesn't like fuss! There's a style to Father, all the same!

ALICE: Yes, in a way!

JUDITH: And I imagine he isn't anxious to see me after that telephone call! . . . Why should he try to get me an old man for a husband? No, it's Allan I want! Allan! (*Throws herself into* KURT's *arms*) I want to go to Allan! (*Tears herself away and runs out to wave*) (KURT *follows and waves, too.*)

ALICE: To think that flowers can grow out of dirt!

(LIEUTENANT *enters from the right.*)

ALICE: Well-l?

LIEUTENANT: Well! Miss Judith . . .

ALICE: Is it so delightful to have her name caress your lips that you forget the dying man?

LIENTENANT: Yes, but she said . . .

ALICE: She? Better say Judith!—But first, how is it in there?

LIEUTENANT: Oh, in there!—It's over!

ALICE: Over?—God, I thank you on behalf of myself and on behalf of humanity for having freed us from that evil! . . . Give me your arm! I want to get out and breathe—breathe! (*The* LIEUTENANT *offers her his arm.* ALICE *checks herself.*) Did he say anything before he died?

LIEUTENANT: Miss Judith's father said a few words.

ALICE: What did he say?

LIEUTENANT: He said: "Forgive them, for they know not what they do." [8]

ALICE: Incomprehensible!

LIEUTENANT: Yes, Miss Judith's father was a good and noble man.

ALICE: Kurt! (KURT *comes in.*) It's over!

KURT: Ah! . . .

ALICE: Do you know what his last words were? No, you don't. "Forgive them, for they know not what they do."

KURT: Can you translate that?

ALICE: I suppose he meant he had always done what was right, and that he died as the one who had been wronged by life.

KURT: He'll get a fine speech at the grave, I suspect.

ALICE: And a lot of wreaths! From the noncommissioned officers.

KURT: Yes-s!

ALICE: A year ago he said something like this: it looks as if life were a big joke on all of us!

KURT: Do you think he has been deceiving us to the last?

ALICE: No! . . . But now, when he is dead, I feel a strange need to speak well of him!

KURT: Let's do that!

LIEUTENANT: Miss Judith's father was a good and noble man!

ALICE (*aside to* KURT): You see!

KURT: "They know not what they do." How many times I asked you if he knew what he was doing. And you didn't think he knew! So, forgive him!

ALICE: Riddles! Riddles! . . . But think of it—there will be peace in the house now! The wonderful peace of death! Wonderful as the solemn anxiety when a child comes into the world! I can hear the silence . . . and I see the marks on the floor from his chair which took him away.—And I feel that my life is over and that I go toward death . . . You know, it's strange—the lieutenant's simple words—and he is a simple soul—haunt me as the truth. My husband, the man I loved when I was young—laugh, if you will—he was a good and a noble man—all the same.

KURT: All the same? And a brave man—who struggled hard for his existence and that of his family?

ALICE: Such worries! Such humiliations! That he crossed out—so he could go on!

KURT: They didn't promote him! That says a great deal. Alice, go to him!

ALICE: No, I can't! For while we have been talking about him, I've seen him as he was when he was young—I have seen him, I see him—now as he was at twenty . . . I must have loved that man!

KURT: And hated him!

ALICE: And hated him! . . . May he rest in peace! (*Goes to the door at the right where she stops with folded hands*)

[CURTAIN]

# Notes on
# 'The Dance of Death II'

1. The Bechstein concert piano, manufactured in Berlin by Karl Bechstein (1826–1900), is considered one of the finest made.

2. The Greek mathematician Archimedes (287–212 B.C.), a native of Syracuse, was not only a theoretical genius but also a practical inventor who provided his native city with weapons of defense, among other things. During the Roman siege of Syracuse in 212 B.C., a Roman soldier is said to have cut him down while he was calmly tracing geometric figures in the sand.

3. Neptune was the Roman god of the sea.

4. The Swedish Order of the Sword (*Svärdsorden*) was created in 1748 along with two other orders, the Order of the Seraphim (*Serafimerorden*) and the Order of the North Star. The Order of the Sword is awarded to officers "for bravery and exceptional performance in war as well as for useful and extended service."

5. The Portuguese Order of Christ was created by King Dionysius in 1318. It is pictured as a royal crown above a white cross within a red one, with a red ribbon below the crown and crosses.

6. See note 7 on page 75.

7. Judith's proposal that they die together is couched in terms reminiscent of *Hedda Gabler* (1890) and of its predecessor "Mot betalning" ("Corinna") in Strindberg's *Giftas* (*Married,* 1884, 1886).

8. "Then said Jesus, Father, forgive them; for they know not what they do" (Luke 23:34).

# Introduction to
# 'Advent'

IN A LETTER to his fellow writer and literary adviser Gustaf af Geijerstam on January 2, 1900, Strindberg made clear his intention in *Advent*:

> Well, I placed myself as you see on a purely Christian childlike basis, and produced the Christ child . . . as the sacrifice of reconciliation. The only One who can undo all our evil, which we can't do ourselves no matter how great our repentance and penitence [may be] . . . I have emphasized this in the Christ child's speech: "Blame me!" Advent is even the coming of the happy news that through Christ's descent into hell, Evil has been forced to serve Good and that the Evil One (legion) is only the *Esprit correcteur,* the Spirit of Correction (Swedenborg's thought!) not an evil principle, through which thought the dualism good and evil is destroyed. In the last Christmas eve scene in Hell, Advent is explained as the hope or the news that the punishments are not eternal! The Judge and his wife are great sinners, who think they can buy "heaven" and illustrate the never-ending ability of the imagination to fool people into believing they are righteous. This notion is a form of punishment (according to Swedenborg) by which a human being is kept in a state of sin in order to suffer the agonies of the damned. Briefly: Evil, the Evil One's, and evil people's problem solved (?) from a monistic point of view.

Strindberg's intention, then, was to write a play that would explain the advent message as he saw it, and to do so with a combination of adult and childlike experience.

Among the notes in the Strindberg collection at the Royal Library are the following jottings:

> *Advent.* Additions and insertions.
> Masters' morality and slave morality. Here there is only one sort.
> The judge's wife has broken up the marriage between Adolf and Amalia.
> Crimes against marriage are punished in the excrement hell.
> . . . They are to confess, fast, and be flogged . . .
> The auction ends with Adolf's reappearance.
> Want to read the Bible, pray, confess, attend mass; but are not permitted to! [In Hades]
> "The punishments are not punishment, but consequences."
> "The punishments are not eternal but can become that if the evil person keeps up his evil eternally . . ."
> The prince suffers at times from torturing others; then becomes sad and sentimental.
> . . . The prince recalls his past, memories of his youth, and the sister he has loved.

While Strindberg did not follow every one of these indications in *Advent,* they suggest the drift of what he has to say.

Strindberg said that *Advent* is a *sagospelstragedi med mystik,* that is, a tragedy that combines modern parallels to the medieval fairy tale, the medieval mystery play, and the medieval morality. It contains elements of the miraculous, events that only the childlike in spirit can accept with appreciation, and a moral message with wide-ranging implications. While it was Strindberg's purpose to emphasize the good news of advent, the very nature of the story directs a reader's or spectator's attention to the evil in which the judge and his wife have indulged and to the effects of that evil.

*Advent* is really an examination of self-righteousness, a highly significant segment of the human experience. The play deals with the human capacity to rationalize, to lie to oneself, to adjust and distort the truth to make life not only bearable but comforting and comfortable as well. *Advent* presents an examination of the problem of human evil: its origin, its nature, its manifestations, and its effects; but it also presents the nature, the manifestations, and the effects of good.

Strindberg illustrates all this by presenting the story of an aging couple and, in the process, he reveals four things primarily:

> What the judge and his wife *do;*
> What the judge and his wife *are;*
> What the judge and his wife *think* or *believe;*
> What the judge and his wife *say.*

Strindberg's problem was how to reveal this on stage, that is, how to express what goes on *within* as well as to include actions and speech that can be observed by the spectator.

His solution was to make use of his dream-play technique, for much of what he felt he had to include was bubbling just beneath the surface of the consciousness of the judge and his wife. *Advent* becomes, then, primarily an expression of inner self-scrutiny. Most of what happens to the characters happens in semiwatchful dream states when the control that permits rationalization is not functioning; in other words, when they are set free of artificial restraint.

As brilliant as Strindberg's contrasts between appearance and actuality are in most of his other works, he has made the contrast even more striking in *Advent.* The judge and his wife may seem to be two highly fortunate aging people, a couple to be envied for their status and position, their wealth, their family, and their growing old together beautifully in comfort and tranquility. They may in their moments of control judge themselves a model couple deserving of all they have and more; they may congratulate themselves at such moments for their superiority over their neighbors in every area of living. But in the flashes of insight that come when the superficial controls are not functioning, they begin to sense that they are two pitiful, hypocritical sinners, fear-ridden, frustrated, self-deceived, isolated not only from their neighbors and family but from their better selves and each other.

Their self-righteousness is common enough. They have operated within the letter of the law, both the Old Testament moral code of "an eye for an eye" and the human law. They have taken advantage of every loophole in both. They have treated their neighbors legally correctly, but they have had no compassion for them and have delighted in their misfortunes. Even worse, perhaps, is their treatment of their own family. They are Christians nominally and think they are good ones, but their religion, humanly enough, is a strange combination of superstitions and superficially accepted and vulgarized notions. There is not a genuine or profound conviction between them. They do have to a striking degree the human knack for reading into and ascribing motives to others that they themselves have but will not admit having.

In this play which, like the medieval morality play, deals with universal human problems, the judge and his second wife find it impossible to reject at all times the evidence of their senses and their insight. Nor have they been able to do so consistently throughout a long lifetime. Even the judge and his wife cannot avoid the knowledge that death is inevitably approaching, and thus they feel the need of a guarantee that they will be secure even after death. Their repressed guilts do insist on popping up into consciousness, however, and it is quite a collection! But as Kurt says in *The Dance of Death* in observing another great sinner: "Perhaps we are all . . . like that." Certainly Strindberg intended to convey that thought in this modern morality play as well as the comforting thought, implicit in *Advent*, that there is hope even for the greatest of sinners.

The points made by C. W. E. L. Dahlström in his *Strindberg's Dramatic Expressionism* (Ann Arbor: University of Michigan Press, 1930)—emanations of the individual ego; expression of the inner man, the unconscious, the dream world; the seeking of the spiritual, the elemental, the ecstatic; the use of lyricism and musical counterpoint; the search for the divine; and the assertion of the dignity of man—can certainly be applied to *Advent* not only as a means of deciding if the play can be labeled expressionistic but for gaining insight into the remarkable skill Strindberg displayed in creating a fairy-tale tragedy on a Christian and *childlike* basis. Other matters noted by Professor Dahlström are also characteristic of *Advent:* deliberate distortions, antitheses, and synthesized characterizations.

Consider the fears the judge and his wife try to suppress: the sunbeam or the reflection of the sun (*solkatten*) which seems to pursue them and torture them, their fear of the evil eye, their fear of counting themselves fortunate, their fear of being overheard, their fear of confiding in each other—to mention a few of the more striking ones. Certainly these are fairly universal in their implications, and Strindberg's devices for expressing them on stage are most effective.

The procession of shadows (Death with his scythe, the White Lady, the Goldsmith, the Beheaded Sailor, the Auctioneer, the Chimney Sweep, the Fool with the pole, the Surveyor, and the Judge with a rope about his neck) are reminiscent of medieval plays as effective externalizations of the deeds that cause pangs of conscience which even the conviction of self-righteousness cannot entirely eliminate. Any child, or any adult who has been fortunate enough to retain something of the childlike, will appreciate this theatrically effective use of allegory combined with visual representation of things that are retained in the memory and never thoroughly repressed or discarded.

The presentation of Satan, the Other One, is not unlike that in *Peer Gynt* except that Strindberg has made his strange devil a rather sympathetic soul, somewhat in keeping with Strindberg's conviction that the old theological sharp distinction between the forces of good and evil is probably not valid. The Other One as a kindly tattered penitent who serves the Eternal One is a Strindberg variation that may well appeal to both reader and spectator, no matter what his age may be.

The scenes in which Erik and Thyra appear are fairly typical of all scenes in which Strindberg includes children. The reader and the spectator do need to exercise complete suspension of disbelief, for Erik and Thyra are not sufficiently "humanized" to begin to compare with the adults in the play. Another way of saying this is that Strindberg tended here as elsewhere to be somewhat sentimental and perhaps a bit uncomfortably uncertain in his interpretation of the very young.

But there is no uncertainty or sentimentality about Strindberg's presentation of his adult characters in the allegorical scenes in Acts IV and V. The ball in Act IV is a dance of death in reverse. With the Other One serving as master of ceremonies, and the seven deadly sins (Pride, Avarice, Lust, Wrath, Gluttony, Envy, and Sloth) in attendance about the throne set aside for royal sinners, the whole becomes a travesty that points up the startling contrast between appearance and horrifying reality. The "royalty" think they are royal, the musicians seem to play but their instruments emit no sounds, and neither Pan nor his worshipers achieve either beauty or joy in this waiting room for release from damnation.

Equally impressive is the brief trial scene in Act IV, the scene in which the judge, while in a dream state, sits in judgment and passes sentence on himself.

If Strindberg had not written as many good plays as he did, *Advent* would probably have been produced far more frequently than it has been. Its companion plays *There Are Crimes and Crimes* and *Easter* have been *Advent*'s most serious rivals; both of them are far pleasanter and far easier to stage; and for generations that have been conditioned to using verisimilitude as the primary criterion for plays, *Advent* has seemed too demanding both in suspension of disbelief and in staging.

But for anyone who appreciates superb revelations of character, challenges to creative response of imagination and emotion from the reader or spectator, and an interesting interpretation of the Christian point of view on crime and punishment, *Advent* is a rewarding experience. The judge and his wife are unforgettable; even the most sophisticated of moderns can afford to respond to allegory; Strindberg's way of looking at crime and punishment is probably not too different from that of any thinking human being; and there is not a little humor, albeit dark and even grotesque, to be enjoyed in *Advent*.

# Advent:[1]
# A Mystery for Children

## Characters

THE JUDGE
THE JUDGE'S WIFE (CAROLINA)
AMALIA
ADOLF
THE NEIGHBOR
ERIK
THYRA
THE OTHER ONE (SATAN)
THE FRANCISCAN (= THE OTHER ONE)
THE PLAYMATE
THE WITCH
THE PRINCE
*Minor characters:* SHADOWS

## Settings

Act I:   The vineyard and the mausoleum
Act II:  The entry
Act III: The wine cellar; the orchard
Act IV:  The crossroads; "the waiting room";
         the crossroads; the courtroom
Act V:   The entry; "the waiting room"

# ACT I

*The background is a vineyard.*

*To the left a mausoleum: a small white plastered brick building with door and window openings in pointed arch style without frames or panes; a red tile roof; a cross on the gable. Clematis with violet cross-shaped flowers climbing the wall. Various flowers at the base of the wall.*

*In the foreground a peach tree with ripe fruit; the* JUDGE *and his* WIFE *are sitting under the tree.*

*The* JUDGE *is dressed in a green hat and costume of the 1820s; yellow knee-length trousers, a blue coat, etc. His* WIFE *is wearing a headcloth; she has a cane, glasses, a snuffbox. She looks like a witch.*

*To the right is a small expiation chapel with an image of the Madonna. The picket fence in front of it has wreaths and bouquets hanging on it. In front of the picket fence is a prayer stool.*

JUDGE: The evening of our lives has finally given us the sunshine the morning promised. Early rain and special rain has blessed our fields and meadows—soon the whole neighborhood will be hearing our servants singing as they tramp out our wine.

WIFE: Don't say it! Someone might hear you!

JUDGE: Who could hear me? And what harm would it do if they heard me thanking God for all His good gifts?

WIFE: No one may talk about his good fortune. Misfortune may be listening.

JUDGE: How could that matter? Why, I was born with a caul! [2]

WIFE: Be careful! Many people envy us, and evil eyes are watching us!

JUDGE: Let them! They always have. But I've managed all the same.

WIFE: So far, yes. But I suspect our neighbor; he's going around the village saying we've cheated him out of his property and saying a lot of such things I don't want to repeat. It doesn't matter, of course, when you have a clear conscience and a spotless life. The slander doesn't hurt me at all: I go to confession and mass and am ready to close my eyes when my hour comes and to open them again to look my Judge in the eye. I know what I'll say to Him!

JUDGE: What?

WIFE: I wasn't free of faults, Lord; I was only a poor sinner, but I was a bit better than my neighbor.

JUDGE: I don't know why you're thinking about all that just now, and I don't find it pleasant. Is it because our mausoleum is to be consecrated soon?

WIFE: Perhaps, for I don't think about death otherwise. Don't I still have all my teeth? Isn't my hair as thick as when I was a bride . . .

JUDGE: Yes, yes, you're eternally young, just as I am, but we'll have to pass away all the same. Since fortune has been kind to us, and we wanted to take advantage of the privilege of lying in our own earth, we built this little mausoleum right here where every tree knows us, where every flower will whisper about our work, our efforts, and our struggles . . .

WIFE: Struggles, yes! Against envious neighbors and ungrateful children . . .

JUDGE: That's right: ungrateful children.—Have you seen Adolf?

WIFE: No, I haven't seen him since he left this morning to try to raise money for the rent.

JUDGE: Money he'll never get . . . and I still less. But his time of grace is up—he knows that—it's the third quarter he's failed to pay.

WIFE: Yes, put him out, out into the world to learn how to work instead of sitting here being a son-in-law. I'll keep Amalia and the children . . .

JUDGE: Do you think Amalia will agree to a separation from Adolf . . . ?

WIFE: Oh, yes, when it's a question of losing her children and her inheritance . . . Well, look at that! It's back again!

(*A "suncat"* [3] *or sunbeam can be seen on the mausoleum wall; it quivers as if it were reflected from running water.*)

JUDGE: What is it? What is it?

WIFE: On our mausoleum! Don't you see it?

JUDGE: The river's reflecting the sun. That means . . .

WIFE: It means we'll see the sun shine for a long time . . .

JUDGE: Or the very opposite. But it doesn't matter. A clear conscience is a fine cushion, and the righteous will receive his reward! See, there's our neighbor.

NEIGHBOR (*enters*): Good evening!

JUDGE: Good evening, neighbor. How are things with you? It's a long time since I had the pleasure . . . How are your grapes doing? I meant to ask.

NEIGHBOR: The grapes! Mildew and the starlings are getting them.

JUDGE: Good heavens! There's no mildew on mine, and I've neither seen nor heard starlings about.

NEIGHBOR: Fate deals us unequal lots: the one is taken up, the other is left behind.

JUDGE: I suspect there are good reasons for that!

NEIGHBOR: I see! The righteous are rewarded, and the unrighteous are punished.

JUDGE: I didn't meant that, quite! But admit it's strange: two farms next to each other—the one has a bumper crop, the other hardly any at all . . .

NEIGHBOR: The one has starlings, the other not. That seems to me stranger still. But not everyone is born with a caul like you, Judge.

JUDGE: That's true, and fortune has favored me. I'm grateful for that and have my moments when I'm proud because I've deserved it.—But you're here as if you'd been sent for . . . The lease is available. Do you want to take it over?

(*The* JUDGE's WIFE *has got up and walked up to the mausoleum, where she putters with the flowers.*)

NEIGHBOR: Well-l! The lease is available! Hm! When did that happen?

JUDGE: This morning!

NEIGHBOR: Hm! Really!—So your son-in-law's leaving?

JUDGE: Yes, that good-for-nothing can't manage.

NEIGHBOR: Tell me one thing: haven't you heard the rumor the state plans to build a military highway across our properties?

JUDGE: I did hear something like that, but it's just talk.

NEIGHBOR: But I read it in the paper. Then this land would be condemned and the renter would be the loser.

JUDGE: I can't imagine their doing it, and I'd never agree to it. Should *I* leave this land where I meant to spend the rest of my days in peace—where I've put up my final resting place so I wouldn't have to lie with the others . . .

NEIGHBOR: Hold it! No one knows where he'll be buried. My father, who owned this land, had thought he would be buried here in his own soil, but that came to nothing. As far as the lease goes, I'll have to say no.

JUDGE: As you wish. The proposal was unselfish on my part since you're an unlucky man. It's no secret you fail in everything you undertake, and people have their own thoughts about anyone who's alone and friendless—like you. Isn't that right: you don't have *one* friend?

NEIGHBOR: That's right! I don't have one friend. And that always looks bad. I can't deny it.

JUDGE: From one thing to another: is the old story that this vineyard was a battlefield in the old days and that's why the wine has its special fire true?

NEIGHBOR: No, I haven't heard that. Father said that this was a place of execution and that the mausoleum stands where the gallows used to.

JUDGE: That was nasty! Why did you tell me?

NEIGHBOR: Why, you asked!—And the last one to be hanged was an unrighteous judge; and he's buried there among many others, among them his innocent victims.

JUDGE: What horrible stories! (*Calls*) Caroline!

NEIGHBOR: And that's why he still has to walk about here as a ghost. Haven't you ever seen him, Judge?

JUDGE: I have never seen anyone.

NEIGHBOR: But I have seen him—he usually comes when the grapes are harvested, and people hear him by the wine press in the cellar!

JUDGE (*calls*): Caroline!

WIFE: What?

JUDGE: Come here!

NEIGHBOR: And he'll never get any rest until he has suffered through all the agony his victims have suffered.

JUDGE: Go away! Go!

NEIGHBOR: Well! I didn't know you were so sensitive, Judge. (*Leaves*)

WIFE: What was that about?

JUDGE: Oh, he was telling stories that upset me! But, oh, he has an evil mind, that man!

WIFE: That's what I've said, but you always have to talk when you see someone . . . What was he chattering about now?

JUDGE: I don't want to talk about it; I get sick when I just think of it! I'll tell you some other time!—Look, there's Adolf!

ADOLF (*enters*): Good evening!

JUDGE (*after a pause*): Well-l?

ADOLF: I'm in bad luck! I haven't raised the money!

JUDGE: I suspect there are good reasons for that.

ADOLF: I can't understand why everything goes well for some and badly for others.

JUDGE: You can't? Take a close look at yourself; examine your acts and thoughts, and you'll see that you yourself are to blame for your misfortunes.

ADOLF: I'm possibly not a righteous man, but I don't have any unforgivable acts on my conscience!

WIFE: Think it over carefully . . .

ADOLF: I don't think I need to—one's conscience surely keeps one awake . . .

JUDGE: One's conscience can be put to sleep . . .

ADOLF: Can it? I've heard of scoundrels who have turned gray in crime whose conscience has been awakened just before death, and I've even heard of criminals whose conscience has awakened only after death.

JUDGE (*shaken*): . . . So they've walked the earth again, you mean. So you, too, have heard that story? It's strange I'm the only one who hadn't heard it . . .

WIFE: What are you two talking about? Stick to business instead.

ADOLF: Yes, that would be more sensible!—Talking about that, I'll give you my proposal . . .

JUDGE: Listen, my boy; I think it's far more proper to tell you my decision. It's this: from today on you're no longer my renter, and you're to be off today to look for work!

ADOLF: Are you serious?

JUDGE: For shame! I never joke! And you can't complain—I've given you two extensions.

ADOLF: And crop failures three times. Am I to blame for that?

JUDGE: I didn't say that, but I'm still less to blame. And I'm not the one who's judging you. Here's the contract, and here's the broken agreement. Have I broken our agreement? No! So I'm without blame, and I wash my hands!

ADOLF: That's the law, but I thought that there would be forbearance between relatives, especially since by the very order of nature this property will be inherited by your daughter, my wife.

WIFE: See! The order of nature! He's just waiting for us to die! But look at me, young man; I can live for twenty years more, and I will just to annoy you.

JUDGE (*to* ADOLF): How low! How unfeeling to say to old people to their face: Aren't you going to die soon? For shame! But now you've broken all ties, and I say only: Get out of here and don't ever let me see you again!

ADOLF: That was plain talk! I'll go, but not alone . . .

WIFE: Oh-h! You think that Amalia, our child, will tramp the highways with you and that you can send one brat after the other to us! We foresaw that and prevented it . . .

ADOLF: Where is Amalia? Where?

WIFE: I might as well tell you! She's at the cloister—on a visit. So there's no point in looking for her here!

ADOLF: You'll pay for this cruelty some day; if you've broken up my marriage, you're going to pay for your crime.

JUDGE: You ought to be ashamed of blaming the innocent. Get out and starve before closed doors until you've learned to be grateful!

ADOLF: May you have the same fate twice over! Just let me say goodbye to my children, and I'll go.

WIFE: Since you don't want to spare your children the pain of parting, I will. I already have!

ADOLF: That, too! Now I can believe every rumor I've heard about your wickedness; now I understand what our neighbor meant when he said that you two . . . can't bear to see the sun!

JUDGE: That's enough! Or you'll feel the law and the hand of justice strike you . . . (*He lifts his right hand so that the audience sees his index finger is missing.*)

ADOLF (*comes up to the* JUDGE, *takes his right hand to examine it*): The hand of justice, the perjurer's hand that lacks the finger that stuck to the Bible when you swore a false oath! Woe unto you! Both of you! The day of retribution has come—your deeds will rise like the dead from their graves to accuse you.

WIFE: What's he saying?—It's as if he were blowing fire on us! Go, you spirit of lies, and may hell be your reward!

ADOLF: May heaven reward you—as you deserve! And may God protect my children! (*Goes*)

JUDGE: What was this? Who said that? The voice seemed to come from a great hall down in the earth.

WIFE: Did you hear it, too?

JUDGE: God help us, then!—Do you remember what he said about the sun? I thought that was the strangest of all! How can he know that . . . that it's so? That I'm so strangely put together the sun always burns me. People say it's because my mother had a sunstroke when she was carrying me . . . but that you, too . . .

WIFE (*frightened*): Sh-h! When you speak of the trolls, then . . . Didn't the sun set?

JUDGE: Of course it set!

WIFE: How can the "suncat" be on the mausoleum still? (*The reflection moves.*)

JUDGE: Mary, Mother of Christ! An omen!

WIFE: An omen! you say; and on our tomb. That doesn't happen every day . . . and only to a few select people who have believed in the highest things . . . (*The "suncat" disappears.*)

JUDGE: It's horrible here tonight, really unpleasant. But what hit me hardest was that good-for-nothing's waiting for us to die so he can get the farm. Do you know I . . . I wonder if I dare to say it . . .

WIFE: Go ahead!

JUDGE: Well, have you heard the story that this was a place of execution?

WIFE: So you *have* heard that, too?

JUDGE: Yes, and you already had?—Well, if we'd give the land to the cloister it would be consecrated soil and we could rest in peace. The income could go to the children until they're grown up. And that would block Adolf's counting on inheriting from us. That seems to me an especially happy solution to the difficult dilemma: giving without taking anything from oneself.

WIFE: Your superior common sense hasn't failed this time either. I agree with you. But assume the land's condemned and expropriated . . . What happens then?

JUDGE: Time enough to think of that when it happens. But: let's first and as soon as possible dedicate the mausoleum . . .

FRANCISCAN (*enters*): God's peace!

WIFE: You come at the right time, Father, to hear an announcement concerning the cloister . . .

FRANCISCAN: I'm glad. (*The "suncat" can be seen on the mausoleum.*)

WIFE: We wanted to ask when the mausoleum could be consecrated.

FRANCISCAN (*fixes her glance*): Oh-h!

JUDGE: Father, look at the omen there . . .

WIFE: Well, isn't it a holy place?

FRANCISCAN: That's seafire . . .

WIFE: Isn't it a good sign? Doesn't it have something to tell us? Doesn't it urge devout minds to meditate? Couldn't this place become a gathering place for pilgrims who seek . . .

FRANCISCAN (*to the* JUDGE's WIFE): May I have a word with you in private? (*He goes to the right.*)

WIFE (*follows him*): Father!

FRANCISCAN (*speaks very quietly*): You have a reputation in the neighborhood you don't deserve, for you're the worst sinner I know. You want to buy forgiveness, and you want to steal heaven. You have cheated the Lord.

WIFE: What's that?

FRANCISCAN: When you were on the verge of death, you promised God to give a monstrance of pure gold to the cloister church if you got well. You got well, and then you gave the sacred vessel, but it was silver, merely gilded. Not because of the gold, but because of the broken promise, you are already damned!

WIFE: I didn't know; the goldsmith deceived me.

FRANCISCAN: You're lying—I have the goldsmith's bill.

WIFE: Can't that be forgiven?

FRANCISCAN: No! For it's a mortal sin to deceive God!

(WIFE *sighs*)

FRANCISCAN: As far as your other sins go, you'll have to settle them with yourself, but if you hurt as much as one hair on the children's heads, you'll find out who protects them, and you'll get to feel the iron whip!

WIFE: Imagine! That damn monk is telling *me* things like that! If I'm damned, I want to be damned! (*Laughs*)

FRANCISCAN: Yes, at least your house won't be blessed, and you won't get peace until you've suffered all the agony you've caused others! May I say something to you, Judge? (*The* JUDGE *comes up.*)

WIFE: Let him have it, too, so we're even.

FRANCISCAN (*to the* JUDGE): Why did you think of building your final resting place on gallows' hill?

JUDGE: The devil must have given us the idea!

FRANCISCAN: Like the idea of driving your children out on the highways and robbing them of their inheritance. But you have been the unrighteous judge, broken your oath, and accepted bribes.

JUDGE: I?

FRANCISCAN: And now you want to *raise* a monument to yourself, build an ever-lasting refuge in heaven! Listen: this land will never be consecrated, and you may count yourself blessed if you may lie in the common cemetery among all the little sinners. This soil is damned, for it has blood guilt and you have acquired it unjustly.

JUDGE: What shall I do?

FRANCISCAN: Repent, and restore what you have stolen!

JUDGE: I have never stolen; I've acquired everything legally.

FRANCISCAN: You see, that's the worst—you consider your crimes legal. Yes, I know you have thought yourself specially favored by heaven because of your righteousness. But you'll see what you'll harvest—thistles and thorns will grow in your vineyard. You shall wander alone and friendless, and the peace of your old age will give way to contention and strife!

JUDGE: What the devil!

FRANCISCAN: Don't call him—he'll come anyway!

JUDGE: Let him come! I'm not afraid, for I have faith!

FRANCISCAN: The devils believe too, and tremble! Farewell! (*Goes*)

JUDGE (*to his* WIFE): What did he say to you?

WIFE: Do you think I'd tell you? What did he say to you?

JUDGE: Do you think I'd tell you?

WIFE: So you're going to keep things from me?

JUDGE: And you? But you always have, and I'll find out about your tricks.

WIFE: Just wait—I'll find out where you've hidden the money that's missing.

JUDGE: So you've hidden money, too! No point in pretending any longer—show yourself in all your ghastliness, you witch.

WIFE: I think you've lost your mind, but that wasn't much of a loss! Save decency at least if you can . . .

JUDGE: And save your beauty if you can! And your eternal youth! (*Laughs*) And your righteousness. You must have been able to turn my sight, for now I see how terribly ugly and old you are.

WIFE (*the "suncat" shines on her*): He's burning me!

JUDGE: Now I get to see what you look like! (*The "suncat" hits the* JUDGE.) Now he's burning me!

WIFE: And how terrible you look! (*Both drag themselves out to the right.*)

(*The* NEIGHBOR *and* AMALIA *enter from the left.*)

NEIGHBOR: There is justice, my child, both human and divine, but we have to be patient.

AMALIA: I want to think what happens is just even if it looks pretty bad; but I can't, I've never been able to love my mother. There's something in me that says she's a stranger to me—even an enemy.

NEIGHBOR: Really? You've come to that!

AMALIA: Why, she hates me, and a mother can't hate her child.

NEIGHBOR: Well!

AMALIA: And I suffer because I can't do what I should—love her.

NEIGHBOR: Oh, well, after you have suffered in *that* way, the moment of truth will soon come when you'll learn the great secret in your life.

AMALIA: I'd be able to bear everything if she only were kind to my children.

NEIGHBOR: You don't have to worry about that. Her power's over. The cup of her unrighteousness has run over.

AMALIA: Do you really believe that? Just today she tore my Adolf away from us, and, as you can see, she has made me a servant to work in the kitchen!

NEIGHBOR: Be patient!

AMALIA: That's easy to say! I understand having to suffer when I deserve it, but when I don't . . .

NEIGHBOR: My dear child, criminals suffer justly in prison and that is no honor, but suffering unjustly is a sign of grace and a test from which a steadfast person harvests golden fruit.

AMALIA: What you say is so attractive I believe you!—Sh-h! There come the children! But I don't want them to see me when I'm dressed like this! (*She and the* NEIGHBOR *step behind a large bush.* ERIK *and* THYRA *enter; the "suncat" falls on the children alternately.*)

ERIK: Look at the suncat!

THYRA: That beautiful sun! But it set just now!

ERIK: Maybe it could stay up later tonight because it has been good today.

THYRA: Silly! The sun can't be good.

ERIK: Of course the sun can be good. Why, it makes the grapes and the peaches grow!

THYRA: But then he can give us a peach, too, if he's kind!

ERIK: He will, too, if we'll only wait. Have any fallen down?

THYRA (*searches the ground*): No, but we could get at the tree.

ERIK: No, Grandmother won't let us.

THYRA: Grandmother said we mustn't shake the tree, but I thought we could play around the tree so the peach would fall anyway—of itself.

ERIK: Silly! That would be the same thing! (*Looks up at the tree*) If a peach would only fall!

THYRA: It won't fall unless we shake the tree!

ERIK: You mayn't say that—it's sin!

THYRA: Shall we ask God to let one drop?

ERIK: We mayn't ask God for anything good—to eat, of course!— Little peach, go ahead, fall! I want you to fall! (*A peach falls from the tree; Erik picks it up.*) Well, look at how good the tree is!

THYRA: Divide it fairly, for I was the one who said first we should shake the tree . . .

JUDGE'S WIFE (*enters with a large switch*): So-o! You've shaken the tree . . . Come here, you brats, and I'll let you have it . . .

ERIK: No, Grandmother, we didn't shake the tree!

WIFE: So you're lying, too! I heard Thyra say you should shake the tree. Come along; I'll lock you up in the cellar so you'll see neither sun nor moon shining . . .

AMALIA (*comes forward*): The children are innocent, Mother!

WIFE: How nice! Standing in back of the bush listening and teaching your own children to lie!

NEIGHBOR (*comes forward*): But they were telling the truth!

WIFE: Two witnesses behind the bush—why, it's just like in court. But I know the tricks, you see, and what I've heard and seen is proof enough for me!—Come, you brats!

AMALIA: Mother, this is sin and shame! (*The* NEIGHBOR *puts a finger to his mouth as a signal to* AMALIA. AMALIA *goes up to the* CHILDREN.) Don't cry, children! Obey Grandmother—it's not dangerous! Better to suffer from what is bad than to do it, and *I* know you're innocent. God protect you! And don't forget to say your evening prayer!

(*The* JUDGE's WIFE *goes out with the* CHILDREN.)

AMALIA: It's hard to believe, but it is a joy to be able to.

NEIGHBOR: Is it so hard to believe God is good even when He wants our very best?

AMALIA: Give me one good and great thought for the night so I may sleep on it as on a good pillow.

NEIGHBOR: Yes, let me think.—This: Isaac *was* to be sacrificed . . .

AMALIA: Oh, no!

NEIGHBOR: Pull yourself together!—Isaac *was* to be sacrificed—but he was not sacrificed!

AMALIA: Thank you! And good-night! (*Goes to the right*)

NEIGHBOR: Good-night, my child! (*Goes slowly to the back*)

.

*

*The procession of shadows come out of the mausoleum, they go to the right with five steps distance between every two figures; they come forward soundlessly.*

DEATH *with his scythe and hourglass. The* WHITE LADY, *blonde, slim; a ring with a gleaming green stone on her finger. The* GOLD-SMITH *with the sham monstrance. The* BEHEADED SAILOR, *with his head in his hands. The* AUCTIONEER *with his gavel and notebook. The* CHIMNEY SWEEP *with line, scraper, and broom. The* FOOL *carrying his cap with jackass ears and bells on a pole with the inscription, "Caul." The* SURVEYOR *with his line and tripod. A* JUDGE *like the judge in facial expression and dress, with a rope around his neck; his right hand lifted showing his index finger is missing.*

*It has turned dark at the start of the procession. The stage is empty while the procession lasts.*

*The* JUDGE *enters from the left. His* WIFE *follows him.*

JUDGE: What are you doing out this late?

WIFE: What are you doing?

JUDGE: I couldn't sleep.

WIFE: Why not?

JUDGE: I don't know! I thought I heard children crying down in the cellar.

WIFE: You couldn't have! Oh, no! You're afraid I'd be searching out your hiding places.

JUDGE: And you're afraid I'm in yours! It'll be a fine old age for Philemon and Baucis! [4]

WIFE: At least no gods will be visiting them.

JUDGE: Not gods exactly!

(*The procession begins again from the mausoleum, this time out forward to the right.*)

WIFE: Mary, Mother of God, what's that?

JUDGE: God save us! (*Pause*)

WIFE: Pray! Pray for us!

JUDGE: I've tried, but I can't!

WIFE: I can't either! I can't remember the words, I can't think! (*Pause*)

JUDGE: How does the Lord's Prayer start?

WIFE: I've forgotten it, but I knew it this morning. (*Pause*) Who is the White Lady?

JUDGE: It's she—Amalia's mother—the one whose memory you wanted to kill.

WIFE: Are they shadows or ghosts, or our own sick dreams?

JUDGE (*takes out his clasp knife*): It's the devil's delusions! I'll throw steel after them!—Open the blade, Caroline. Can't you see I can't?

WIFE: No, I understand—it isn't so easy without an index finger!— Well, I can't either! (*Drops the knife*)

JUDGE: Steel won't help here! There's the beheaded sailor! Let's go!

WIFE: That's easy to say! I can't move!

JUDGE: And it's as if I were fixed to the ground! No, I don't want to see more! (*Covers his eyes*)

WIFE: But what *is* this? Are they vapors from the earth, or are they shadows of the trees?

JUDGE: No, it's hallucinations! Why, I'm walking over there, but I'm standing here! If I could only sleep one night I'd stick my tongue out at the whole lot!—The devil! Won't the joke ever come to an end?

WIFE: Why do you keep looking at it?

JUDGE: Why, I see through my hand; I see in the dark through closed eyelids!

WIFE: But it's over now!

(*The procession has left the stage.*)

JUDGE: Praised be . . . I can't say it! How will I ever get to sleep tonight? We'll have to send for the doctor!

WIFE: Or maybe Father Colomba!

JUDGE: He can't help, and the One who could, won't!—Well, let the Other One do it then!

(OTHER ONE *enters from in back of the Madonna's chapel. He is extremely thin and moth-eaten; thin, parted snuff-brown hair; beard thin as hemp; poor outgrown clothes, no shirt; a red woolen scarf wound around his throat; wears glasses; has a cane under his arm.*)

JUDGE: Who's there?

OTHER ONE (*softly*): I'm the Other One!

JUDGE (*to his* WIFE): Make the sign of the cross! I can't!

OTHER ONE: The sign of the cross doesn't frighten me, for I'm just going through my time of testing to be able to carry it!

JUDGE: Who are you?

OTHER ONE: I became the second one because I wanted to be the first. I was evil—my punishment is to serve what is good.

JUDGE: Then you're not the evil one?

OTHER ONE: Oh, yes, and I have the task of torturing you to the cross where we'll meet once again.

WIFE (*to* JUDGE): Don't listen to him! Ask him to go!

OTHER ONE: That won't help! You've summoned me so now you'll have to put up with me!

(*The* JUDGE *and his* WIFE *go to the left; the* OTHER ONE *follows them.*)

[CURTAIN]

# ACT II

*A large whitewashed room with a black timbered ceiling, small deep-set windows with iron bars. Furniture of various kinds: cabinets, chiffoniers, bureaus, chests, and tables heaped up. On the furniture are silver services, candelabra, candlesticks, beakers, centerpieces, vases, statuettes, and so forth.*

*A door at the back; on one side of the door a portrait of the* JUDGE, *on the other one of his* WIFE.

*By a little sewing table with an elbow chair is a harp.*

AMALIA *is standing next to a table to the right polishing a silver coffee service.*

*The sun is shining through the windows at the back.*

NEIGHBOR (*enters*): Well, child, how's your patience?

AMALIA: Not bad, thank you! The hardest job I've had is polishing this silver service. I've been at it for half an hour without success.

NEIGHBOR: That's strange, but I suppose there are good reasons for that, as the judge says. Did you sleep last night?

AMALIA: Beautifully! But Father was out in the vineyard with his rattle all night . . .

NEIGHBOR: Yes, I heard him . . . What sort of crazy idea was that?

AMALIA: He thought he heard the starlings had come to eat the grapes!

NEIGHBOR: Poor man! The starlings aren't out at night!—How about the children?

AMALIA: She still has them locked up in the cellar. Just so she doesn't forget to give them something to eat.

NEIGHBOR: The One who feeds the birds doesn't forget the children! I'm going to tell you something one mustn't otherwise tell.— There's a little opening between my wine cellar and the judge's. When I was down airing the cellar this morning, I heard voices. When I looked through the opening, I saw Erik and Thyra playing with a little boy I didn't know!

AMALIA: You did? Were they . . .

NEIGHBOR: Happy and healthy . . .

AMALIA: Who was the playmate?

NEIGHBOR: I can't imagine.

AMALIA: This terrible house is filled with secrets.

NEIGHBOR: That's true, but it's not our task to search them out!

JUDGE (*enters carrying a rattle*): So you're here plotting! Isn't it enough that you set the starlings on my vineyard wtih your evil eye! You do have an evil eye, but we'll soon put that out of commission! I can do magic tricks, too!

NEIGHBOR (*to* AMALIA): Is there any point in trying to explain to him? He doesn't believe what one says! (*Going*)

AMALIA: We can't do anything about that!

JUDGE: Amalia, have you seen where Mother usually searches when she thinks she's alone?

AMALIA: No, Father!

JUDGE: I see by your eyes that you know! You looked in this direction. (*He goes up to a bureau, but gets into the sunlight.*) That damned sun! That always has to burn me. (*He goes over to the window, pulls down a shade, and returns to the bureau.*) It should be here. Let's see . . . We should look for the stupidest place for that's the cleverest—for example, here in the perfume basket! Absolutely right! (*Picks up bills and securities*) What's this? Twelve English banknotes. Twelve! Then I can imagine the rest! (*Stuffs*

Tora Teje, Poul Reumert, and Gabriel Alw in *The Dance of Death*
(Royal Dramatic Theater, Stockholm)

Uno Henning, Tora Teje, and Bernt Callenbo in *Advent*
(Royal Dramatic Theater, Stockholm)

Signe Hasso as Eleonora in *Easter*
(Royal Dramatic Theater, Stockholm)

Harriet Bosse as Eleonora in *Easter*
(Royal Dramatic Theater, Stockholm)

Eva Dahlbeck and George Rydeberg in *There Are Crimes and Crimes*
(Royal Dramatic Theater, Stockholm)

*the papers into his pockets*) But what do I hear out there?—It's
the starlings again! (*Goes to the open window and shakes the
rattle*) Get out of there!

WIFE (*enters*): What are you up to?

JUDGE: Aren't you in the kitchen?

WIFE: No, as you see! (*To* AMALIA) Are you through polishing?

AMALIA: No, Mother. I can't get this polished—it must be imitation.

WIFE: Imitation! Let me see!—My word, the silver is black! (*To the*
JUDGE, *who has pulled down the other shade*) Where did you get
this service?

JUDGE: That one?—I got it from a dead man's heirs.

WIFE: Because you drew up the inventory! The gift suited the act!

JUDGE: You shouldn't use insulting words that are punishable by
law.

WIFE: Is he crazy, or did I say anything crazy?

JUDGE: Besides it's silver—hall-marked silver.

WIFE: Then Amalia's to blame!

VOICE (*from outside the window*): The judge can make white black,
but he can't make black white!

JUDGE: Who said that?

WIFE: I thought it was a starling that spoke!

JUDGE (*pulls down the last shade*): Now the sun's here—a moment
ago it was there.

WIFE (*to* AMALIA): Who was it that spoke?

AMALIA: I think it was the strange schoolmaster with the red tie.

JUDGE: Ugh! Let's talk about something else!

MAID (*enters*): Dinner's served. (*Goes. A pause*)

WIFE: Go down and eat, Amalia.

AMALIA: Thank you, Mother. (*Goes*)

(JUDGE *sits down on a chair next to a chest.*)

WIFE (*goes over to the bureau on which the perfume basket stands*):
Aren't you going to eat?

JUDGE: No, I'm not hungry.—Aren't you going?

WIFE: I've just eaten. (*Pause*)

JUDGE (*takes a piece of bread out of his pocket*): Then you'll excuse me if I eat.

WIFE: There's a venison roast on the table!

JUDGE: Really!

WIFE: Do you think I'm poisoning the food?

JUDGE: Yes, I thought it tasted of creosote this morning!

WIFE: What I ate had a metallic taste . . .

JUDGE: If I assure you I haven't put anything in your food . . .

WIFE: I won't believe you! And if I swear . . .

JUDGE: I won't believe you! (*Eats the bread*) Venison is very good. I can smell it way in here, but bread isn't bad. (*Pause*)

WIFE: Why are you watching that chest?

JUDGE: For the same reason you're watching the perfumes.

WIFE: So you've been there, you house thief!

JUDGE: Corpse robber!

WIFE: What words between us! *Us!* (*Weeps*)

JUDGE: Yes, the world is evil, and people are evil.

WIFE: Yes, you can say that justifiably—and ungrateful above everything! Ungrateful children who steal while they're renting, ungrateful grandchildren who steal the fruit from the tree. You are right: the world is evil . . .

JUDGE: I who have seen everything ought to know that best—I who have had to hand down the death penalty. But that's why the riffraff hate me—as if I had written the laws . . .

WIFE: What people say doesn't mean anything if one only has a clear conscience . . . (*Three raps sound from the largest cabinet.*) What's that? Who's there?

JUDGE: It was the cabinet—it always creaks when it's going to rain. (*Three distinct raps again*)

WIFE: It's some trick that that wandering charlatan is up to!

(*The lid on the coffee pot that* AMALIA *has just polished jumps up and bangs shut a few times.*)

JUDGE: What is that?

WIFE: It's that magician who knows his tricks, but he doesn't frighten me.

(*The pot bangs shut again.*)

JUDGE: You think he's a magnetist?

WIFE: Yes, whatever it is they call him . . .

JUDGE: Maybe, but how can he know our secrets?

WIFE: Secrets? What do you mean?

(*The clock strikes innumerable times.*)

JUDGE: Now I am afraid!

WIFE: The devil take me if I'll stay here! (*The "suncat" falls on her portrait.*) See! He knows that secret, too!

JUDGE: You mean there's a portrait of *her* under yours?

WIFE: Let's go down to eat; then we can talk about selling the farm and everything at auction afterward . . .

JUDGE: Yes, you're right—sell every blessed thing, make a clean start, and begin life anew!—Let's go eat!

(THE OTHER *appears in the doorway; the* JUDGE *and his* WIFE *shrink back.*)

JUDGE: He's no ordinary person!

WIFE: Talk to him!

JUDGE( *to the* OTHER): Who are you?

OTHER: I have told you twice! Your not believing me is one of your punishments, for if you believed me, it would shorten your suffering.

JUDGE (*to his* WIFE): I think . . . it's he! For I'm turning to ice! How will we get rid of him? They say impure spirits can't bear music. Play the harp for him, Carolina!

(WIFE, *frightened, sits down by the table, takes the harp, and plays a somber melody in a minor key. The* OTHER ONE *listens reverently; he is touched.*)

WIFE (*to the* JUDGE): Has he gone?

OTHER: Thank you for the music! It quiets my pain and awakens memories of a better life even in one damned . . . Thank you!—

As far as the auction goes, I think you're doing absolutely the right thing though I think a regular bankruptcy would be better— yes, hand over your wealth to your creditors, and let every one of them get what is rightfully his.

JUDGE: Bankruptcy? I have no debts . . .

OTHER: No debts!

WIFE: My husband *has* no debts!

OTHER: No debts! To be that lucky!

JUDGE: Yes, that's how it is! But other people owe me . . .

OTHER: Forgive them, then!

JUDGE: It isn't a question of forgiveness but of payment . . .

OTHER: Fine! Then you're going to pay!—Farewell for the time being! We'll often see each other again, the last time at the big auction! (*Backs out*)

JUDGE: You're afraid of the sun, you, too! (*Laughs*)

OTHER: For yet a while, yes. But when I've once got used to the light, I'll hate the darkness! (*Goes*)

WIFE: Do you think he's . . . the Other One?

JUDGE: He may not look like it, but times change, and we with the times. They used to say he gave gold and honor, but this one goes about dunning . . .

WIFE: He's a fool and a charlatan, that's all. A coward who doesn't dare to bite though he'd like to very much!

OTHER (*in the door*) Watch out for me! Watch out!

JUDGE (*lifts his hand*): Watch out yourself!

OTHER (*lifts his hand, pretending to shoot as if with a pistol*): For shame!

(JUDGE *frozen in the gesture. Sighs with horror*)

OTHER: You have never believed in what is good. Now you are going to believe in that Evil One. You see the Eternal One can do no harm, so he lets wretches like me do that! To get more certain results you two will get to torture each other and yourselves!

WIFE (*kneels before the* OTHER ONE): Spare us! Help us! Mercy!

OTHER (*as if he wanted to rend his clothes*): Get up, woman! There's

only One you should pray to! Get up, or . . . Well, now you believe though I don't have a red cape and a sword and a money bag
and can crack jokes; but take care you don't take me for a joke.
I'm as serious as sin and strict as retribution! I haven't come to
tempt you with gold and honor but to discipline you with whips
and scorpions! . . . (*The clock strikes as before; it turns dark.*)
Your time is drawing to an end, so put your house in order for
you shall die! (*There is a stormlike sound.*) Whose voice is speaking now? Speak His name and try to frighten Him with your
rattle when He blows across your vineyard! Storm and hail—
those are His names—and He bears destruction under His wings
and your punishment in His grasp. Put on your caul now and
dress yourself in your clear conscience . . . (*The hailstorm can be
heard pattering.*)

JUDGE: Mercy!

OTHER: Yes, if you promise to change for the better!

JUDGE: I promise and swear . . .

OTHER: You can't swear, for you're already forsworn! But promise
to set the children free first of all . . . and then all the rest!

JUDGE: I promise that before the sun sets the children will be free!

OTHER: The first step forward, then! But if you turn back, you shall
see I deserve my name, for I am . . . Legion! (*Lifts his cane,
whereupon the* JUDGE *is released from his state*)

[CURTAIN]


# ACT III


*A wine cellar with vats in a row to the right, another row to the
left. An iron door at the back.*

*The vats have serious notations; on those nearest the audience are small trays above the spouts, and on these are glasses.*

*To the right in the foreground are a wine press and a couple of chairs.*

*Bottles, funnels, siphons, baskets, and so forth here and there.*

ERIK *and* THYRA *are sitting next to the wine press.*

ERIK: This isn't any fun.

THYRA: That's because Grandmother is bad.

ERIK: We mustn't say that.

THYRA: No, maybe not, but she is bad.

ERIK: You mustn't say that, Thyra. If you do, the little boy won't come back to play with us.

THYRA: Then I won't say it again! If it only weren't so dark.

ERIK: Don't you remember the boy said we shouldn't complain . . .

THYRA: Then I won't . . . (*The "suncat" appears on the floor.*) Look! There's the "suncat"! (*She jumps up and stands on the "suncat."* )

ERIK: You mustn't step on the sun! That's a sin!

THYRA: But I'm not stepping on him hard—I just want to have fun with him. Look! Now he's in my arms, and now I'm patting him . . . Look! He's kissing my mouth!

(*The Playmate appears from behind a wine vat. He is dressed in a white garment that extends below his knees; he has a blue belt around his waist, sandals on his feet. He is blond, and, when he enters, the cellar becomes light.*)

ERIK (*goes up to him*): Hello!—Come here, Thyra, and say hello to him. (*To the* PLAYMATE) What's your name? You have to tell us today. (*The* PLAYMATE *looks at him.*)

THYRA: You mustn't be inquisitive, Erik, or he'll be embarrassed.— But who is your father? What does he do?

PLAYMATE: Don't be so inquisitive! When you know me better, I'll tell you all that—But we'll play a game now!

THYRA: But not anything useful—that's so boring! Let's play something pleasant!

PLAYMATE (*smiles*): Shall I tell you a story?

THYRA: Yes, but not out of Bible history—we know that by heart
. . . (*The* PLAYMATE *smiles.*)

ERIK: Don't make him sad, Thyra . . .

PLAYMATE: No, I won't get sad . . . But if you're really good, we'll
go outside to play . . .

ERIK: Yes, let's!—But Grandmother won't let us . . .

PLAYMATE: But Grandmother has said you may, so we'll go before
she changes her mind. Come along!

THYRA: Wonderful! Look . . .

(*The door at the back opens; they see outside a sunlit yellow
rye field with cornflowers and daisies.*)

PLAYMATE: Come along! Out into the sunlight to have fun!

THYRA: May we take the "suncat" with us? It's a shame if he has
to be here in the dark.

PLAYMATE: Yes, if he wants to. Call him!

(ERIK *and* THYRA *go toward the door; the "suncat" follows them
on the floor.*)

ERIK: Look! Isn't he nice? (*To the "suncat"*) Kitty, kitty, kitty!

PLAYMATE: Put him on your arm, Thyra; otherwise he won't get over
the threshold!

(THYRA *puts the "suncat" on her arm. They all go out. The door
shuts by itself. Pause. The* JUDGE *comes in with a lantern, his* WIFE
*with a switch.*)

WIFE: It's cool and comfortable in here, and the sun can't torture
me.

JUDGE: And it's quiet, too. But where are the brats? (*They look for
the children.*) I think they've taken us at our word!

WIFE: Us? I didn't promise anything, for he—you know who I
mean—was talking only to you toward the end.

JUDGE: Perhaps, but this time we'll have to obey him, for I don't
want any more nonsense with hailstones and the like.—But the
children aren't here.—They'll be back when they're hungry.

WIFE: And then I'll "congratulate" them! (*The switch is jerked out *of her hand and dances away behind a vat.*) Now that's starting again!

JUDGE: Well, but give in and do what he—you know!—says. For my part I don't dare do anything unjust any more. Our grapes have been destroyed; we'll have to be glad we had got some harvested. Come here, Carolina, and we'll get a lift from something good! (*He taps on a barrel and pours a glass.*) This is from 1869, the year of the big comet . . . they said it meant there'd be a war. And there was a war! (*Offers his* WIFE *a filled glass*)

WIFE: You drink first!

JUDGE: No, really! Did you think this is poisoned, too?

WIFE: No, I didn't really . . . but . . . well, there'll be neither peace nor happiness for us any more.

JUDGE: Do as I do! Submit! (*Drinks*)

WIFE: I want to, and I try, but when I think of how badly other people have treated us, I feel I'm as good as they are. (*Drinks*) That's really good wine! (*Sits down*)

JUDGE: The wine is good and gives me a lift . . . The wise man says we're all about the same, so I can't understand why the one should be going about telling the other what to do. (*Drinks*) For my part, I've always done everything legally, that's to say according to the letter of the actual laws; if other people haven't known the law, it's their fault, for no one may be ignorant of the law! So if Adolf doesn't pay the rent, he has broken the law, not I.

WIFE: But you'll be blamed all the same and be treated as a criminal. Isn't it as I say: there isn't any justice in the world. If you did the right thing, you'd sue Adolf and kick his family out . . . it isn't too late yet . . . (*Drinks*)

JUDGE: Yes, if I wanted to proceed all the way legally, I could insist on the breaking up of his marriage, and then he couldn't inherit . . .

WIFE: But do it, then!

JUDGE (*looks about*): Well-l—that would probably be going too far.

I don't suppose a divorce would be granted, but one could get the marriage annulled because of some flaw in the form . . .

WIFE: And if there weren't any?

JUDGE (*somewhat high*): There's always a flaw if you look for it.

WIFE: Well, then! Think of that good-for-nothing who's waiting for us to die, but now he'll see how nature drives its drones to wander the highways . . .

JUDGE (*laughs*): You're so right, so right! And, you know, when I think about it carefully, what do we have to accuse ourselves of? What evil have we done? That monstrance! That's pretty small-minded to talk about, and it hasn't hurt a single human being. And that I've sworn falsely is quite simply a lie. I got a felon in my finger—that's all and quite natural . . .

WIFE: I ought to know that best . . . and I want to add that that hailstorm was as obvious as if it had been in the almanac!

JUDGE: There you are! I think so, too. That's why, Carolina, we'd do best to forget all this latest talk, and if you agree with me we'll go to another priest and have him consecrate the mausoleum.

WIFE: Why shouldn't we?

JUDGE: Why shouldn't we? Probably because that hypnotist is going around here talking superstition?

WIFE: Tell me, do you think that's all he is?

JUDGE (*blusters*): All he is? He's a first-class charlatan! A char-la-tan!

WIFE (*looks about*): I'm not so sure!

JUDGE: But I am sure! S-u-r-e! And if he shows up once more, I'll drink a toast to him and say: Here's to you, you old joker! (*His lifted glass is jerked out of his hand and glides out through the wings.*) What's wrong? (*The lantern is extinguished.*)

WIFE: Help us! (*A storm wind can be heard outside; then it becomes silent.*)

JUDGE: Just get some matches, and I'll manage this. Just now I'm afraid of nothing. Nothing!

WIFE (*goes*): Oh, oh! If you get out of this alive, then . . .

JUDGE: Don't say it! Don't!

THE OTHER (*steps out from in back of a vat*): Now we'll talk privately.

JUDGE (*frightened*): Where did you come from?

OTHER: That's none of your business!

JUDGE (*straightens up*): What sort of talk is that?

OTHER: It's yours!—Off with your cap! (*Blows on the* JUDGE, *whose cap is lifted off and falls to the floor.*) Listen to the pronouncement of the sentence: You have wanted to put asunder what the One whose name I may not mention has joined together. Now you shall be parted from the one who should have been a support for your old age, and you shall run your gauntlet alone. You shall suffer the agony of sleepless nights alone.

JUDGE: Is that merciful?

OTHER: It's justice; it's the law: an eye for an eye and a tooth for a tooth! The New Testament is different, but you don't want to hear about that! Up and on your way now! (*Swings his cane*)

\*

*The setting is an orchard with cypresses and yews in the form of obelisks, candelabra, vases, and so forth; underneath roses, hollyhocks, digitalis. In the center a fountain over which a gigantic fuschia ("drops of Christ's blood") is in bloom. The background is a ripening rye field with cornflowers and daisies; in the center a scarecrow; way in the distance a vineyard (on hills) and cliffs of light yellow slate with a beech forest and ruins of medieval castles.*

*The highway toward the back; to the right a vaulted covered passage in Gothic style. In front of it a Madonna with the Child.*

ERIK *and* THYRA *enter, holding the* PLAYMATE *by the hand.*

ERIK: Isn't it beautiful!

THYRA: Who lives here?

PLAYMATE: The one who feels at home here lives here!

THYRA: May we play here?

PLAYMATE: Anywhere except in the walk to the right.

ERIK: May we pick the flowers, too?

PLAYMATE: Yes, you may pick the flowers, but you mustn't touch the tree by the spring.

THYRA: What sort of tree is it?

ERIK: Why, it's . . . (*lowers his voice*) the fuschia, the drops of Christ's blood!

THYRA: Cross yourself when you mention God by name.

ERIK (*makes the sign of the cross*): Tell me, why mayn't we touch that tree?

THYRA: Don't be inquisitive, Erik—just obey! (*To the* PLAYMATE) But why does that ugly scarecrow have to be there? Can't we take it away?

PLAYMATE: You certainly may; then the birds will come and sing for us!

   (ERIK *and* THYRA *hurry over to the scarecrow and pull it down.*)

ERIK: Away with you, you ugly scarecrow! Come, little birds, and eat now! (*The golden bird comes flying in from the right and sits down in the fuschia.*) Look! The golden bird! Look, Thyra!

THYRA: How beautiful it is! Can it sing, too?

   (*The bird calls like the cuckoo.*)

ERIK (*to the* PLAYMATE): Can you understand what he's singing?

PLAYMATE: No, the birds have their little secrets, and they have the right to keep them.

THYRA: That's right, Erik; otherwise, children would tell where their nests are and steal their eggs, and the bird would be so sad and couldn't have any young any more.

ERIK: My, you're sensible, Thyra!

PLAYMATE (*puts a finger to his mouth*): Sh-h! Someone's coming! Let's see if he likes to be with us or not.

   (CHIMNEY SWEEP *enters, stares in amazement.*)

PLAYMATE: Don't you want to play with us?

CHIMNEY SWEEP (*takes off his cap; embarrassed*): You don't want to play with me!

PLAYMATE: Why not?

CHIMNEY SWEEP: Why, I'm covered with soot—besides I can't play— I don't know how.

THYRA: Poor boy! He has never played.

PLAYMATE: What's your name?

CHIMNEY SWEEP: Name? They call me Olle . . . but . . .

PLAYMATE: What's your other name?

CHIMNEY SWEEP: Other? I don't have any other.

PLAYMATE: What's your father's name then?

CHIMNEY SWEEP: I don't have a father.

PLAYMATE: Your mother's name?

CHIMNEY SWEEP: I don't know.

PLAYMATE: He doesn't have a father or a mother! Come over to the spring, and you'll become as white as a little prince.

CHIMNEY SWEEP: If anybody else said so, I wouldn't believe that . . .

PLAYMATE: How can you believe me?

CHIMNEY SWEEP: Well, I don't know—but I think you look as if it's true.

PLAYMATE: Thyra, give him your hand!—Do you want to give him a kiss, too?

THYRA (*hesitates; then*): Well, since you ask me! (*Kisses the* CHIMNEY SWEEP)

PLAYMATE (*The* PLAYMATE *dips his hands into the spring and sprinkles the boy's face; his black mask falls in such a way as not to be noticed by the audience*): There, now you're white! Go in back of that rosebush and you'll get new clothes!

CHIMNEY SWEEP: Why do I get all this that I haven't deserved?

PLAYMATE: Because you believe you haven't deserved it!

CHIMNEY SWEEP (*goes behind the rosebush*): Thank you, but I don't understand what it means.

THYRA: Has the boy been bad since he's a chimney sweep?

PLAYMATE: No, but he had a bad guardian, who took all his money, and he had to support himself somehow . . . Look, how nice he is now!

(*The* CHIMNEY SWEEP *comes back dressed in light-colored summer garments.*)

PLAYMATE (*to the* CHIMNEY SWEEP): Go over to the archway and you'll meet someone whom you love . . . and who loves you!

CHIMNEY SWEEP: Who can love me?

PLAYMATE: Take a look!

(*The* CHIMNEY SWEEP *goes toward the archway where he is met by a* WHITE LADY *who embraces him.*)

THYRA: Who lives in there?

PLAYMATE (*his finger in his mouth*) Inquisitive! But who's coming over there?

(*The* JUDGE'S WIFE *comes trudging on the highway with a sack on her back and a stick in her hand.*)

ERIK: It's Grandmother! Now we'll get it!

THYRA (*sighs*): It is Grandmother!

PLAYMATE: Pull yourselves together! I'll take the blame.

ERIK: No, you mustn't; then she'll beat you.

PLAYMATE: Well, can't I take a beating for my friends?

ERIK: No! I will!

THYRA: I, too!

PLAYMATE: Sh-h! We'll hide—then we won't get a scolding! (*They hide.*)

JUDGE'S WIFE: (*up to the spring*): Here's the famous spring that they say can cure everything! Since the angel stirred its waters, of course!—But I suspect that's only a lie! Well, I can always quench my thirst—and water's water! (*She bends over the spring.*) But what's this I see?—Erik and Thyra with a boy! What does that mean? They aren't here. It must be a magic spring. (*She takes a beaker and fills it; then drinks.*) Terrible—it tastes like copper . . . so he has been here and poisoned this water, too! Everything's poisoned! Everything!—I am weary, though the years haven't taken their toll . . . (*She uses the spring as a mirror; primps*)

Why, I look quite young . . . but walking is hard, and getting up
still harder . . . (*She tries desperately to get up.*) My God, my
God, have mercy, or I'll have to lie here . . .

PLAYMATE (*signals to the children to stay where they are; goes up
to the* JUDGE's WIFE *and wipes the perspiration for her forehead*):
Stand up, and do not be evil any more!

WIFE (*gets up*): Who is it?—So it's you, who lead my children
astray!

PLAYMATE: Go, ungrateful woman! I wipe the sweat of anguish from
your brow and raise you up when you have collapsed, and you
reward me thus. Go!

    (WIFE *looks at him wiith amazement; then lowers her eyes,
turns away, and goes.* ERIK *and* THYRA *come forward*)

ERIK: But it's a shame about Grandmother all the same though she
is bad!

THYRA: I don't like this—I want to go home!

PLAYMATE: Wait a little! Don't be impatient!—There comes someone else you know! (*The* JUDGE *on the highway*) He mustn't
come here and make this spring impure! (*He waves his hand; the
"suncat" falls on the* JUDGE *so that he turns and goes out.*) It's very
nice you pity your grandparents, children, but you must believe
I'm doing the right thing. Do you?

ERIK AND THYRA: Yes! Yes, we do!

THYRA: But I want to go home to Mother!

PLAYMATE: Yes, you may! (*The* OTHER ONE *appears at the back, then
disappears behind the bushes.*) For I have to go now; the bells
will soon be ringing for Angelus.

ERIK: Where are you going?

PLAYMATE: I have other children to play with—far away where you
may not go with me. But when I leave you here, don't forget I
said you can't touch that tree!

ERIK: We won't! But don't leave—then it'll turn dark right away.

PLAYMATE: Well-l! If you have a clear conscience and can say your evening prayer, you won't have anything to be afraid of.

THYRA: When will you come back to us?

PLAYMATE: I'll be back at Christmas . . . every Christmas!—Good night!

(*He kisses them on their foreheads and goes toward the back between the bushes. When he reappears at the back, he is carrying a little cross with a banner in the way the child Jesus is usually portrayed when he stands by the Lamb. The bells ring for Angelus. Now he lifts the banner and waves it to the children. As he goes out a strong white light envelops him.* ERIK *and* THYRA *fall to their knees and pray while the bells ring.*)

ERIK (*making the sign of the cross*): Do you know who he is?

THYRA: He's the Savior!

(THE OTHER *comes forward.*)

THYRA (*frightened, runs to* ERIK, *who protects her with his arms*): Ugh!

ERIK (*to the* OTHER ONE): What do you want of us? You nasty thing!

OTHER: I wanted only . . . Look at me!

ERIK: Yes.

OTHER: I look like this because I touched that tree once—then I wanted very much to make others do it, too. But now that I'm old, I've repented, and I'm going about among people to warn them. But no one believes me any more—no one, because I used to be . . .

ERIK: You don't need to warn us, because you can't fool us anyway!

OTHER: There, there! Don't be so sure! Otherwise, it's fine.

ERIK: Go away, then, for I don't want to listen to you! And you're frightening my sister.

OTHER: I will go—I'm not at home here, and I have other things to do elsewhere! Farewell, children!

AMALIA's (*voice from the right*): Erik! Thyra!

CHILDREN: It's Mother!

(AMALIA *enters, takes them in her arms.* THE OTHER *is visibly moved; turns away.*)

[CURTAIN]


# ACT IV


*A crossroad in a spruce forest. Moonlight.*
WITCH *standing waiting.*

JUDGE's WIFE (*enters*): At last! There you are!

WITCH: You've made me wait! Why have you summoned me?

WIFE: Help me!

WITCH: How?

WIFE: Against my enemies.

WITCH: There's only one help against your enemies: do good to them.

WIFE: Well! I think the world's turned upside down.

WITCH: Yes, it looks like it.

WIFE: Even the Other One—you know who I mean—has been converted.

WITCH: Then it may be about time for you, too!

WIFE: About time! You mean I'm getting old. About three weeks ago I danced at a wedding.

WITCH: And that's happiness and bliss for you. If that's all you want, you'll get your fill. There's going to be a ball here tonight though I can't take part.

WIFE: Here?

WITCH: Right here! It'll start when I wish . . .

WIFE: It's a shame I don't have my gown with the plunging neckline along!

WITCH: You can borrow one from me . . . and dancing slippers with red heels.

WIFE: Gloves and a fan, too?

WITCH: Everything! And especially many young men, who'll make you the queen of the ball.

WIFE: You're joking!

WITCH: I don't joke, and I know that at balls of this kind they have enough taste to select the right queen of the ball—by *right* I mean the most deserving . . .

WIFE: You mean the most beautiful?

WITCH: No, I don't, but the most deserving! If you wish, I'll sound the start of the ball right away.

WIFE: Fine as far as I'm concerned!

WITCH: Step over there and you'll find a maid. I'll have the hall readied . . .

WIFE (*goes out into the right wing*): Imagine! I get a maid, too . . . you know that was the dream of my youth that was never fulfilled.

WITCH: You see, "What you want in your youth you get in your old age." (*Blows a pipe*)

## Change of Scene

*The setting is changed to the floor of a valley surrounded on all sides by mountains; the back and the sides are steep dark mountain walls without vegetation. To the left, in the foreground the throne of the Queen of the Ball. To the left the orchestra's platform.*

*In the center of the stage a statue of Pan, surrounded by potted plants: henbane, burdock, thistles, onions, and so forth.*

*The musicians enter dressed in gray; their faces are chalk white and sad; their gestures, weary. They seem to be tuning their instruments, which do not make any sound.*

*The* ORCHESTRA LEADER *enters.*

*The* GUESTS (*cripples, beggars, criminals*) *enter, pulling on black gloves. Slow movements, funereal miens.*

*The* OTHER ONE (*the same person as the* MASTER OF CEREMONIES): *a seventy-year-old fop with a black wig that is too small so that the gray hair underneath shows; waxed mustache, a single lorgnette, outgrown tails* (*costume*), *tall boots. He looks sad and is obviously suffering because of his role.*

THE SEVEN DEADLY SINS (PRIDE, AVARICE, LUST, WRATH, GLUTTONY, ENVY, SLOTH) *enter and station themselves about the throne.*

*The* PRINCE *enters; a hunchback; a soiled velvet jacket with shiny buttons, sword, lace collar, boots with spurs.*

*The whole of the following scene is played with an unwavering melancholy gravity without a trace of irony, satire, or humor; all the figures have a touch of death masks, walk soundlessly, and make embarrassed gestures as if they had been memorized.*

PRINCE (*to the* MASTER OF CEREMONIES): Why do you disturb my rest at this midnight hour?

MASTER OF CEREMONIES: So you're still asking why. Hasn't the light gone up for you yet?

PRINCE: Only in part. I see a connection between my suffering and my guilt, but I don't understand why I should suffer eternally since *He* has suffered in my stead.

MASTER: Eternally! You died yesterday. Time ceased for you then, so a few hours seem eternal to you.

PRINCE: Yesterday?

MASTER: Yes!—But since you were proud and didn't want help in your suffering, you'll have to suffer it alone.

PRINCE: What is it I have been doing, then?

MASTER: A sublime question!

PRINCE: Tell me!

MASTER: Since it's our task to torture each other with the truth— we were called heroes of truth when we were alive, weren't we?— I'll tell you part of your secret. You were and still are a hunchback . . .

PRINCE: What's that?

MASTER: You see! You don't know what others know. But everyone else felt sympathy for you, so you never heard the word, the name of your defect . . .

PRINCE: What defect? You probably mean my "weak chest," but that's not a defect.

MASTER: "Weak chest." Yes, that's your name for it. But people concealed your bodily defect, and they tried to mitigate your misfortune through mercy and friendliness, but you took their kindness as tribute you had coming, their encouraging words as admiration of your physical superiority; and you finally went so far in your self-love that you considered yourself exceptionally handsome. When woman finally gave you her favor out of pity, you believed you were an irresistible conqueror.

PRINCE: What right do you have to insult me like this?

MASTER: Right? I'm fulfilling the Evil One's sad duty of punishing the evil; and you're going to have the same cruel duty to a woman who's insane with vanity, a person who resembles you very, very much.

PRINCE: I don't want to!

MASTER: Try to do anything but what you must and you'll experience an inner disharmony you can't explain.

PRINCE: What?

MASTER: This: that you can't stop being immediately what you are: and you are what you wanted to be! (*Strikes his hands together*)
    (JUDGE'S WIFE *enters; an aging awkward figure but "painted" and wearing a powdered rococo wig; dressed in a rose-red gown with a plunging neckline, red shoes, a fan of peacock feathers*)

WIFE (*somewhat uncertainly*): Where am I? Am I in the right place?

MASTER: You're in the absolutely right place—you're in what we call the Waiting Room. It's called that since we—(*sighs*) spend our time here waiting . . . Waiting for something that will come sometime . . .

WIFE: Well, it's rather nice . . . and there's the orchestra . . . and there's a bust . . . Whose?

MASTER: A pagan idol, called Pan because he was everything to the ancients; and since we here are ancient, or more or less old-fashioned, he has been brought here for us to look at.

WIFE: Surely we're not old . . .

MASTER: Yes, my queen, when the new time came—(*sighs*) we couldn't keep up but were left behind . . .

WIFE: The new time . . . What's that? . . . When did that begin? . . .

MASTER: It's easy to figure out when the year one started . . . As far as that goes, it was a night, the stars were shining in a clear sky, and it must have been mild, for the shepherds were out in the open . . .

WIFE: There, there . . . Isn't there a ball here tonight?

MASTER: Of course there is. The prince is waiting to ask for the first dance.

WIFE: Is he a real prince?

MASTER: A real prince, my queen; that is, he is absolutely real in a certain way . . .

WIFE (*to* PRINCE): You don't look happy, Your Highness.

PRINCE: No, I'm not happy!

WIFE: I can't say it's very gay here either . . . and it smells just as if the glazier had just been here. What sort of strange fragrance of linseed oil is it?

PRINCE (*horrified*): What are you saying? Do you mean it smells of the dead?

WIFE: Apparently I said something impolite, but it's not up to the lady to say polite things—that's up to the man . . .

PRINCE: What shall I say that you don't already know?

WIFE: That I don't already know? Let me think . . . No, *I* had better tell *you* that you are handsome, Your Highness . . .

PRINCE: Now you're exaggerating, Your Majesty; I'm not handsome, but I have always been thought to have what people call a good appearance . . .

WIFE: That's just like me . . . I wasn't any beauty . . . I mean I *am* not, but considering my years . . . How stupid I am! What was I going to say?

MASTER (*to the orchestra*): Start playing!

  (MUSICIANS *can be seen playing, but not a sound can be heard.*)

MASTER (*to the* PRINCE): Well? Aren't you going to dance?

PRINCE (*mournfully*): No, I haven't any desire to dance.

MASTER: But you have to—you're the only presentable man on the floor.

PRINCE: That's probably true . . . (*thoughtfully*).—But is that anything for me?

MASTER: How do you mean?

PRINCE: Sometimes I have the feeling I have something else to think about, but then I forget what it is.

MASTER: Don't brood . . . enjoy life while you're still young and your cheeks are rosy from the joy of life. There! Straighten up and get your legs going . . .

  (PRINCE *smiles broadly; offers his hand to the* JUDGE's WIFE; *they dance a couple of minuet steps.*)

WIFE (*stops the dance*): Ugh! Your hands are as cold as ice! (*Goes toward the throne*) Why aren't the seven ladies over there dancing?

MASTER: How did Your Majesty like the orchestra?

WIFE: It was superb, but it could have played a little louder . . .

MASTER: Well, they're soloists, all of them, and wanted to outplay each other, so they have to tune down now . . .

WIFE: But I asked why the seven sisters didn't want to dance. Can't you make them?

MASTER: No, I doubt I could—they're as stubborn as sin . . . But won't you, Your Majesty, take your place on your throne? We're putting on a little play in honor of the day . . .

WIFE: What fun! But the Prince must conduct me . . . !

PRINCE (*to the* MASTER): Do I have to?

WIFE: Why, you hunchback!

PRINCE (*spits in her face*): Mind your manners, you old she-devil!

WIFE (*slaps the* PRINCE): There, take that!

PRINCE (*leaps at her and knocks her down*): And you take that!

ALL (*cover their eyes with their hands*).

PRINCE (*tears the wig off the* JUDGE's WIFE *revealing that she is bald*): Here's the false scalp—now we'll take out her false teeth!

MASTER: That's enough! (*Helps the* JUDGE's WIFE *to get up and gives her a cloth with which to cover her head*)

WIFE (*weeping*): To think I've let myself be fooled like this. I don't deserve any better, if I must admit it!

PRINCE: No, you deserve much worse, but you shouldn't have mentioned my hunched back—then all hell breaks loose.—It's ghastly to see an old woman sunk so low and so foolish. You're to be pitied as we're all to be pitied!

ALL: We're all to be pitied!

PRINCE (*scornfully*): Queen!

WIFE (*responding in kind*): Prince!—But haven't we met before?

PRINCE: Yes, perhaps when we were young. For even I am old. You were so decked out a bit ago . . . but now we've seen each other as we are . . . Certain features begin to show up . . .

WIFE: Don't say any more . . . Don't say any more . . . Where am I? What's happening to me?

PRINCE: Now I know—you're my sister!

WIFE: But . . . my brother's dead. Have they lied to me? Or do the dead come back?

PRINCE: Everything comes back.

WIFE: Am I dead or am I alive?

PRINCE: You may well ask, for I don't know there's any difference. But you haven't changed at all since I saw you last; just as vain and just as dishonest.

WIFE: Do you think you're any better?

PRINCE: Perhaps! I have the seven deadly sins, but you've invented the eighth—stealing from the dead.

WIFE: What do you mean?

PRINCE: Twelve years running I sent you money for a wreath for Mother's grave. You kept the money—you didn't buy any wreath.

WIFE: How do you know?

PRINCE: The only thing that interests you right now is how I know about your sin.

WIFE: Prove it!

PRINCE (*takes bills from his pocket*): Here are the bills!

(WIFE *collapses.*)

(*A church bell rings; all bend their heads, but no one kneels.*)

WHITE LADY (*enters; goes up to the* JUDGE'S WIFE *and helps her get up*): Do you know me?

WIFE: No.

WHITE LADY: I'm Amalia's mother. You've stolen her memory of me from her. You have blotted me out of her life, but you're now going to be blotted out, and I'll win back my child's love and her prayers that I need.

WIFE: So they've told that minx . . . I'll put her to watching the pigs . . .

(PRINCE *slaps her across the mouth.*)

WHITE LADY: Don't hit her!

WIFE: You put in a good word for me!

WHITE LADY: Yes, I've learned to do that.

WIFE: Hypocrite, you'd wish me as far down in the earth as it is to the sun if you only dared!

MASTER (*touches the* JUDGE'S WIFE *with his staff; she falls to the ground*): Down, you damned bitch!

(*Change of scene without lowering the curtain. The statue of Pan sinks through the ground; the* MUSICIANS, *the throne, and the* SEVEN DEADLY SINS *are concealed by lowered scenery and disappear. Finally: the crossroad in the forest is restored. The* JUDGE'S WIFE *is lying by the road sign. The* WITCH *is standing beside her.*)

WITCH: Get up!

WIFE: I can't! I've turned to ice!

WITCH: The sun will soon rise, the cock has crowed, and the bells for morning services are ringing.

WIFE: I don't care about the sun.

WITCH: Then you shall wander in darkness!

WIFE: My eyes! What have you done?

WITCH: I merely put out the light since it tortures you. Get up and go now—in cold and darkness until you collapse!

WIFE: Where is my husband?—Amalia! Erik and Thyra! My children!

WITCH: Where are they? Where you won't see them until your pilgrimage is fulfilled. So: get up and go! Otherwise: I'll set my dogs loose!

(WIFE *gropes about, and goes.*)

*

*The courtroom. At the back the chairman's tribune in white and gold with the emblems of justice. In the center of the floor in front of the tribune is the judgment table with writing utensils, a copy of the Bible, a clock, a gavel.*

*On the wall in back the hangman's ax; under it handcuffs; above, a large black crucifix.*

*The* JUDGE *enters, steals forward slowly; the clock strikes; the gavel strikes once; all the chairs are shoved up to the table in unison; the Bible is opened; the candles are lighted.*

*The* JUDGE *stands still, striken with horror. Then he approaches the cupboard.*

*The cupboard door opens; the papers are thrown at the* JUDGE, *who picks them up.*

JUDGE (*becomes calm*): That was lucky! Here are the accounts of my guardianship; here is the rent contract and the inventory of that estate . . . Fine! (*The handcuffs on the wall rattle.*) Go ahead, rattle! As long as the ax doesn't move, I'm not afraid. (*He puts the papers on the judgment table and goes back to shut the cupboard door, but it refuses to stay shut though he closes it again and again.*) There's a reason for everything: *ratio sufficiens.* This door has a spring I don't know about so I'm amazed because I don't, but I'm not frightened. (*The ax on the wall moves.*) The ax is moving; that has always meant an execution, but today it simply means it's off balance. No, when I see my spirit, I'll begin reflecting, for that charlatan can't do magic about my spirit.

(SPIRIT *comes from behind the cupboard; he is exactly like the* JUDGE *except that he has eyes without pupils and entirely white as in a plaster statue.*)

JUDGE (*frightened*): Who are you?

SPIRIT: I no longer am; I have been. I have been the unjust judge who has come to receive his judgment.

JUDGE: Poor fellow, what did you do?

SPIRIT: Everything an unjust judge can do by way of evil . . . Pray for me . . . you, who have a clear conscience . . .

JUDGE: Shall I pray . . . for you?

SPIRIT: Yes, you who have never spilled innocent blood . . .

JUDGE: That's true—I never really have; besides I've followed the letter of the law so I can for good reason accept the title, the just judge . . . yes, yes, without irony!

SPIRIT: The moment would be a bad one to joke in, when the invisible powers are sitting in judgment . . .

JUDGE: What do you mean? Who are sitting in judgment?

SPIRIT (*points at the judgment table*): You don't see them, but I do! (*The clock strikes. A chair is pushed away from the table.*) Pray for me!

JUDGE: I don't want to—justice must be done! You must be a big criminal to have come so late to a consciousness of your guilt.

SPIRIT: You are as strict as a good conscience.

JUDGE: Yes, indeed! Strict but just!

SPIRIT: No mercy, then?

JUDGE: None!

SPIRIT: No grace?

JUDGE: No grace.

(*The gavel falls; the chairs are shoved away from the table.*)

SPIRIT: The judgment was handed down! Did you hear it?

JUDGE: I don't hear anything!

SPIRIT (*points at the table*): And see nothing? Don't you see the decapitated sailor, the surveyor, the chimney sweep's boy, the white lady, the renter . . .

JUDGE: No, I see absolutely nothing!

SPIRIT: Woe be unto you, then, when your eyes have once been opened as mine have been! The verdict was just now handed down: Guilty! (*The candles on the table are snuffed out.*)

JUDGE: Guilty!

SPIRIT: You pronounced it . . . yourself! And you are already sentenced! Now all that's left is the big auction!

[CURTAIN]


# ACT V


*The same room as in scene 1, Act II. The room has been prepared for an auction with benches in the middle of the room. On the auctioneer's table is the silver service, the pendulum clock, vases, branched candlesticks, and so forth.*

*The portraits of the judge and his wife have been taken down; they are leaning against the table.*

AMALIA (*dressed for scrubbing*): Before Mother left, she told me to scrub the entrance and the stairs. I can't say I've enjoyed carrying out her orders in this cold winter weather . . .

NEIGHBOR: Oh-h, you haven't enjoyed it! You know, child, you do expect a lot of yourself. But now you've obeyed and stood the test, the time of your trials will be over—and I'll tell you the secret of your life.

AMALIA: Tell me—I can't rely on my good will any longer.

NEIGHBOR: The woman you call "Mother" is your stepmother! Your father married her when you were a year old. Your mother died when you were born.

AMALIA: So that's it!—To have had a mother but never to have seen her! Did you ever see her?

NEIGHBOR: I knew her!

AMALIA: What did she look like?

NEIGHBOR: What did she look like?—Her eyes were blue as flax blossoms, and her hair golden as wheat straw . . .

AMALIA: And she was tall and slim; and her hand as small and white as if it had sewed only silk all her days, and her mouth looked like a heart and as if only good words had passed her lips . . .

NEIGHBOR: How do you know all that?

AMALIA: She's the one I used to dream about when I had been angry . . . she'd lift her hand in warning, and it had a ring with a green jewel that glowed.—Wasn't there a picture of her in this house?

NEIGHBOR: There used to be, but I don't know if it's still here.

AMALIA: So this is my stepmother. God is good. He let me keep my mother's image untarnished. From now on I'll find it right that my stepmother is cruel to me.

NEIGHBOR: Cruel stepmothers make children kind. And you weren't, Amalia, but you have become so. So I'll give you a Christmas present in advance. (*He takes the judge's wife's portrait, loosens the frame, and reveals a water-color portrait of Amalia's mother— as described above.*)

AMALIA (*kneeling before the portrait*): My mother! The mother of my dreams! (*Gets up*) But I won't get that portrait—it's to be auctioned off.

NEIGHBOR: Yes, you'll get it—the auction's over.

AMALIA: When? Where?

NEIGHBOR: It was held in a place you may not know about. They're going to fetch the things today!

AMALIA: How strangely everything happens! And so many secrets in this house!—But where is my stepmother? She has been gone a long time.

NEIGHBOR: Well, I'll have to tell you: She's in a place from which one doesn't return.

AMALIA: Is she dead?

NEIGHBOR: She's dead. They found her frozen to death in a swamp in which she had got stuck.

AMALIA: Merciful God, have mercy on her!

NEIGHBOR: He most likely will in time. Especially if you pray for her.

AMALIA: Of course I will!

NEIGHBOR: See, child, how good you've become! Because she got so evil!

AMALIA: Don't say that when she's dead . . .

NEIGHBOR: Right! May she rest in peace!

AMALIA: But where is Father?

NEIGHBOR: None of us knows. But it's nice that you ask about him before you ask about your Adolf.

AMALIA: Adolf? Yes, where is he? The children are asking for him, and Christmas Eve is almost here! And what will Christmas be like?

NEIGHBOR: Let each day have its burden. Take your Christmas gift and go! Things have to be cleared up after the auction, and then you'll get news.

AMALIA (*takes her mother's portrait*): I'll go, not alone any more. I think something good will happen to—I don't know what! (*Goes out to the right*)

NEIGHBOR: *I* know! But what's going to happen now is not for children to see.

(*He opens the door at the back and rings the auction bell. People gather in the following order: A whole crowd of poor people; the*

SAILOR; *the* CHIMNEY SWEEP; *the* NEIGHBOR *up in front; the* WIDOW
*and the* ORPHANS, *the* SURVEYOR.)
   (*The* OTHER ONE *with the auctioneer's gavel and a pile of paper.*)
   (*The* OTHER *is at the auction table; strikes his gavel.*)
THE OTHER: This bankruptcy auction is held in the courthouse because these items, which should now be assumed or taken over by
the proper parties, were set aside by the court . . . for the creditors.
JUDGE (*enters, old and decrepit*): Stop in the name of the law!
THE OTHER (*pretends to throw something at the* JUDGE, *who stands
there amazed and silent*): Don't mention the law; here we bring
the gospel, but not to you, who wanted to buy your way into
heaven with your stolen money!
   First: the widow and the orphans. (*Addressing them*) There
you have the silver service the judge took as his fee in his false
appraisal of your estate. The silver did get rather tarnished in his
unclean hands, but I hope it will become shining again in yours!
Then we have the ward who had to learn to become a chimney
sweep because he was robbed of his inheritance! (*To him*) There
you have your funds and the receipts. You needn't thank your
guardian! Then there's the surveyor, who got false maps and set
up an illegal division of land and had to sit innocently in the house
of correction for two years. Can you (*to the* JUDGE) undo that or
recompense him for his lost reputation?
JUDGE: Give the fool a trifling sum so he'll be satisfied. His reputation
wasn't worth two cents to start with.
THE OTHER (*strikes the* JUDGE *on the mouth. The people spit at him
and mumble, their fists clenched*): Here we have the innocently
beheaded sailor's brother. (*To the* JUDGE) Can you restore his
brother's life? No! And you can't pay with your own life for that
isn't worth as much as his! Finally, the neighbor's time has come
—the property the judge cheated him out of in an absolutely legal
way has been returned to him. But since your neighbor has no
legal experience he has—contrary to existing law—rented the

property to the judge's son-in-law for life, canceled his debts, and made him his heir!

JUDGE: I'll appeal to a higher court!

THE OTHER: You've gone through every court but the Very Highest, and you can't get there yet with your official papers! If you tried, all these poor people you've robbed of their means of support would cry out: Guilty! All this is what we have been able to straighten out, but all that has not been cleared up will go to the poor: clocks, vases, jewels, and the other things that have been used as bribes, souvenirs, "gifts"—all acquired in a legal fashion since witnesses and proof are lacking. Poor people! Take what is yours: your tears have washed the guilt from the unjustly acquired things! (*The poor rush to take the things.*) And now the last item I have to sell! The penniless ex-judge who will go to the person who bids least to support him at the expense of the parish! How much am I offered? (*Silence*) No offer! (*Silence*) Going, going— no offer! (*To the* JUDGE) Did you hear that? No one wants you! Well, I'll take you! And see to it you get the punishment you deserve!

JUDGE (*bent*): Isn't there any forgiveness?

OTHER ONE: Yes, punishment brings forgiveness! Drive him into the forest and stone him! According to the Mosaic Law! The judge doesn't know any other! Out with him! (*The people throw themselves on the* JUDGE, *pushing him out.*)

*

"*The waiting room.*"[5] *The same scenery as in scene 2, Act IV: a low valley surrounded by high black mountains.*

*At the back a large scale, on which new arrivals are weighed.*

*The* JUDGE *and his* WIFE *are sitting directly across from each other at a little table.*

JUDGE (*staring ahead as if dreaming*): Sh-h! I was dreaming some-

thing! They were throwing stones at me . . . but I can't feel any
pain . . . then everything got dark and empty until now . . .
how long it lasted I can't say . . . But I'm beginning to hear
again . . . and feel. Now it feels as if they were carrying me . . .
ugh, how cold it is; they're washing me, I think . . . I'm lying in
a box as if in a funeral parlor, and it smells of carpentry . . . they
carried me . . . and a bell is ringing [6] . . . wait, I'm riding now
but not in a streetcar though it's always ringing . . . Now I'm
sinking down, down as if I were drowning . . . bang, bang, bang,
three blows on the ceiling . . . and the lesson begins . . . the
teacher reads first . . . and now the boys are singing . . . What *is*
this? . . . And there are blows on the ceiling again, endlessly,
endlessly . . . bang, bang, bang, bang bang, bang bang, bang
. . . Silence . . . It's over! (*Wakes up*) Where am I? I'm choking; it's so heavy and close!—Is it you?—Where are we? Whose
bust is that?

WIFE: They say it's the new god's.

JUDGE: Why, he looks like a goat!

WIFE: Perhaps it's the god of the goats.

JUDGE: "The goats on the left" . . . What am I remembering?

PRINCE: It's the god Pan! [7]

JUDGE: The devil?

PRINCE: Yes! They're the same! And when the shepherds at night—
no, no, not *those* shepherds [8]—see one hair of his pelt they're
panic-stricken!

JUDGE (*gets up; sighs with horror*): I don't want to be here any
more! Can't one get out of here? I want to get out! (*Wanders
about seeking an exit in vain*)

THE OTHER (*clad as a Franciscan*): Here there are only entrances but
no exits!

JUDGE: Are you Father Colomba?

THE OTHER: No, I'm the Other One . . .

JUDGE: As a monk . . . ?

THE OTHER: Yes. Didn't you know that when the Other One gets old, he becomes a monk, and it's probably a good thing, don't you think, that he finally does? But seriously talking, for everything is serious here: this is my festive garb, which I'm allowed to wear only this day each year so I may recall what I once had and what I've lost.

JUDGE (*frightened*): What day is this?

THE OTHER (*sighs; inclines his head*): It's Christmas eve!

JUDGE (*approaches his* WIFE): It's Christmas eve! You know, I don't dare to ask where we are . . . I don't dare, but let's go home, home to the children, to our own home . . . (*Weeps*)

WIFE: Yes, let's leave here, go to our home, and begin a new life in peace and harmony . . .

THE OTHER: It's too late!

JUDGE (*in despair*): Help us, have mercy, forgive us!

THE OTHER: It's too late!

JUDGE (*takes his* WIFE's *hand*): I'm suffering so! Don't ask him where we are! I don't want to know! But one thing I'd like to know: will there never be an end to this!

THE OTHER: Never!—We don't know the word *end* here!

JUDGE (*crushed*): Never an end! (*Looks about*) Doesn't the sun ever penetrate into this damp, cold room?

THE OTHER: Never, for the ones who live here have not loved the sun.

JUDGE: That's true! I've cursed the sun! Would you hear my confession?

THE OTHER: No! You're to carry your sins within yourself until they swell up and choke you!

WIFE (*falls to her knees, amazed*): Imagine, I can't pray! (*Gets up, walks about uneasily, twisting her hands*)

THE OTHER: Because for you there is no one to whom to pray!

WIFE (*in despair*): My children, send someone here who will say one word about hope and forgiveness.

THE OTHER: That won't happen. Your children have forgotten you and are rejoicing because you are gone.

(*On the mountain wall is seen a tableau: the home with* ADOLF, AMALIA, ERIK, THYRA *around the Christmas tree; in the background the* PLAYMATE)

JUDGE: They're sitting at the Christmas table rejoicing over our misfortune! No, you're lying, for they were better than we!

THE OTHER: New tones! I had heard you were a just man . . .

JUDGE: I? I was a big sinner . . . the biggest there ever has been!

THE OTHER: Hm, hm!

JUDGE: And if you say anything bad about the children, you're sinning! I know they're praying for us!

WIFE (*on her knees*): I can hear them saying the rosary: sh-h, I hear them!

THE OTHER: You're absolutely mistaken: what you're hearing is the workmen's song when they tear down the mausoleum!

JUDGE: The mausoleum! Where we were to have rested in peace!

PRINCE: Under the shadow of twelve wreaths!

JUDGE: Who's that?

PRINCE (*points at the* JUDGE's WIFE): She's my sister, so you're my brother-in-law!

JUDGE: Oh, you're that good-for-nothing!

PRINCE: Listen: here we're all good-for-nothings!

JUDGE: But not all hunchbacks!

PRINCE (*slaps him on the mouth*): Don't mention the hump or all hell will break loose!

JUDGE: Imagine, that's how they treat a deserving man of my high position in the community! What a Christmas eve!

PRINCE: You probably are expecting Christmas fish and cake . . .

JUDGE: Not exactly, but I should certainly get something to eat . . .

PRINCE: Here there's fasting on Christmas eve, you see . . .

JUDGE: How long do we fast?

PRINCE: How long? Time isn't measured here, for time has come to an end . . . a minute can last an eternity . . .

WIFE: We suffer according to our sins . . . so don't complain . . .

PRINCE: Just try to complain, and you'll really see something . . .

We're not particular at all here, but let 'em have it without legal distinctions.

JUDGE: Are they beating clothes out there on a day like this?

PRINCE: No, that's extra treatment with the switch as a reminder for those who've forgotten the significance of this day.

JUDGE: Do they violate one's person? Is it possible that educated people lay hands on each other?

PRINCE: Badly educated people are educated here—the ones who've behaved like rascals are treated as such!

JUDGE: That's beyond all limits!

PRINCE: Because the limit has been passed!—Get ready—I've already been out there to get what I had coming.

JUDGE (*shrinks with horror*): What a humiliation! But that's robbing one of all human dignity!

PRINCE (*laughs*): Human dignity!—(*Laughs*) Look at the scale over there; that's where human dignity is weighed; and everyone's is too slight!

JUDGE (*sits down at the table*): I never would have believed . . .

PRINCE: No, you believed only in your righteousness and your caul! Still you had Moses and the prophets and others besides, for the dead came back to you!

JUDGE: The children! The children! Can no one get to them with a greeting and a warning?

PRINCE: No! Never!

(WITCH *comes up with a basket filled with stereopticons.*)

JUDGE: What's that?

WITCH: They're Christmas presents for the righteous! They're viewers! (*Gives him one*) There you are! Doesn't cost anything.

JUDGE: One friendly human being at least; and a little attention at my age and for a man in my position shows good taste and a good heart . . .

WITCH: You're too polite, Judge; but don't feel disappointed because I've thought of the others, too!

JUDGE (*disappointed*): Damn hag, are you making fun of me?

WITCH (*spits in his face*): Watch it, you shyster.

JUDGE: Imagine what company I've got into!

WITCH: If it isn't good enough for you, you old perjurer, you receiver of bribes, you robber of heirs, you word twister! Look in the viewer and you'll see your whole history: "From the cradle to the grave." There you have the story of your whole life and all your victims . . . Take a look . . . there!

(JUDGE *looks in the viewer; gets up horror-stricken.*)

WITCH: I hope the little attention will add to your Christmas joy!

(*She gives his* WIFE *a viewer and proceeds to distribute others to the rest.*)

JUDGE (*has sat down at the table; his* WIFE *sits down across from him*): What do you see?

WIFE: Everything's there; everything!—Did you notice that it's all black? The long bright life is dark, and the moments I thought were innocent joy show up as something nauseating, nasty, almost criminal. It's as if my memories, even the most beautiful, have rotted . . .

JUDGE: Yes, you're right; not one memory can brighten up in this darkness. When I see her—my first love—I see a corpse. When I recall Amalia, who was good, there appears—a whore; the little children make faces at me like street brats; my home is a pig pen, my vineyard a garbage dump with thistles growing on it, and the mausoleum—ugh, no—a privy! When I think about the green forest, the leaves turn snuff-brown and the trunks white as masts on a ship; the blue river flows as if from a barnyard pool, and the blue vault above is like a sooty roof . . . The sun itself I remember only by name, and what was called the moon and shone like a watchlight over bays and groves on evenings of love in my youth I remember only as . . . no, I don't remember it any more! But I still remember the words though they're only sounds without meaning . . . Love, wine, song! Flowers, children, joy—Don't the words sound beautiful? And that's all that's left.—Love! What was that?

WIFE: What that was?—Two cats on a privy roof!

JUDGE (*foolishly*): Yes, that's what it was! That's what it was! And three dogs in a gutter! That's "pleasant" to remember!

WIFE (*presses his hand*): It is pleasant!

JUDGE (*looks at his watch*): The watch has stopped. I'm very hungry . . . and thirsty . . . and long for tobacco. But I'm tired too, and want to sleep. All my desires can't satisfy one! We are damned! Damned!

WIFE: And I'm longing for a cup of tea, longing beyond words!

JUDGE: Warm, green tea. That's exactly what I'd like; and a little, little bit of rum, too!

WIFE: No, not rum! I'd prefer coffee cake . . .

PRINCE (*who has come up and heard them*): With sugar on it!—If you sing out, yes!

WIFE: This crude talk tortures me more than everything else!

PRINCE: That's because you don't know how the rest will torture you.

JUDGE: What's that?

WIFE: No, don't say it—we don't want to know. Sh-h!

PRINCE: Yes, I'll say it! It begins with . . . . *s.*

WIFE (*covers her ears and screams*): Mercy! Don't say it, don't!

PRINCE: No, no, I won't keep still, and brother-in-law is curious, so I'll tell him! The second letter is *u!*

JUDGE: This uncertainty tortures me more than anything . . . Speak out, you devil, or kill me!

PRINCE: Kill! (*laughs*) Here we're all immortal, body and soul, the little that's left. However: the third letter is . . . now you won't find out any more!

GRAY-CLAD ONE (*a little thin man in gray costume, a gray face, black lips, gray beard, and gray hands; speaks softly*): May I speak with you a little, ma'am?

WIFE (*gets up, terrified*): What about?

GRAY-CLAD ONE (*smiles in a ghastly, mean fashion*): I'll tell you—out there!

WIFE (*weeps*): No, no, I don't want to!

GRAY-CLAD ONE (*laughs*): It isn't dangerous! Come along! I just want to *talk* with you! Come! (*They go toward the back.*)

PRINCE (*to the* JUDGE): A little Christmas gift helps a lot!

JUDGE: Are you going to mistreat a woman?

PRINCE: All wrongs are canceled here, and a woman is treated as the equal of man!

JUDGE: You devil!

PRINCE: Call me that but not a hunchback, for that's the last pretense I have!

OTHER ONE (*comes up to the table*): Well, what do you think of animal magnetism? That can perform miracles on scoundrels!

JUDGE: I don't understand any of this!

OTHER ONE: That's exactly what's intended—it's nice that you admit there's something you don't understand!

JUDGE: I assume I'm in the kingdom of the dead, then . . .

OTHER ONE: Say hell—that's its name!

JUDGE (*stammers*): Then I want to remind you that the One who descended to this place once to save the damned . . .

PRINCE (*at the* OTHER ONE's *gesture slaps the* JUDGE *across the mouth*): No reasoning!

JUDGE: They don't listen to me! This is pure despair! Without mercy, without hope, without end!

OTHER ONE: True! Here there's only justice and retribution above all justice: an eye for an eye, a tooth for a tooth! Exactly as you wanted it.

JUDGE: But among human beings there is pardon—there isn't any here!

OTHER ONE: Only princes can pardon! And as a lawyer you ought to know there has to be a plea for pardon if it's to be granted!

JUDGE: There isn't any pardon for me!

OTHER ONE (*gestures to the* PRINCE *so that he goes aside*): So you think your guilt is too great?

JUDGE: Yes!

OTHER ONE: Then I'll speak nicely to you! You see: there's an end if there's a beginning, and you've made a beginning! But what's ahead is long and hard!

JUDGE: God is good!

OTHER ONE: That's right!

JUDGE: But . . . there is one thing that can't be straightened out . . . there is one.

OTHER ONE: You mean the monstrance that should have been of gold but became silver! Well: don't you think the One who could change water to wine can change silver to gold?

JUDGE (*on his knees*): But my sin is greater, greater than any that can be forgiven.

OTHER ONE: You're overestimating yourself again! But get up—we're going to celebrate Christmas eve in our way.—The sun never reaches this place, as you know, nor the moon, but this night, only this one, a star rises so high over the mountains that we can see it. It's the star that guided the shepherds across the desert, and *that* is the morning star! (*He claps his hands; Pan sinks into the ground; the* JUDGE's WIFE *comes out looking calm and quietly happy; goes up to the* JUDGE *and extends her hand to him in trust.*)

(*The stage is filled with shadows, figures, all of whom look up toward the mountain at the back.*)

(*Off stage two sopranos and an alto sing to the accompaniment of stringed instruments and a harp:*

> *Puer natus est nobis;*
> *Et filius datus est nobis,*
> *Cujus imperium super humerum ejus;*
> *Et vocabitur nomen ejus*
> *magni consilii Angelus.*

(*Chorus of soprano, alto, tenor, and bass*):

> *Cantate Domino canticum novum*
> *Quia mirabilia fecit!*

(*The star appears over the mountain at the back. All fall to their knees. A fragment of the mountain is moved to the side*

*revealing a tableau: the Manger with the Child and the Mother:*
*the shepherds worship to the left, the Three Kings to the right.*
*(A chorus of two sopranos and two altos sings):*

> *Gloria in excelsis Deo*
> *Et in terra pax*
> *Hominibus bonae voluntatis!*

[CURTAIN]

# Notes on 'Advent'

1. In a play dealing with the four Sundays before Christmas, and therefore with the coming of Christ to save human beings, it is not surprising that Strindberg made use of many biblical allusions. Most important is the sharply drawn contrast between the Old Testament doctrine of guilt and punishment and the New Testament doctrine of love and forgiveness. During the Advent season, the Church of Sweden as well as many other Christian churches emphasizes the significance of Christ as Saviour and the need for Christians to prepare themselves to receive Him properly and to be reconciled with God before they face Him at the Last Judgment.

2. The old superstition was that anyone born with a caul (a portion of the membrane surrounding a fetus which sometimes covers its head at birth) would be lucky.

3. The Swedish term is *solkatten* (literally, "the suncat"); it has obvious significance as a disturbing factor for the judge and his wife.

4. See any translation of Ovid's Metamorphoses for the tale of the generous and hospitable old Phrygian couple Baucis and Philemon, who were so well mated that they wished to die at the same time.

5. "Now there is at Jerusalem by the sheep market a pool . . . having five porches. In these lay a great multitude of impotent folk, of blind, halt, withered, waiting for the moving of the water. For an angel went down at a certain season into the poor, and troubled the water: whosoever then first after the troubling of the water stepped in was made whole of whatsoever disease he had" (John 5:2–5).

6. The Angelus bell calls believers to worship morning, noon, and evening. The Angelus commemorates the Incarnation ("The Word became flesh"), that is, Christ's taking the form of a human being.

7. The Greek god Pan, worshiped by goatherds and shepherds, had a

goat's hoofs, ears, and horns. Pan loved the wilderness, pursued wood-land nymphs, and in general represented the animal aspects of life. He was known for his skill as a musician, his physical ugliness, and the fear he inspired in human beings. See H. J. Rose's *A Handbook of Greek Mythology* (New York: E. P. Dutton & Co., 1959; available in paper-back) for information about Pan and other mythological characters.

8. See preceding note. "Not *those* shepherds" refers to the shepherds who found and adored the infant Jesus. See Luke 2:8–20 for a biblical account of the Advent of Christ.

# Introduction to 'Easter'

*Easter* (*Påsk*, 1900) is a play about which even Strindberg's most violent enemies and his severest critics have never been unkind. Audiences and readers have been in essential agreement that it is a literary and dramatic gem. Even those who judge plays primarily and exclusively in terms of realism-naturalism—or, if you will, verisimilitude or truth-to-life—have refrained from questioning its quality both for reading and theater.

The play was not intended to be purely realistic, but is a modern combination of the miracle and the morality play. *Easter* presupposes that the universe is a moral universe, not deterministic or mechanistic. It is an expression of the acceptance of certain basic teachings of Christianity: that there is a Creator who cares for His creatures; who not only is able to do something for them but is also more than willing to do so; and who has, moreover, given them a pattern of behavior (figuratively and, to an appreciable degree, literally) to follow. The concept of the world in which the action of the play takes place is of one in which there can be miracles and in which self-sacrifice, suffering, atonement, faith, reconciliation, salvation, and resurrection are not merely terms out of an obsolete romantic and religious mythology but have very real meaning for human beings of any age and of any place.

The ideational content consists of the application to human beings of the themes involved in Christ's final suffering, death, and resurrection. Implicit, of course, is the Christian admonition: lead the Christ-like life; that is, practice self-sacrifice even if you as a finite human being are not capable of achieving self-negation. The testimony Strindberg here offers concerns the acceptance of resignation to the facts of the human condition, but not resignation in the sense of apathetic passivity or utter defeat and helplessness; it concerns the achievement of humaneness implicit in compassion, *caritas,* and control of the ego.

The Christianity we find expressed in *Easter* is that of simple faith, not one of hair-splitting dogmas. It is a Christianity that is applied to human experiences that are—aside perhaps from Eleonora's—fairly representative. It is a Christianity expressed within the framework of the church of Sweden with its Lenten and Easter customs. It is, moreover, supported by the music of Josef Haydn's *The Seven Last Words of Christ* (1788).

Strindberg himself stated simply and firmly his choice of the structure of the play designed to present the core of Christ-like living: "The form is my invention, comprising the three acts of the passion play." An expansion of this statement in terms of the church becomes:

> Act I (*Reningsdagen* = the Day of Purification; *Skärtorsdag* = Sheer Thursday) Maunday Thursday or the Day of Purification, the partaking of the flesh and blood at communion services.
>
> Act II (*Långfredag* = Long Friday), the long, long, Good Friday of suffering and death, a suffering that can ennoble.
>
> Act III (*Påskafton* = Easter evening). The evening before the resurrection with the fulfillment of the promise and the bringing of hope.

Holy Week is, of course, the week before Easter Sunday—Passion Week or the Week of Suffering.

Strindberg was keenly aware of the fact that Easter has close ties with the northern spring, a season that is not merely Christian in its significance. The human joy over such "miracles" as the melting and disappearance of snow and ice, the increase in sunlight and warmth, the budding of leaves and the blooming of flowers, and the relief over the passing of a long, long winter are matters that do not essentially conflict with the Christian concept of Easter but rather complement it.

The plot of *Easter* is a simple one that traces in broad terms and in telling detail the story of the misfortunes of the Heyst family and shows the crucial final period in which a stubborn and arrogant human being is forced to learn his Easter lessons. It is a plot that reveals the chastening of several human beings, most of whom have resented bitterly the misfortunes that have been meted out to them. In presenting the agony of the Heysts, Strindberg thought he presented the agony of most human beings: suffering stemming more from egotistic concern with self than from external blows. In all this, Strindberg placed his major emphasis on his characters, each of whom is presented impressionistically.

Mrs. Heyst is a motherly soul concerned about her family, hiding her shame from them, both believing and not believing in her husband's innocence, but really whistling in the dark. While she may talk about such things as apple soup, Elis' overcoat, and Benjamin's behavior, and may hit out at Lindkvist, she is really devoting herself to homely tasks in order to keep life going—in spite of everything.

Mrs. Heyst may pretend even to herself, but her prospective daughter-in-law Kristina knows very well what she is doing and saying. She had been a sleepwalker when she went away, but she has returned as an interpreter who has accepted life. She, too, devotes herself to homely tasks; she is extremely human in her patience, understanding, and compassion; she serves as the interpreter of the central idea, "Even the good repeats itself."

The most challenging role is that of Eleonora—challenging because, in an age conditioned to the criteria of realistic analysis, she has to be accepted on faith and not subjected to searching objective analysis. Strindberg thought of her as a very special human being, "a poetic figure of light in a world heavy with bitterness."

On the one hand, one can consider her a precocious and sensitive sixteen-year-old, who had reacted so unrestrainedly when her father was sentenced that she had to be "put away" in the asylum up north. Just how unrestrained her reactions had become is merely hinted at, but Elis' fears that her return would make his burdens unbearable suggest that the reactions had not at that time led to quiet suffering and resignation.

The extreme sensitivity is there: she can't bear anything harsh. But even though it looks as if she is the one who needs protection above all the others, she is the strongest one of all. It is as if she had a sixth sense, the gift of clairvoyance, the ability to understand others and their problems intuitively rather than through objective analysis, and even extrasensory perception. The one who leads the Christ-like life, she is a Christ figure who feels the need for punishment and suffering and who takes on the burdens of others' suffering. She is an angel of peace and tranquility, an "innocent" who is well on the way to self-sacrifice and self-negation.

Eleonora is reflected in several characters in Pär Lagerkvist's fiction and dramas. Take, for example, his mother and his sister Signe as presented in *The Guest of Reality* (*Gäst hos verkligheten*, 1925) or Anna in *Allowed to Live His Life Over Again* (*Han som fick leva om sitt liv*, 1928). They share with Eleonora a quiet acceptance of life and the gift for living so that light radiates from them for the comfort and sustenance of those about them. It is the need for making light seem to emanate from within that makes the role of Eleonora one of the most difficult Strindberg ever created. It is also, however, one of the most challenging and rewarding roles an actress can accept.

Kristina's comment, "Don't touch the butterfly's wing," applies not only to Eleonora but to Benjamin as well. "The youngest and the most favored of my friends" has the human capacity to restrain his ego, to fear for another human being, and to be willing to sacrifice and suffer for others. While he may be defiant and resentful because of disappointment, he is not frozen in a mold. His sulking gives way to gentleness and dignified nobility. As Kristina, the interpreter, says, "Suffering ennobles."

Strindberg's interpretation of Lindkvist is a startlingly effective illustration of the many ways in which a human being can be looked at and judged. Mrs. Heyst, fighting to protect her family, calls him a swindler, but there is no proof that she means it. Elis indulges in very human distortion and ambivalence about Lindkvist. Instead of objectively analyzing Lindkvist, as one might expect of a scholar on the verge of getting his doctorate, Elis "sees" Lindkvist as a poor man who needs his money, as a spider watching flies, as a creditor with an evil eye on his prey, as a gigantic shadow, and as a giant ready to pounce on his victims.

But in reality Lindkvist is a highly articulate aging man, humane and resigned, who wants to repay a great debt. Lindkvist knows what the world is like, he knows what people are like, and he knows what has to be done about the Elises of this world if they are not to go under or to defeat themselves. He knows that they need to have the truth spelled out for them (Peter's invitation to Kristina and Peter's inviting the governor to the doctoral dinner), and that they must be forced to bow in humility when giving up their false pride. Lindkvist's weapons are represented by the white documents and the blue forms, the one set promising, the other threatening.

If any character may be said to represent humanity's need to learn the Easter lessons best, it is Elis. Although he is a graduate student, a doctoral candidate, and a teacher, Elis has never analyzed himself, his problems, or other people objectively. In spite of his claims to being an intellectual, he examines no one and no thing in depth; when he does analyze his problems, he does so with a bias, incompletely; he sees only the darkest possible side. He has, moreover, a very active imagination with an inclination to unnecessary distortion.

Elis does, however, have very human problems and troubles: the postponement of his marriage, the postponement of taking his Ph.D., his father's disgrace, Eleonora's having to be put away, Benjamin's failure in Latin, Peter Holmblad's apparent triple disloyalty, creditors' claims, exile from his native city, having to support the family, having to go through the legal documents time and again, and imagined threats from Lindkvist and others. It is a heavy burden, but perhaps no heavier than most other people have to bear, according to Strindberg's way of looking at it. Instead of facing his problems calmly with a view to solving them, he works himself into a state of anguish, bitterness, and frustration. To be sure, he does appreciate much that life has meted out to him—nature, Kristina, the "new" Eleonora, Stockholm—but he fears people and the nature of things. He takes on responsibility willingly, but not cheerfully. He is at best superficially patient. One of those who are in danger of being frozen in a mold of fear-induced frustrations and permanent defeat, he has to be driven to his "salvation"—to faith in the existence of good as well as bad. Exposed to Job-like test upon test, Elis surrenders his false pride and stubborn egotism only when forced, figuratively, to his knees.

Strindberg's selection of music from Haydn's *The Seven Last Words of Christ* emphasizes the dominant mood and atmosphere of the play. The precurtain music for Act I is the majestic, slow music of Haydn's introduction; preceding Act II is the very slow music of Haydn's first section: "Father, forgive them, for they know not what they do"; and Act III is introduced by the easy, graceful music of Haydn's fifth section: "I thirst." For the full impact of the Haydn oratorio on Strindberg's conception of Easter in terms of human experience and his play, one should listen to the whole oratorio from the introduction to the concluding section: "Father, into Thy hands I commend my spirit." It is highly appropriate music for a play that deals with man's suffering as a human (and therefore limited) parallel to that of Christ.

It is not only Strindberg's selection of music that has made many scholars and critics consider *Easter* an expressionistic play. There are other elements that support such a conclusion, though it might be more accurate to say that *Easter* belongs with what Strindberg called his dream plays. The mood and atmosphere of fear, anxiety, and anguish; the prisonlike isolation of the family; the exaggeration and intensification of basically realistic details; and the lyrical use of the folktale motif are all characteristic of the Strindbergian dream play. Also characteristic are the distortion of Lindkvist by Elis and his mother, and the interpretation of Eleonora, who shares many qualities with Agnes of *A Dream Play*—intuitive understanding and essential constancy, for example: "I was born old; I knew everything when I was born, and whenever I learned something it was only to be reminded of it."

*Easter* has a magic about it that is revealed both by reading and by seeing the play. The natural dialogue with its frequently poetic overtones, the dominantly reflective mood, the profoundly human story, the ease with which one can identify oneself or the people one knows with the various characters, and the Strindbergian interpretation of the Easter message all contribute toward making *Easter* a very special experience.

*Easter*

## Characters

MRS. HEYST
ELIS, *her son, a teacher*
ELEONORA, *her daughter*
KRISTINA, *Elis' fiancée*
BENJAMIN, *a schoolboy*
LINDKVIST

*The entire foreground is a first-floor glass-enclosed veranda fur-nished as a living room. In the center is a large door leading to the front yard with its picket fence and a gate opening to the street. Across the street—on the same level as the Heyst house—can be seen a low picket fence enclosing a garden sloping down toward the city. The background represents this garden's treetops in spring foliage. Beyond them a church tower and a monumental gable of a house.*

*The glass windows of the porch that extends across the stage have light yellow flowered cretonne curtains, which can be drawn. A mirror hangs on a window post next to the door; below the mirror is a calendar.*

*To the right of the door at the back is a large writing desk with books, writing utensils, and a telephone. To the left of the door are a dining table, a stove with mica panes, and a sideboard. In the right foreground is a sewing table with a lamp. Next to it two easy chairs. A lamp hangs from the ceiling.*

*Outside next to the street is a gas street lamp.*

*To the right is a door leading to the kitchen, to the left a door leading to the rest of the house.*

*The action takes place in our day [1901].*

# ACT I

## *Maundy Thursday* [1]

Precurtain music: Haydn's *Seven Last Words,*[2] Introduction: Maestoso adagio

*A ray of sunlight falls directly across the room from the left and strikes one of the chairs by the sewing table.* KRISTINA *is sitting on the other chair pulling cords through a pair of newly ironed curtains.* ELIS *comes in, his winter overcoat unbuttoned, carrying a large bundle of documents which he puts on the desk. Then he takes off his coat and hangs it up to the left.*

ELIS: Good morning, dear!

KRISTINA: Good morning, Elis!

ELIS: The double windows down; the floor scrubbed, clean curtains . . . it *is* spring again! . . . And they've chopped up the ice, and I can put away my winter coat . . . You know, it's as heavy (*weighs the coat in his hand*)—as if it has soaked up all the troubles of winter, the sweat of anguish, and the dust of the schoolroom . . . (*Sighs*)

KRISTINA: And you have vacation now!

ELIS: Easter vacation! Five wonderful days to enjoy, to breathe again, to forget! (*Shakes* KRISTINA's *hand and sits down in the easy chair*) Well, the sun's back again . . . it went away in November; I remember the day it disappeared back of the brewery directly across the street . . . What a winter! What a long, long, winter!

KRISTINA (*gestures toward the kitchen door*): Sh-h-h!

ELIS: I will keep still, and I will be glad it's over . . . That wonderful sun . . . (*He rubs his hands and pretends he's washing himself.*) . . . I want to bathe in sunshine, wash myself in light after all this dark filth . . .

KRISTINA: Sh-h-h!

ELIS: You know, I think peace is returning and our misfortunes have wearied . . .

KRISTINA: Why do you think so?

ELIS: Well, just because a white dove came flying along when I passed the cathedral a while ago—it came down on the sidewalk and dropped a branch it was carrying in its beak right in front of my feet.

KRISTINA: Did you see what kind of branch it was?

ELIS: It can't very well have been an olive branch,[3] but I think it was a symbol of peace, and just now I feel a blessed, sunny calm . . . Where is Mother?

KRISTINA (*gestures toward the kitchen*): In the kitchen.

ELIS (*softly, his eyes closed*): I hear it is spring! I hear the double windows are out. Do you know how I hear it?—Mostly in the carriage wheels . . . but what's that? The finch is singing! And they're hammering away on the shipyard, and it smells of oil paint from the steamboats, from the red lead.

KRISTINA: Can you tell that all the way from here?

ELIS: Here? That's true—we are *here,* but I was *there,*[4] up there in the north, where our home is . . . How did we ever come to this terrible town where everyone hates everyone else and where one is always alone? Well, bread and butter showed us the way . . . but there were our misfortunes, too: Father's criminal acts and my little sister's illness.—Did Mother get to visit Father at the prison?

KRISTINA: I think she's even been there today!

ELIS: What did she say?

KRISTINA: Nothing! She talked about other things.

ELIS: We have gained one thing, though: after the sentence, we've had certainty and a strange calm, since the newspapers have quit bringing up the accounts. A year has passed; in a year he'll be free, and then we'll have to start again.

KRISTINA: I admire your patience in suffering.

ELIS: Don't! Don't admire anything about me; I have only short-comings! Now you know! If you'd only believe that!

KRISTINA: Yes, if you were suffering because of your own mistakes, but it's because of others'!

ELIS: What are you sewing?

KRISTINA: They're kitchen curtains, dear!

ELIS: It looks like a bridal veil . . . You'll be my bride this fall, won't you, Kristina?

KRISTINA: Yes, but let's think about summer first!

ELIS: Summer, yes! (*Takes out his checkbook*) See, I already have the money in the bank! And when school's over, we'll go north to our country—to Lake Mälare.[5] The cottage is ready there just as it was in our childhood; the lindens are there, the rowboats by the willows on the shore . . . If it were only summer so I could bathe in the lake! Our family's disgrace has hit me body and soul so I long for a lake in which to wash myself clean.

KRISTINA: Have you heard anything about your sister Eleonora?[6]

ELIS: Poor thing, she's restless and writes letters that tear me to pieces. She wants to get out and come home, naturally, but the superintendent of the institution doesn't dare let her go, because she does things that could lead to prison. You know, I'm conscience-stricken sometimes; most of all because I favored her being put in.

KRISTINA: You blame yourself for everything, but in this case it was a good thing she got care, poor girl.

ELIS: That's true, and I think it's calmer the way it is, of course. Yes, she's as well off as she can be! And when I think how she went about here darkening every hint of happiness, how her lot depressed us like a nightmare, tortured us to despair, I really feel a selfish relief that resembles joy. And the biggest misfortune I can imagine would be to see her walk into this house. That's how low I am!

KRISTINA: That's how human you are!

ELIS: And just the same . . . I suffer, suffer at the thought of her agony, and my father's!

KRISTINA: Some people seem to be born to suffer . . .

ELIS: You poor thing, that got into this family, condemned from the beginning . . . and damned!

KRISTINA: Elis! You don't know if these are tests or punishment! [7]

ELIS: I don't know what all this is for you, for you're innocent if anyone is!

KRISTINA: Tears in the morning, joy in the evening! Elis, maybe I can help you through . . .

ELIS: Do you think Mother has a white tie?

KRISTINA (uneasy): Are you going out?

ELIS: I'm going to a dinner. Peter defended his dissertation [8] yesterday, you know, and he's giving a dinner today.

KRISTINA: Do you want to go to that?

ELIS: You think I should stay away because he proved to be such an ungrateful pupil of mine.

KRISTINA: I don't deny his ingratitude bothered me. He had promised to quote your dissertation, but he plundered it without citing his source!

ELIS: That's common enough, and I'm happy in the knowledge that "I did this."

KRISTINA: Has he invited you?

ELIS: Why, no, he hasn't! That's really strange; for years he's kept talking about that dinner as if I would be invited without question, and I've talked about it to others. If I'm not invited, I'll be publicly insulted. All right, it isn't the first time, nor the last! (Pause)

KRISTINA: Benjamin's late! Do you think he'll pass?

ELIS: I surely hope so—in Latin with the highest grade!

KRISTINA: He's a good boy, Benjamin.

ELIS: Exceptional, but he's inclined to brooding. You know why he's living with us, don't you?

KRISTINA: Is it because . . .

ELIS: Because . . . his guardian, my father, embezzled his means like so many others'! You see, Kristina, that's the terrible thing: in school I have to see these orphans who've lost everything suffer the humiliation of having to be charity pupils. And you can understand how they look at me. I have to remember their misery to be able to forgive them their cruelty.

KRISTINA: I think your father is really better off than you!

ELIS: Yes!

KRISTINA: Elis, we should think about this summer, not about the past!

ELIS: Yes, about summer!—You know, I woke up last night when they were singing the student song: "Yes, I'm coming. Happy winds, tell the country, the birds, I love them. Tell the birch and the lindens I want to see them. See them as I saw them as a child . . ." [9] (*Gets up, stirred up*) Will I get to see them, will I get to leave this horrible town, this Ebal, this cursed mountain, and see Garizim [10] again? (*Sits down by the door*)

KRISTINA: Yes, yes! You shall!

ELIS: But do you think I'll get to see *my* birches and lindens as I saw them before? Don't you think the same black veil will cover them as it's covered nature and life down here ever since that day . . . (*Points at the easy chair, which now is in shadow*) See, the sun has gone away!

KRISTINA: It will come back—to stay longer!

ELIS: That's true; the days will get longer, the shadows shorter.

KRISTINA: We're going toward light, Elis; believe me.

ELIS: Sometimes I think so, and when I think of the past and compare it with the present, I'm happy. Last year you weren't sitting there—you had left me and broken our engagement! You know, that was the worst of all. I literally died, bit by bit; but when you came back, I came alive. Do you remember why you left?

KRISTINA: No, I don't—now it seems as if there weren't any reason.

I just felt I should, so I left—as in sleep. When I saw you again, I woke up and was happy!

ELIS: And you'll never leave again, for if you did, I'd really die! . . . There comes Mother! Don't say anything; spare her in her imagined world, where she lives thinking Father's a martyr, and all his victims are rascals.

MRS. HEYST (*enters from the kitchen wearing a kitchen apron and peeling an apple; speaks in a friendly, somewhat simple fashion*): Hello, children! Do you want the apple soup cold or warm?

ELIS: Cold, Mother.

MRS. HEYST: That's fine, my boy; you always know what you want and say it, but Kristina can't. Elis learned that from his father; he always knew what he wanted and what he was doing, and people can't stand that, so things went wrong for him. But his day will come, and he'll be proved right, and the others proved wrong! . . . Wait a minute, what was I going to say? Yes! Did you know Lindkvist has moved to town? Lindkvist, the biggest of all the rascals.

ELIS (*gets up, beside himself*): Is he here?

MRS. HEYST: Yes, he's living right across the street.

ELIS: Then we'll have to see him walk past every day. Even this!

MRS. HEYST: Let me talk to him once, then he'll never come back and show himself again, for I know his little quirks! . . . Well, Elis, how did it go for Peter?

ELIS: Beautifully!

MRS. HEYST: I can believe that. When are you going to defend your dissertation?

ELIS: When I can afford to, Mother! [11]

MRS. HEYST: When I can afford to! That's no real answer! . . . And Benjamin! Did he pass his examinations?

ELIS: We don't know yet, but he should be here soon.

MRS. HEYST: Well, I don't quite like Benjamin—he goes about pretending he has privileges . . . but we'll cure him of that! . . . A good boy in any case. Well, and there's a package for you, Elis. (*Goes into the kitchen to get the package*)

ELIS: Imagine how Mother keeps up on everything; sometimes I think she's not so simple as she pretends.

MRS. HEYST (*comes back*): Here's the package. Lena took it in.

ELIS: A present! I've been afraid of presents ever since I got a box filled with stones.[12] (*Puts the package on the table*)

MRS. HEYST: I'm going out into the kitchen again.—Won't it get cold if you keep the door open?

ELIS: Not at all, Mother.

MRS. HEYST: You shouldn't hang your overcoat there—it looks so careless! . . . Well, Kristina, will you have my curtains ready soon?

KRISTINA: In a few minutes, Mother!

MRS. HEYST: I really like that Peter: he's my favorite . . . Aren't you going to his dinner, Elis?

ELIS: Yes, of course, I am.

MRS. HEYST: Well, why did you say you wanted the apple soup cold when you were going out? There's really no depending on you, Elis. But one can on Peter! . . . Shut the door when it gets cool, so you don't catch cold. (*Goes out to the right*)

ELIS: What a good woman! . . . And always Peter . . . Is she trying to tease you about Peter?

KRISTINA: Me?

ELIS: You know older women get notions like that!

KRISTINA: What sort of present did you get?

ELIS (*tears the package open*): A Lenten switch![13] . . .

KRISTINA: From whom?

ELIS: Anonymous! . . . Well, it's innocent enough, and I'll put it in water so it'll turn green as Aaron's staff![14] "Birch . . . which in my childhood days" . . . and Lindkvist[15] has come.

KRISTINA: What is special about him?

ELIS: We owe him more than anyone else.

KRISTINA: But you don't owe him anything, do you?

ELIS: Yes, we—one for all, and all for one; the family name is dis-honored as long as there is any debt.

KRISTINA: Change your name!

ELIS: Kristina!

KRISTINA (*puts aside her work, now finished*): Thank you, Elis! I only wanted to test you!

ELIS: But you mayn't tempt me! . . . Lindkvist is a poor man and needs his . . . Where my father went is like a battlefield with dead and wounded . . . and Mother thinks he's the victim! . . . Do you want to go for a walk?

KRISTINA: To find the sun? Very much!

ELIS: Can you understand that the Saviour has suffered for our sins, yet we still have to keep on paying? No one pays for me!

KRISTINA: But if someone did, would you understand . . . ?

ELIS: Yes, then I would! . . . Sh-h! There comes Benjamin. Can you tell if he looks happy?

KRISTINA (*looks out the door at the back*): He's walking very slowly . . . Now he's stopping at the fountain . . . and washing his eyes . . .

ELIS: Even this!

KRISTINA: Wait . . .

ELIS: Tears, tears!

KRISTINA: Patience!

(BENJAMIN *comes in; friendly, respectful, but disturbed; he is carrying a few books and a briefcase.*)

ELIS: Well, how did Latin go?

BENJAMIN: Badly!

ELIS: May I see your exam? What did you do?

BENJAMIN: I wrote *ut* with the indicative, though I knew it should be conjunctive.

ELIS: Then you're lost! But how could you?

BENJAMIN (*resignedly*): I can't explain it . . . I knew how it should be, wanted to write the right form, but didn't! (*Sits down crushed at the dining table*)

ELIS (*sinks down by the desk and reads* BENJAMIN's *copy*): Yes, it's in the indicative. My God!

KRISTINA (*with an effort*): Well, better luck next time: life is long—so terribly long!

BENJAMIN: Yes, it *is!*

ELIS (*sadly, but without bitterness*): That everything has to come at once, too!—And you were my best pupil [16]—what can I expect from the others?—I'll lose my reputation as a teacher, I'll get no tutoring any more, and then . . . everything will crash! (*To* BENJAMIN) Don't feel bad . . . it isn't your fault . . .

KRISTINA (*with an extreme effort*): Elis, courage. Courage, for God's sake!

ELIS: Where shall I get it?

KRISTINA: Where you got it before!

ELIS: It isn't as it was! I seem to be in disfavor!

KRISTINA: It is a special grace to suffer innocently . . . Don't be fooled into impatience . . . Bear the test, for it is only a test, I feel . . .

ELIS: Can a year be shorter than 365 days for Benjamin?

KRISTINA: Yes, a happy spirit shortens time!

ELIS (*smiles*): Blow on the sore and it'll heal, they tell children!

KRISTINA: Be a child, then, and I'll say that to you . . . Think of Mother . . . how she stands everything!

ELIS: Give me your hand; I'm sinking!

(KRISTINA *takes his hand.*)

ELIS: Your hand is trembling . . .

KRISTINA: Not that I can feel . . .

ELIS: You're not as strong as you seem . . .

KRISTINA: I don't feel any weakness . . .

ELIS: Why don't you give me some of your strength?

KRISTINA: I haven't any to spare!

ELIS (*looks out the window*): Do you know who's coming now?

KRISTINA (*looks out the window; falls to her knees, crushed*): This is too much!

ELIS: The creditor, the one who can take our furniture any time
he wants to—Lindkvist who moved here to sit like a spider in the
middle of his web to keep an eye on the flies . . .

KRISTINA: Flee!

ELIS (*gets up*): No, I won't flee! . . . Now, when you became weak,
I grew strong . . . he's coming up the street . . . and he has already cast his evil eyes on his prey . . .

KRISTINA: Step out of his way at least!

ELIS: No, he amuses me now . . . He seems to glow as if he saw
his prey in the trap . . . [*Toward* LINDKVIST] Come on! . . . He's
counting the steps to the gate and has seen by our open door we're
home . . . Now he met someone and has stopped to speak . . .
He's talking about us for he's looking this way . . .

KRISTINA: Just so he doesn't meet Mother so that her violent words
may make him merciless . . . Prevent that, Elis!

ELIS: Now he's shaking his stick as if he were swearing he'd not
let mercy replace justice! . . . He's unbuttoning his overcoat to
show we haven't stripped his clothes off his body yet . . . I can
see on his lips what he's saying . . . What shall I say to him . . .
"Sir, you're right! Take everything—it belongs to you!" . . .

KRISTINA: That's all you should say!

ELIS: Now he's laughing! A good laugh, not an evil one! Maybe
he isn't so bad, even if he wants his money! . . . If he'd only
come *now,* and stop that blessed talk . . . now his stick is moving
again . . . They always have sticks, the ones who have debts to
collect . . . and leather overshoes that say "swish, swish" just like
whips in the air . . . (*Puts* KRISTINA's *hand above his heart*) . . .
Can you feel how my heart is beating . . . I hear it myself like
an ocean liner in my right ear . . . Now he said good-bye . . .
those overshoes! "Swish, swish" like the Easter switch . . . but
he has a watch chain with charms! Then he isn't penniless!
They always have carnelian charms like old flesh they cut from
their neighbors' backs . . . listen to those overshoes . . . "wolves,
wolves, mad, madder, maddest, swish, swish!" Watch it! He sees

me! He sees me! . . . (*Bows toward the street*) . . . He greeted
me first! He's smiling! He's waving his hand . . . and . . .
(*Sinks down by the desk weeping*) He went by!

KRISTINA: God be praised!

ELIS: He went by! . . . But he'll be back! . . . Let's go out into the
sunlight.

KRISTINA: And Peter's dinner?

ELIS: Since I've still not been invited, I won't go! Besides, what
would I have to do there in the midst of his joy. Meeting a faithless friend! I'd only suffer on his account so that I couldn't be
hurt on my own!

KRISTINA: Thank you for staying with us!

ELIS: That's what I prefer! As you know! . . . Are we going out for
a walk?

KRISTINA: Yes, this way! (*Going out to the left*)

ELIS (*when he passes* BENJAMIN, *pats him on his head*): Courage,
my boy! (BENJAMIN *puts his face in his hands.* ELIS *takes the
Easter switch from the dining table and puts it behind the mirror.*) It wasn't an olive branch the dove brought me—it was a
birch switch! (*Goes out*)

(ELEONORA *enters from the back; a sixteen-year old girl with a
braid down her back. She is carrying a yellow daffodil—the Swedish Easter lily—in a pot.*[17] *Without looking at* BENJAMIN, *or
pretending not to see him, she takes a water carafe from the sideboard and waters the plant, puts it on the dining table, sits down
by that table directly across from* BENJAMIN, *observes him, and
imitates his actions.*)

(BENJAMIN *observes her with amazement.*)

ELEONORA (*points at the Easter lily*): Do you know what *that* is?

BENJAMIN (*childishly, simply*): It's an Easter lily, of course . . . But
who are you?

ELEONORA (*in a friendly but sad fashion*): Yes, who are you?

BENJAMIN (*as before*): My name is Benjamin, and I'm boarding
here with Mrs. Heyst!

ELEONORA: Oh! I'm Eleonora—I'm her daughter.

BENJAMIN: Strange . . . they've never mentioned you!

ELEONORA: People don't talk about the dead!

BENJAMIN: The dead!

ELEONORA: I'm legally dead, for I've committed a very bad crime.

BENJAMIN: You!

ELEONORA: Yes, I've embezzled my guardian's funds—that didn't matter so much, because what's unjustly gained shall be lost— but that my old father got the blame and was put in prison, you see, can never be forgiven.

BENJAMIN: How strangely and beautifully you speak . . . and I've never thought about that, that my inheritance could have been unjustly gained.

ELEONORA: People should not be bound; they should be set free.

BENJAMIN: Well, you've freed me from the worry about having been cheated . . .

ELEONORA: So you're Father's ward . . .

BENJAMIN: Yes, and I have the sad lot of having these poor people let me live with them to pay their debt.

ELEONORA: You may not use harsh words—then I'll go away; I'm so delicate, I can't bear anything harsh! But . . . you're enduring this for my sake?

BENJAMIN: For your father's sake.

ELEONORA: That's the same thing, for he and I are one and the same person [18] . . . (*Pause*) I've been very ill . . . Why are you so sad?

BENJAMIN: I've had a piece of bad luck!

ELEONORA: Should you be sad about that? "Correction is grievous unto him that forsaketh the way: and he that hateth reproof shall die." What bad luck have you had?

BENJAMIN: I failed my exam in Latin—though I was absolutely sure I'd pass.

ELEONORA: So, you were absolutely sure, so sure, you could bet you'd pass!

BENJAMIN: I did bet!

ELEONORA: I believe it! You see, you failed because you were sure.

BENJAMIN: Do you think that was why?

ELEONORA: Of course it was! Pride goes before a fall!

BENJAMIN: I'll remember that next time.

ELEONORA: That's right; and the sacrifice which pleases God . . . is a sorrowful spirit.

BENJAMIN: Are you a pietist?

ELEONORA: Yes, I'm a pietist!

BENJAMIN: A believer, I mean!

ELEONORA: Yes, that's what I mean. So if you speak ill of God, my protector, I won't sit at the same table as you!

BENJAMIN: How old are you?

ELEONORA: For me there's neither time nor space; I'm everywhere at all times! I'm in my father's prison and in my brother's schoolroom, I'm in my mother's kitchen and in my sister's store far away in America. When things go well for my sister and she gets to sell a lot, I feel her joy, and if it goes badly for her, I suffer, but I suffer most when she does wrong. Benjamin. Your name is Benjamin, because you are the youngest of my friends [19] . . . Yes, all people are my friends . . . if you want me to take you up, I will suffer for you, too.

BENJAMIN: I don't really understand the words you speak, but I seem to grasp the meaning of your thoughts! And I want everything you want!

ELEONORA: To begin with, do you want to stop judging people, even those who are convicted criminals . . .

BENJAMIN: Yes, but I want a reason for it! You see, I've studied philosophy!

ELEONORA: Oh, have you? Then you'll help me interpret what a great philosopher said: "They that hate the righteous shall be desolate."

BENJAMIN: According to logic that means one could be condemned to commit crimes . . .

ELEONORA: And that the crime itself is a punishment.

BENJAMIN: That's really deep! Kant or Schopenhauer [20] could have said that.

ELEONORA: I don't know them.

BENJAMIN: What book did you read it in?

ELEONORA: In the Holy Scriptures!

BENJAMIN: Really? Are there things like that in the Bible?

ELEONORA: What an ignorant, neglected child you are! If I might bring you up!

BENJAMIN: You little thing!

ELEONORA: But there certainly isn't any evil in you! You look good . . . Who's your Latin teacher?

BENJAMIN: Mr. Algren! [21]

ELEONORA: I'll remember that! . . . (*Sighs*) Now Father is suffering very much! They're cruel to him. (*Stands still as if she were listening*) Do you hear the telephone wires singing . . . they're the harsh words, that the delicate beautiful red copper can't bear . . . When people speak evil of each other on the telephone, the copper laments, and complains . . . (*harshly*) and every word is recorded in the book . . . and at the end of time will come the judgment!

BENJAMIN: How strict you are!

ELEONORA: Not I, not I! How would I dare to be? I? I? (*She goes up to the stove and opens its door; takes out some torn-up pieces of white statonery.* BENJAMIN *gets up and looks at the papers which* ELEONORA *pieces together on the dining table. She speaks to herself*) That people can be so thoughtless that they put their secrets into stoves . . . Wherever I come, I go to the stove right away! But I never misuse what I find, I wouldn't dare to, for then I'd suffer! . . . What's this? (*Reads*)

BENJAMIN: It's Dr. Peter, who has written to make an appointment with Kristina . . . I've expected that for a long time.

ELEONORA (*puts her hand over the papers*): You! What have you expected? Tell me, you evil person, who believe only evil! This letter will bring only good, for I know Kristina, who's going to be my sister-in-law. And their meeting will prevent a misfortune for Elis . . . Will you promise me to say nothing about it, Benjamin?

BENJAMIN: I think I wouldn't dare mention it!

ELEONORA: What unjust things people who have secrets do . . . They think they're wise and are fools! . . . But what did I have to do there?

BENJAMIN: Yes, why are you curious?

ELEONORA: It's my illness that I have to know everything; otherwise I get uneasy . . .

BENJAMIN: Know everything?

ELEONORA: It's a fault I can't overcome. But I know what the starlings say all the same.

BENJAMIN: They can't talk, can they?

ELEONORA: Haven't you heard starlings that people have taught to talk?

BENJAMIN: Yes, that they've taught!

ELEONORA: So starlings can learn to talk! And there are some who teach themselves . . . of course, they sit listening without our knowing, and they imitate. Just now when I came home I heard two of them sitting talking in a walnut tree.

BENJAMIN: You're fun! But what did they say?

ELEONORA: Well! "Peter," said one. "Judas," [22] said the other. "The same thing," said the first.—"Fie, fie, fie," said the second. But have you noticed that the nightingales sing only in the garden of the deaf and dumb near here?

BENJAMIN: Yes, that's right! Why's that?

ELEONORA: Because those who can hear can't hear what the nightingales say, but the deaf and dumb can!

BENJAMIN: Tell me more stories!

ELEONORA: Yes, if you're good.

BENJAMIN: How good?

ELEONORA: Well, you must never catch at my words, and never say
that you said so and so then, and then you said so . . . Shall I tell
you more about birds? There's a bad bird called the rat-buzzard;
as you can tell by his name, he lives on rats. But since he's bad,
he has a hard time catching rats. So he can say only one single
word, and it sounds like a cat's "Meow." When the buzzard says
"Meow," the rats hide . . . but the buzzard doesn't understand
what he himself says—but he's often without food because he's
mean!—Do you want to hear more? Or shall I talk about flowers?
. . . You know, when I was sick, I had to take a drug made from
henbane, which makes one's eye a magnifying glass . . . The
belladonna does the opposite—it makes one see everything much
smaller . . . Well, now I can see farther than other people, and I
can see the stars in broad daylight!

BENJAMIN: But the stars aren't up then, are they?

ELEONORA: You're funny! The stars are always up . . . now I'm
facing north looking at the constellation Cassiopeia which resembles a W and sits right in the middle of the Milky Way . . . Can
you see it?

BENJAMIN: No, I can't!

ELEONORA: Notice that one person *can* see what the next one can't
. . . Don't trust *your* eyes so much! . . . Now I should tell about
the plant on the table . . . It's an Easter lily that has its home in
Switzerland . . . it has a chalice that has been drinking sunlight
so it's yellow and soothes pains . . . I was walking by a florist's
shop, saw it, and wanted to give it to Elis . . . When I was going
to go in, the door was locked . . . it's confirmation today . . . As
I had to have the plant, I took out my keys and tried them . . . Can
you imagine, my door key fitted . . . I went in . . . Well, do you
understand the silent language of flowers? Every fragrance ex-
presses a host of thoughts, and these thoughts came upon me; and
with my magnifying eye I saw in their workshops what no one
has seen. And they told me about the sorrows the ignorant gar-

dener had caused them—I don't say cruel—because he's only thoughtless! . . . Then I put a crown and my card on the counter —took the plant and left.

BENJAMIN: That was thoughtless! What if they miss the plant and don't find the coin?

ELEONORA: That's true! You're right.

BENJAMIN: It's easy enough for a coin to get lost, and, if they find only your card, you're lost!

ELEONORA: Surely no one can think I wanted to steal anything?

BENJAMIN (*stares at her*): No-o?

ELEONORA (*looks at him, then gets up*): Oh! I know what you mean! Like father, like daughter! How thoughtless I've been! . . . Well! What's going to happen, will happen! (*Sits down*) Let it!

BENJAMIN: Can it be straightened out? . . .

ELEONORA: Sh-h! Talk about something else! . . . Dr. Algren! . . . Poor Elis! Poor all of us! But it's Easter, and we're to suffer. There's a concert tomorrow, isn't there? And they're giving Haydn's *Seven Last Words!* "Mother, behold thy Son!" (*She weeps, her hands covering her face.*)

BENJAMIN: What sort of illness did you have?

ELEONORA: It isn't fatal—it's in God's honor! "When I looked for good, then evil came unto me: and when I waited for light, there came darkness." [23] . . . What was your childhood like, Benjamin?

BENJAMIN: I don't know. Boring! And yours?

ELEONORA: I never had any. I was born old . . . I knew everything when I was born, and when I learned something it was only like remembering something. I knew people's . . . thoughtlessness and ignorance when I was four years old, and that's why people were mean to me.

BENJAMIN: Everything you say I seem to have thought, I, too!

ELEONORA: You most likely have! . . . Why did you think my coin would be lost in the florist's shop?

BENJAMIN: Because what's annoying is always bound to happen!

ELEONORA: So you've noticed that, too! . . . Sh-h, someone's coming!

(*Looks toward the back*) I hear . . . that's Elis! . . . Oh, what fun! My only friend on earth! . . . (*She becomes depressed.*) But . . . he's not expecting me. And he won't be happy to see me. No, he won't! . . . Surely not!—Benjamin, Benjamin, look friendly and be cheerful when my poor brother comes. I'll go in there so you can prepare him for my return. But no harsh words—they hurt me very much. Promise me! (*They shake hands on it.* ELEONORA *kisses the top of his head.*) There! Now you're my little brother! God bless you and keep you! (*Goes toward the left and in passing pats* ELIS' *overcoat on the sleeve*) Poor Elis! (*Goes out*)

ELIS (*worried, enters from back;* MRS. HEYST *comes in from the kitchen*): There you are, Mother!

MRS. HEYST: Was it you? I thought I heard a strange voice.

ELIS: I have news! I met the lawyer on the street!

MRS. HEYST: Well?

ELIS: The case is to go to a higher court . . . and to gain time I have to read through all the trial proceedings.

MRS. HEYST: Well, you can do that quickly!

ELIS (*points at the documents on the desk*): I thought it was over, and now I have to suffer through this whole story of suffering— all the accusations, all the testimony, all the evidence! Over again!

MRS. HEYST: Yes, but then he'll be acquitted in the next court.

ELIS: No, Mother—he confessed!

MRS. HEYST: Yes, but there can be a technical error, the lawyer said the last time I saw him.

ELIS: He said that to comfort you.

MRS. HEYST: You're not going to that dinner?

ELIS: No!

MRS. HEYST: You've changed your mind again!

ELIS: Yes!

MRS. HEYST: That's bad.

ELIS: I know, but I'm tossed like a chip between breakers.

MRS. HEYST: I did think I heard a strange voice that I recognized.—

But I suppose I didn't. (*Points at his overcoat*) That coat shouldn't be hanging there, I said. (*Goes out to the right*)

ELIS (*goes slowly to the left; sees the Easter lily on the dining table. To Benjamin*): Where did that plant come from?

BENJAMIN: A young woman brought it!

ELIS: Woman? What's that? Who was it?

BENJAMIN: It was . . .

ELIS: Was it . . . my sister?

BENJAMIN: Yes!

ELIS (*sinks down by the dining table. Pause*): Did you speak with her?

BENJAMIN: Oh, yes!

ELIS: Oh, God, isn't it enough soon? Was she unkind to you?

BENJAMIN: She? No, she was very kind! Very kind!

ELIS: Strange! . . . Did she say anything about me? Was she very angry with me?

BENJAMIN: No! On the contrary! She said you were her best and only friend on earth . . .

ELIS: What a strange change!

BENJAMIN: And when she went, she patted your coat over there on the sleeve . . .

ELIS: Went? Where did she go?

BENJAMIN (*points to the left door*): In there.

ELIS: She's in there?

BENJAMIN: Yes.

ELIS: You look so happy and friendly, Benjamin.

BENJAMIN: She talked so beautifully to me . . .

ELIS: What did she talk about?

BENJAMIN: She told stories, and she said a lot about religion . . .

ELIS (*gets up*): That made you happy.

BENJAMIN: Yes!

ELIS: Poor Eleonora, who's so unhappy herself and can make others happy! (*Goes slowly to the left*) God help me!

[CURTAIN]

# ACT II

## *Good Friday*

Music before this act: Haydn's *Seven Last Words*, Largo No. 1:
"Pater dimitte illis" [24]

*The same setting, but the curtains are drawn shut and the gas-light outside shines through them. The ceiling lamp is lit; on the dining table is a small lighted kerosene lamp. There is a fire in the stove.*

ELIS *and* KRISTINA *are sitting by the sewing table doing nothing.*
BENJAMIN *and* ELEONORA *are sitting at the dining table directly across from each other with the lamp between them.* ELEONORA *has a shawl over her shoulders.*

*All are dressed in black;* ELIS *and* BENJAMIN *have white ties.*

*On the desk are spread the documents concerning the court proceedings. The Easter lily is on the sewing table. An old pendulum clock is on the dining table.*

*Now and then the shadow of someone passing can be seen on the curtains.*

ELIS (*softly to* KRISTINA): Yes, Good Friday! But so terribly long! And the snow lies on the paving stones like straw outside the home of someone dead; there isn't a sound—except the basses of the organ that I can hear way up here . . .

KRISTINA: I think Mother went to evening services . . .

ELIS: Yes, because she didn't dare to go to high mass . . . She's hurt by people's looking at her . . .

KRISTINA: It's strange about these people; they expect us to keep out of sight; they think that's proper . . .

ELIS: Yes, and they're right perhaps . . .

KRISTINA: Because of one person's slip, the whole family's outlawed . . .

ELIS: Yes, that's how it is!

    (ELEONORA *shoves the lamp toward* BENJAMIN *so he'll see better.*)

ELIS (*gestures toward* ELEONORA *and* BENJAMIN): Look at those two!

KRISTINA: Isn't it nice! . . . How well they get along!

ELIS: How fortunate that Eleonora is so calm. If it will only last!

KRISTINA: Why shouldn't it?

ELIS: Because . . . good fortune doesn't generally last very long! I'm afraid of everything today!

    (BENJAMIN *shoves the lamp slowly toward* ELEONORA *so she can see better.*)

KRISTINA: Look at them!

ELIS: Have you noticed how changed Benjamin is! Sullen defiance has given way to quiet resignation . . .

KRISTINA: How lovely she is in all her being—I don't want to use the word beautiful!

ELIS: And she has brought an angel of peace who goes about invisible breathing a quiet tranquillity . . . Even Mother was calm when she saw her, calm in a way I hadn't expected.

KRISTINA: Do you think she has recovered now?

ELIS: Yes, if it weren't for her extreme sensitivity. She's reading about the suffering of Christ and weeps now and then.

KRISTINA: Well, I remember I did, too, in school on Wednesdays during Lent . . .

ELIS: Don't speak so loudly—she hears so well!

KRISTINA: Not now. She's far away!

ELIS: Have you noticed something dignified, noble has come over Benjamin?

KRISTINA: That comes from suffering; happiness makes everything commonplace.

ELIS: More likely it's probably . . . love! Don't you think those youngsters . . .

KRISTINA: Sh-h . . . don't touch the butterfly's wings! Then it'll fly away!

ELIS: They're most likely looking at each other, only pretending to read—I can't hear that they're turning any leaves.

KRISTINA: Sh-h!

ELIS: See, now she can't sit still . . .

(ELEONORA *gets up, goes up to* BENJAMIN, *and puts her shawl about his shoulders.* BENJAMIN *resists mildly but gives in; thereupon* ELEONORA *sits down again and shoves the lamp over to* BENJAMIN'*s side.*)

KRISTINA: Poor Eleonora. She doesn't know how well she wishes him.

ELIS (*gets up*): Now I'm going back to my documents.

KRISTINA: Can you see any point to reading them?

ELIS: Just one: to keep Mother's hope alive! But though I, too, only pretend to read, some of the words remain like thorns in my eye. The testimony of witnesses, figures, Father's confessions . . . like this: "The defendant admitted with tears" . . . So many tears, so many tears. And these papers . . . with their stamps that remind me of counterfeit money or prison locks; and the cords and the red seals . . . They look like Christ's five wounds . . . and the clauses that never end, the eternal agony . . . It's work for a long, long Good Friday . . . Yesterday the sun shone, we went out into the country, in our thoughts . . . Kristina . . . What if we have to stay here this summer!

KRISTINA: We'd save a lot of money . . . but it would be too bad.

ELIS: I couldn't live through it . . . I've been here for three summers . . . and it's like a grave. At high noon, one sees the long gray street twist like a trench . . . not one human being, and not a horse, not a dog . . . But out of the sewer openings the rats come, because the cats are away at summer places . . . And some people left behind sit by their gossip mirrors[25] spying on their neighbor's clothes . . . "Look, that fellow's wearing his winter clothes!" . . . and their neighbor's worn-down heels . . . and their neighbor's faults . . . And out of the poor people's neighborhood creep cripples who've hidden themselves before, people without noses and ears, mean people and unfortunate ones . . . And they sit along the great promenade sunning themselves just as if they'd taken over the town . . . where beautiful well-dressed children played while their beautiful mothers spoke tender encouraging words, hosts of ragged ones who curse and torture each other roam about . . . I remember a Midsummer Day[26] two years ago!

KRISTINA: Elis, Elis! Look ahead! Ahead!

ELIS: Is it brighter there?

KRISTINA: Let's believe it will be!

ELIS (*sits down at the desk*): If it would only stop snowing! So we could go out walking!

KRISTINA: Dear, last night you wished the darkness would return, so people couldn't see us . . . "Darkness is so beautiful, so wholesome," you said; "it's like pulling the blanket over one's head!"

ELIS: See, misery is just as great in any case . . . (*Reading in the documents*) The worst about the trial are the impertinent questions about my father's way of life . . . It says, we gave brilliant parties . . . One witness says he drank! . . . No, it's too much! I can't keep on with this! . . . But I have to all the same . . . to the end! . . . Aren't you freezing?

KRISTINA: No, but it isn't warm . . . Lina isn't at home, is she?

ELIS: No, she went to communion, you know.

KRISTINA: Mother will surely be home soon?

ELIS: I'm always afraid when she goes, she'll have heard so much, and seen so much . . . and all of it bad.

KRISTINA: Your family is unusually morbid.

ELIS: That's why only morbid people have wanted to associate with us! Cheerful ones have avoided us!

KRISTINA: Mother just came into the kitchen!

ELIS: Don't be impatient with her, Kristina!

KRISTINA: Oh, no! I suspect she's having the hardest time of all. But I don't understand her.

ELIS: She conceals her shame as well as she can; that's why she's impossible to understand. Poor Mother!

MRS. HEYST (*enters; dressed in black with a psalmbook and a handkerchief in her hand*): Good evening, children.

ALL (*with the exception of* BENJAMIN, *who greets her silently*): Good evening, Mother.

MRS. HEYST: You're all dressed in black as if you were in mourning. (*Silence*)

ELIS: Is it still snowing?

MRS. HEYST: Yes, it's sleet. It's cold in here! . . . (*Goes up to* ELEONORA *and pats her*) Well, my dear, you're studying, I see. (*To* BENJAMIN) And you should be! (ELEONORA *takes her mother's hand and brings it to her lips.* MRS. HEYST *suppresses the fact that she is touched.*) There, my child! There, there . . .

ELIS: You went to evening services, Mother.

MRS. HEYST: Yes, it was the curate, and I don't like him.

ELIS: Did you see anyone you knew?

MRS. HEYST (*sits down by the sewing table*): It would have been better if I hadn't!

ELIS: Then I know who . . .

MRS. HEYST: Lindkvist! And he came up to me . . .

ELIS: That was cruel . . . very.

MRS. HEYST: He asked how I was . . . and, imagine my horror, he asked if he could visit us tonight.

ELIS: On a holiday?

MRS. HEYST: I was speechless! And he took my silence as consent! (*Pause*) He may be here any time!

ELIS (*gets up*): Here? Now?

MRS. HEYST: He said he wanted to leave a document that should be looked at right away.

ELIS: He wants to take the furniture.

MRS. HEYST: But he looked so strange . . . I didn't understand him!

ELIS: Let him come. Justice is on his side, and we'll have to agree. We'll have to receive him in a proper way when he comes.

MRS. HEYST: Just so I don't have to see him!

ELIS: Well, you can stay in there . . .

MRS. HEYST: But he must not take the furniture. What would we do if he took all our things? We can't live in empty rooms! Can we?

ELIS: Foxes have dens, and birds nests . . . There are homeless people living in the forest.

MRS. HEYST: That's where the rascals should live, not respectable people.

ELIS (*at the desk*): I'm reading these, Mother.

MRS. HEYST: Have you found any error?

ELIS: No, I don't think there is any.

MRS. HEYST: But I met the city clerk, and he said there could be a technical error, a witness who could be challenged, an unproved assertion, or a contradiction. You must not be reading carefully enough!

ELIS: Yes, Mother, but it's very painful . . .

MRS. HEYST: Listen, I met the city clerk—but I told you that—and he told me about a burglary here in town yesterday—in broad daylight. (ELEONORA *and* BENJAMIN *prick up their ears.*)

ELIS: Burglary? Here in town? Where?

MRS. HEYST: In a florist's shop on Cloister Street. But it was very strange, the whole thing. It's supposed to have been like this: the florist shut his store to go to church, where his son . . . maybe it was his daughter, was to be confirmed. When he came back about three, maybe it was four, but that makes no difference . . . well, the door was open, and there were flowers missing, a whole lot, especially a yellow tulip that he noticed first!

ELIS: A tulip! If it had been a lily, I'd have been afraid.

MRS. HEYST: No, it was a tulip; that's quite certain. Well, the police are on the lookout. (ELEONORA *has got up as if she wanted to speak, but* BENJAMIN *goes up to her and whispers something.*)

MRS. HEYST: Imagine, on Maundy Thursday itself to break in when the young people are to be confirmed . . . Rascals only, the whole town! And that's why they put innocent people in prison.

ELIS: Do they suspect anyone?

MRS. HEYST: No. But it was a strange thief, for he didn't take any money from the cash drawer! . . .

KRISTINA: If this day were only over!

MRS. HEYST: And if Lina would only come home! . . . Well, I heard them talking about Peter's dinner yesterday. The governor himself was there.

ELIS: That amazes me, for Peter was always considered an opponent of the governor's party.

MRS. HEYST: I suppose he's changed sides.

ELIS: His name isn't Peter [27] for nothing, it seems.

MRS. HEYST: What do you have against the governor?

ELIS: He's an obstructionist! He stands in the way of everything: he blocked the folk high school, he blocked the young people's military drills, he wanted to block harmless bicycles, the attractive vacation colonies [28] . . . and he has blocked me!

MRS. HEYST: I don't understand all that . . . and it probably doesn't matter. But the governor held a speech . . . and Peter thanked him . . .

ELIS: . . . touched, I suppose, and denied his teacher and said: "I do not know that man." And the cock crowed again! Wasn't the governor's name Pontius Pilate? [29]

(ELEONORA *moves as if she wanted to speak, but calms herself.*)

MRS. HEYST: Don't be so bitter, Elis. People are people, and we have to put up with them.

ELIS: Sh-h! I hear Lindkvist coming!

MRS. HEYST: Can you hear that in the snow?

ELIS: I can hear his cane hitting the stones . . . and his leather overshoes. Go out, Mother!

MRS. HEYST: No, now I want to stay so I can tell him something!

ELIS: Please, Mother, go out! It will be too painful!

MRS. HEYST (*gets up; shaken*): May the day I was born be forgotten!

KRISTINA: Don't curse!

MRS. HEYST (*with an expression of spiritual greatness*): "Is not destruction to the wicked? and a strange punishment to the workers of iniquity?" [30]

ELEONORA (*with a cry of anguish*): Mother!

MRS. HEYST: "My God, why hast Thou forsaken me?" [31] And my children! (*Goes out to the left*)

ELIS (*listening intently*): He has stopped! . . . Maybe he thinks it's improper . . . or all too cruel! . . . That's unlikely—he could write such terrible letters! Always on blue paper,[32] and since then I can't look at a blue letter without trembling!

KRISTINA: What are you going to say to him, what are you going to suggest?

ELIS: I don't know! I've lost all my ability to think clearly . . . Shall I get down on my knees and beg him for mercy? . . . Can you hear him? I can hear only my blood surging in my ears!

KRISTINA: Let's consider the worst that can happen. He'll take everything . . .

ELIS: Then the landlord will come and want security that I can't find . . . He'll want security since the furniture won't be a guarantee for the rent any longer.

KRISTINA (*who has been looking out behind a curtain*): He isn't there any more! He has gone!

ELIS (*sighs*): You know, Mother's indifferent resignation bothers me more than her anger!

KRISTINA: Her resignation is only pretended or imagined. There was something of the lioness' roar in her last words . . . Did you see how dignified she became?

ELIS: You know, when I think about Lindkvist, I see him like a good-natured giant who only wants to frighten children! How can I think so?

KRISTINA: Thoughts come and go . . .

ELIS: How fortunate I wasn't at the dinner yesterday . . . I'd cer-

tainly have given a speech attacking the governor . . . then I'd
have destroyed everything for myself and us! That was very fortunate!

KRISTINA: So you understand that!

ELIS: Thanks for your advice. You did know your Peter!

KRISTINA: My Peter!

ELIS: I meant . . . mine! There, he's here again! (*On the curtain
can be seen the shadow of a man approaching hesitantly. The
shadow is gradually magnified until it becomes gigantic. All of
them become extremely anxious.*) The giant! Look at the giant,
who wants to devour us!

KRISTINA: Something to smile at—just as in fairy tales!

ELIS: I can't smile any more! (*The shadow becomes smaller and
disappears.*)

KRISTINA: Look at the switch, then, and you'll have to laugh!

ELIS: He left! Now I want to breathe, because he won't come back
until tomorrow! Ah-h!

KRISTINA: And the sun will shine tomorrow—it will be the evening
of resurrection, the snow will be gone, and the birds will be
singing.

ELIS: Tell me more things like that! I *see* everything you say.

KRISTINA: That you could see into my heart, see my thoughts, my
good intentions, my innermost prayer, Elis, Elis, now when I
. . . (*Stops herself*)

ELIS: What? Tell me!

KRISTINA: When I now . . . ask you for one thing.

ELIS: What?

KRISTINA: It's a test! Think of it as a test, Elis!

ELIS: Test! Trial? Well?

KRISTINA: Let me . . . No, I don't dare! It *can* fail! (ELEONORA
*pricks up her ears.*)

ELIS: Why do you torture me?

KRISTINA: I'll regret it; I know that! . . . Well, let it! Elis, let me
go to the concert tonight.

ELIS: Which concert?

KRISTINA: Haydn's *Seven Words on the Cross* in the cathedral.

ELIS: With whom?

KRISTINA: With Alice . . .

ELIS: And?

KRISTINA: Peter!

ELIS: With Peter?

KRISTINA: See, you're angry! . . . I'm sorry, but it's too late!

ELIS: Yes, it's pretty late! But explain yourself!

KRISTINA: I prepared you for not being able to explain, but that's why I asked for your full confidence.

ELIS: Go ahead! I rely on you, but I'll suffer all the same for your seeking that traitor's company!

KRISTINA: I understand that. But it is a test!

ELIS: That I can't pass!

KRISTINA: You're going to!

ELIS: I want to, but I can't—But you're to go in any case!

KRISTINA: Your hand!

ELIS (*they shake hands*): There! (*The telephone rings.* ELIS *answers it.*) Hello . . . No answer! . . . Hello! . . . My own voice answers! . . . Who is this . . . Strange! I can hear my own voice like an echo!

KRISTINA: That sort of thing can happen!

ELIS: Hello! . . . This is ghastly! (*Hangs up*) Go ahead, Kristina! Without explanations, without detailed explanations. I will pass the test!

KRISTINA: If you do, it will go well for us.

ELIS: I will!

(KRISTINA *goes to the right.*)

ELIS: Why are you going in that direction?

KRISTINA: I have my clothes out there. So! Farewell! (*Goes*)

ELIS: Farewell, dear! (*Pause*) Forever! (*Rushes out to the left*)

ELEONORA: God help us, what have I done this time? The police are looking for the thief, and if I'm found—poor Mother, and Elis!

BENJAMIN (*childishly*): Eleonora, you must say I did it!

ELEONORA: You! Can you bear another's guilt, child?

BENJAMIN: Surely that's easy to do when one knows one is innocent.

ELEONORA: One should never lie!

BENJAMIN: Well, let me call the florist to tell him how it was!

ELEONORA: No, I've done wrong, and I have to be punished with anxiety. I have awakened their fear of burglary, and I'm to be frightened.

BENJAMIN: But if the police come . . .

ELEONORA: That will be hard, of course . . . but then it's to be! If this day were only over! (*Takes the clock on the dining table and moves the hands*) . . . Dear clock, go a little faster! Ticktock, ping, ping, ping! Now it's eight! Ping, ping, ping . . . Now it's nine! Ten! Eleven! Twelve! Now it's Easter eve! Now the sun will soon rise, and we'll write on our Easter eggs! I'll write like this: "Satan hath desired to have you, that he may sift you as wheat." [33]

BENJAMIN: Why do you hurt yourself so, Eleonora?

ELEONORA: I! hurt myself! Benjamin, think of all the blooming flowers, the anemones, the buttercups, that have had to stand in the snow all day and all night—freezing out in the darkness! Imagine how they have to suffer! Night's most likely worst since it's dark, and they become afraid of the dark but can't run away . . . and they stand waiting until daylight comes. Everything, everything suffers, but the flowers most! And the birds of passage that have come. Where are they going to sleep tonight?

BENJAMIN (*childishly*): They'll sit in hollow trees; you must know that.

ELEONORA: There aren't enough hollow trees for all of them. I've seen only two hollow trees in the parks, and owls that kill little birds live in them . . . Poor Elis, who thinks Kristina left him! But I know she'll come back!

BENJAMIN: If you knew that, why didn't you say so?

ELEONORA: Because Elis has to suffer; everybody has to suffer on

Good Friday, because they have to recall Christ's suffering on the cross. (*The sound of a police whistle can be heard from the street.*)

ELEONORA (*jumps up*): What was that?

BENJAMIN: Don't you know?

ELEONORA: No!

BENJAMIN: That was the police!

ELEONORA: Oh! . . . Yes, that's what it sounded like when they came to get Father . . . and then I became ill! And now they're coming to take me!

BENJAMIN (*facing the door at the back stations himself in front of* ELEONORA): No, they mustn't take you! I'll defend you, Eleonora!

ELEONORA: That's nice, Benjamin, but you mayn't . . .

BENJAMIN (*looks out through the curtains*): There are two of them! (ELEONORA *wants to shove* BENJAMIN *out of the way, but he resists gently.*) Not you, Eleonora, then—I wouldn't want to go on living!

ELEONORA: Go on—sit down in that chair, child! Go on—sit down! (BENJAMIN *obeys unwillingly.* ELEONORA, *without concealing herself, looks out behind the curtains.*) It was only two boys! Oh, we of little faith! Do you think God is so cruel, when I haven't done anything bad, only acted thoughtlessly . . . I deserved it! Why did I doubt?

BENJAMIN: But the one who'll take the furniture will come tomorrow.

ELEONORA: Let him come! And we'll have to leave! Everything . . . all the old furniture Father has gathered for us, and that I've seen since I was a little child! Well, one shouldn't own anything that binds one to the earth. Out on the stony highways, wandering with sore feet, for that way leads upward, and that's why it's so hard . . .

BENJAMIN: Now you're torturing yourself again, Eleonora!

ELEONORA: Let me! . . . Do you know what will be hardest to part from? That clock there! It was present when I was born, and it has measured my hours and my days . . . (*She lifts the clock from the table.*) Listen to it beating like a heart . . . just like a heart . . . and it stopped on the hour when Grandfather died, because it was present even then! Good-bye, little clock, may you stop soon again! . . . You know it used to speed up when it wanted to get past the evil, for *our* sake, of course! But when times were good, it slowed down so we could enjoy ourselves longer. It was the good clock! But we had a bad one . . . That has to hang in the kitchen now. It couldn't stand music—as soon as Elis began to play the piano it began to strike—we all noticed it, not only I; and that's why it has to be in the kitchen now, for it was mean! But Lina doesn't like it, either, for it isn't silent at night, and she can't boil eggs by it . . . Lina says they always get hardboiled! Yes, you're laughing!

BENJAMIN: Yes, what should I do? . . .

ELEONORA: You're a good boy, Benjamin, but you should be serious! Think of the switch behind the mirror!

BENJAMIN: But you talk so amusingly, I have to smile . . . and why should one always weep?

ELEONORA: Where should we weep if not in this vale of tears?

BENJAMIN: Hm!

ELEONORA: You'd like to smile all day, but that's why you've been hit, too! And I like you only when you're serious. Remember that!

BENJAMIN: Do you think we'll get out of all this, Eleonora?

ELEONORA: Yes, most of it will clear up once Good Friday is over, but not everything! Today the switch, tomorrow the Easter eggs! [34] Today snow, tomorrow thaw! Today death, tomorrow the resurrection!

BENJAMIN: How wise you are!

ELEONORA: Yes, I already feel it clearing up into beautiful weather; the snow will melt . . . it already smells of melted snow in here . . . and tomorrow the violets along the south wall will burst into bloom! The clouds have lifted; I can tell by my breathing . . . I know so very well when the way's open to heaven! Go, Benjamin, draw the curtains aside; I want God to see us! (BENJAMIN *gets up and obeys; moonlight falls into the room.*) Look at the full moon! It is Easter's! And now you know the sun is still there though the moon casts its light!

[CURTAIN]

# ACT III

## *Easter Eve*

Music preceding Act III: Haydn's *Seven Last Words,* No 5 ("I thirst"), Adagio

*The same setting. The curtains have been drawn aside. The landscape outside is the same, but it is gray. The stove has been lighted; the doors at the back are shut.*

ELEONORA *is sitting in front of the stove with a bouquet of anemones in front of her.* BENJAMIN *enters from the right.*

ELEONORA: Where have you been so long, Benjamin?

BENJAMIN: It wasn't long, was it?

ELEONORA: I've been longing for you!

BENJAMIN: Where have you been, Eleonora?

ELEONORA: I've been at the market place buying anemones, and I'm warming them—they've been freezing, poor things.

BENJAMIN: Where's the sun?

ELEONORA: Behind the fog; there aren't any clouds today, just fog from the sea—it smells salty . . .

BENJAMIN: Did you see that the birds are still alive out there?

ELEONORA: Yes, and not one falls to the ground unless God wishes. But on the square there were dead birds . . .

ELIS (*enters from the right*): Has the paper come?

ELEONORA: No, Elis. (ELIS *is crossing the stage; when he gets half-way,* KRISTINA *enters from the left.*)

KRISTINA (*without noticing* ELIS): Has the paper come?

ELEONORA: No, it hasn't. (KRISTINA *crosses the stage to the right, passes* ELIS, *who exits to the left. They do not look at each other.*) How cold it has got! Hate has come into our house. As long as there was love, one could bear everything, but now it's so cold, so very cold!

BENJAMIN: Why do they want the paper?

ELEONORA: Don't you understand? That's where it'll say . . .

BENJAMIN: What?

ELEONORA: Everything! The breaking in, the police, and still more . . .

MRS. HEYST (*enters from the right*): Has the paper come?

ELEONORA: No, Mother dear!

MRS. HEYST (*as she goes out to the left*): Tell *me* first when it does.

ELEONORA: The paper, the paper!—If only the press had gone to pieces, if the editor had become ill . . . no, one mustn't say anything like that! You know, I was with Father last night . . .

BENJAMIN: Last night?

ELEONORA: Yes, in my sleep . . . and I was with my sister in America . . . the day before yesterday she sold thirty dollars' worth, so she had earned five.

BENJAMIN: Is that much or just a little?

ELEONORA: It's quite a lot!

BENJAMIN (*slyly*): Did you meet anyone you knew when you were at the marketplace?

ELEONORA: Why do you ask? Don't be sly with me, Benjamin; you want to know my secrets, but you mayn't.

BENJAMIN: And you think you get to know mine that way!

ELEONORA: Do you hear the telephone wires singing? So the paper's printed, and people are telephoning! "Have you read it?" "Yes, I have!" Isn't it terrible?

BENJAMIN: What's terrible?

ELEONORA: Everything! Everything in life is terrible! But we have to be satisfied all the same! . . . Think of Elis and Kristina: they love each other, and they hate each other all the same, so the thermometer falls when they walk through the room! She was at the concert yesterday, and they're not talking to each other today . . . Why, why?

BENJAMIN: Because your brother is jealous!

ELEONORA: Don't mention that word! Besides, what do you know about it, except it's a sickness and therefore a punishment? You mustn't touch evil for then it'll hit you! Just look at Elis! Haven't you noticed how changed he is since he started to read those documents . . .

BENJAMIN: Concerning the trial?

ELEONORA: Yes. Isn't it as if all the evil in that has forced its way into his soul and shone through his face and eyes . . . Kristina senses that, and to keep his evil away from her she has made herself armor of ice! Ah, those papers—if I could only burn them up! They radiate meanness and falseness and revenge. That's why you should keep what's evil and unclean away from you, away from your lips and your heart!

BENJAMIN: How you do notice everything!

ELEONORA: Do you know what's ahead of me if Elis and the rest find out that it was I who bought the Easter lily in that unusual way?

BENJAMIN: What will they do to you?

ELEONORA: I'll be sent back . . . to that place from which I came, where the sun doesn't shine, where the walls are white and naked as in a bathroom, where all you hear is weeping and complaining, where I've wasted a year of my life!

BENJAMIN: Where do you mean?

ELEONORA: Where one is tortured, worse than in prison, where the damned live, where anxiety is at home, where despair keeps watch day and night, and from where no one returns.

BENJAMIN: Worse than prison! Where do you mean?

ELEONORA: One is condemned in prison, but in that place one is
damned! In prison one is questioned, and heard; in that place one
is unheard! . . . Poor Easter lily which is to blame. I meant so
well and did so badly!

BENJAMIN: But why don't you go to the florist and say, "That's how
it was"? You're just like a lamb being led to slaughter.

ELEONORA: When it knows it *is* to be slaughtered, it doesn't complain
and try to flee. What else can it do!

ELIS (*enters from the left, a letter in his hand*): Hasn't the paper
come yet?

ELEONORA: No, Elis!

ELIS (*turns, speaking to someone in the kitchen*): Have Lina go get
a paper!

(MRS. HEYST *enters from the right.* ELEONORA *and* BENJAMIN *are
frightened.*)

ELIS (*to* ELEONORA *and* BENJAMIN): Please step out, children, for a
moment. (*They go out to the left.*)

MRS. HEYST: You've received a letter?

ELIS: Yes!

MRS. HEYST: From the institution?

ELIS: Yes!

MRS. HEYST: What do they want?

ELIS: They insist that Eleonora must be brought back.

MRS. HEYST: We won't! She's my child!

ELIS: My sister!

MRS. HEYST: What do you mean?

ELIS: I don't know! I can't think any more!

MRS. HEYST: But I can! . . . Eleonora, my child of sorrow, has come
with joy, not this world's, though; her restlessness has been
changed to peace which she shares! Sane or not! To me she's wise,
for she understands how to bear the burden of life better than I,
than we. Besides, Elis, am I sane, was I sane when I believed my
husband was innocent? I knew he was convicted by substantial
telling evidence and that he had confessed! . . . And you, Elis,

are you crazy enough not to see Kristina loves you? When you think she hates you?

ELIS: It's a strange way to love!

MRS. HEYST: No! Your coldness turns her to ice inwardly, and you're the one who hates. But you're wrong, and that's why you have to suffer!

ELIS: How can I be wrong? Didn't she go with my faithless friend last night?

MRS. HEYST: Yes, she did, and with your knowledge. But why did she go? Well, you ought to be able to sense that!

ELIS: No, I can't!

MRS. HEYST: Fine! Then you deserve what you're going through! (*The kitchen door opens; a hand reaches in a paper which* MRS. HEYST *takes and gives to* ELIS.)

ELIS: This was the only real misfortune! With her I could bear the others. But my last support is being torn away, and I'm falling!

MRS. HEYST: Fall, but fall properly so you can get up again afterward! . . . What's the news in the paper?

ELIS: I don't know; I'm afraid of the paper today.

MRS. HEYST: Give it to me; I'll read it.

ELIS: No! Wait a minute! . . .

MRS. HEYST: What are you afraid of? What do you expect? . . .

ELIS: The worst of all!

MRS. HEYST: That has already come many times . . . and, child, if you knew my life . . . if you had been there when I saw your father take step after step toward ruin without my being allowed to warn the many people he brought to misfortune. When he fell, I felt like an accomplice, because I knew about his crime, and if the judge hadn't been a sensible man who understood my difficult position as wife, I would have been punished, too!

ELIS: What caused Father's fall? I've never quite understood that.

MRS. HEYST: Pride as with the rest of us!

ELIS: Why should we innocent ones suffer for his mistakes?

MRS. HEYST: Be quiet! . . . (*Pause, during which she takes the paper and reads.* ELIS *at first stands uneasy, then he walks back and forth.*) What's this? . . . Didn't I say it was a yellow tulip among other things that had been stolen at the florist's shop?

ELIS: Yes, I remember that distinctly.

MRS. HEYST: But here it says . . . an Easter lily!

ELIS (*frightened*): Does it?

MRS. HEYST (*collapses in a chair*): It was Eleonora! Oh, God! my God!

ELIS: So it's not over!

MRS. HEYST: Prison or the asylum!

ELIS: It's impossible she did it! Impossible!

MRS. HEYST: And our family name's to be dishonored again . . .

ELIS: Do they suspect her?

MRS. HEYST: It says their suspicions are taking a certain direction toward . . . It's quite clear where.

ELIS: I'll talk with her!

MRS. HEYST (*gets up*): Talk gently! For I can't any more! . . . She is lost . . . found and lost . . . Talk with her! (*Goes out to the right*)

ELIS (*sighs; then goes to the door at the left*): Eleonora dear! May I speak with you?

ELEONORA (*comes in; her hair is down*): I was just putting up my hair.

ELIS: Let it be . . . Tell me, dear, where did you get that plant?

ELEONORA: I took it . . .

ELIS: Oh, God!

ELEONORA (*her head bent, crushed, with her arms crossed over her chest*): But I put the money alongside . . .

ELIS: So you paid for it?

ELEONORA: Yes and no! It's always so irritating . . . but I didn't do any wrong . . . I only meant well . . . Do you believe me?

ELIS: I believe you, dear, but the paper doesn't know you're innocent!

ELEONORA: Then I'll have to suffer that, too, dear . . . (*She bends her head so her hair hangs down in front.*) What do they want to do with me now? Let them!

BENJAMIN (*comes in from the left, beside himself*): No, you may not touch her, for she hasn't done any wrong. I know, for it was I, I, I—(*weeps*)—who did it!

ELEONORA: Don't believe what he says . . . it was I!

ELIS: What shall I believe? Whom shall I believe?

BENJAMIN: Me! Me!

ELEONORA: Me! Me!

BENJAMIN: Let me go to the police . . .

ELIS: Sh-h, sh-h . . .

BENJAMIN: No, I want to go, I *want* to go . . .

ELIS: Quiet, children! Mother's coming!

MRS. HEYST (*enters, extremely upset, takes* ELEONORA *in her arms and kisses her*): Child, child, my beloved child! You're here with me, and you're going to stay with me!

ELEONORA: You kissed me, Mother! You haven't done that for many years. Why now?

MRS. HEYST: Because now . . . because the florist is out there begging our pardon because he stirred up so much trouble . . . the coin has been found, and your name . . .

ELEONORA (*leaps into* ELIS' *arms and kisses him; then she embraces* BENJAMIN *and kisses him on top of his head*): You dear who wanted to suffer for me! How could you want to?

BENJAMIN (*shyly, childishly*): Because I like you so much, Eleonora!

MRS. HEYST: Put on your things, children, and go out into the garden. It's clearing up!

ELEONORA: Oh, it's clearing up! Come, Benjamin! (*She takes his hand; they go, hand in hand, out to the left.*)

ELIS: May we throw the switch on the fire soon?

MRS. HEYST: Not yet! There's a little left!

ELIS: Lindkvist?

MRS. HEYST: He's out there! But he's very strange and inexplicably gentle. It's a shame he's so talkative and talks so much about himself.

ELIS: Now that I've seen one ray of sunshine I'm not afraid to meet the giant. Let him come!

MRS. HEYST: But don't irritate him . . . Providence has put our destiny in his hands, and the meek . . . well, you know where the arrogant go!

ELIS: I know! . . . Listen: those galoshes: wolf, wolf, switch, switch! [35] Does he intend to keep them on? Why not? It's his rugs and furniture . . .

MRS. HEYST: Elis! Think of all of us! (*Goes out to the right*)

ELIS: I do, Mother!

LINDKVIST (*enters from the right. He is an older serious man with a terrifying appearance. He has gray hair with a toupee and military sideburns. Large black bushy eyebrows. Small closely clipped black whiskers. Round glasses with black bows. Large carnelian charms on his watch chain; a Spanish cane in his hand. Dressed in black with his overcoat on; his top hat in his hand; tall boots with leather galoshes, which squeak. When he enters he stares at* ELIS *with curiosity and remains standing all the time*): My name is Lindkvist!

ELIS: (*defensively*): Mine is Heyst! . . . Please sit down.

(LINDKVIST *sits down on the chair to the right of the sewing table and looks hard at* ELIS. *Pause*)

ELIS: What may I do for you?

LINDKVIST (*with dignity*): Hm!—I had the honor of announcing my intended visit last night; but after thinking it over, I thought it improper to take up business matters on a holiday.

ELIS: We are very grateful . . .

LINDKVIST (*sharply*): We are not grateful! Well! (*Pause*) However: the day before yesterday I happened to pay a visit to the governor . . . (*Pauses, and looks to see what impression the word makes on* ELIS) . . . do you know the governor?

ELIS (*carelessly*): I don't have that honor!

LINDKVIST: Then you'll get that honor! . . . We talked about your father!

ELIS: That I can believe!

LINDKVIST (*takes up a* [*white*] *paper and puts it on the table*): [36] And there I got this document!

ELIS: I've expected that for a long time! But before we go on, let me ask one question.

LINDKVIST (*short*): Go ahead.

ELIS: Why don't you hand this document to the executors, then we'd at least be spared this painful and slow execution?

LINDKVIST: So that's it, young man!

ELIS: Young or not, I don't ask for any mercy, only justice!

LINDKVIST: Oh-h! No mercy, no mercy!—Look at this document I've put here on the table. Now I'll put it away again . . . So it's justice you want! Only justice! Listen, old friend: once I was robbed of my money in an unpleasant way. When I wrote to you politely and asked how much time you needed, you answered impolitely! And treated me as if I were a usurer who wanted to strip widows and fatherless children though I was the one who had been stripped, and you belonged to the party of robbers. But, since I had more sense, I was content to answer your impolite letter with a polite but sharp one. You know my blue paper, eh? I'll put official stamps on it when I want to, but I don't always want to! (*Looks about the room*)

ELIS: Go ahead, the furniture is at your disposal!

LINDKVIST: I wasn't looking at the furniture! I was looking to see if your mother is about. She apparently likes justice as much as you do!

ELIS: I hope so!

LINDVIST: Good! . . . You know if the justice you value so highly had been carried through, your mother, who knew about the criminal act, could have been hit by human justice!

ELIS: Oh, no!

LINDKVIST: Oh, yes, and it's not too late yet!

ELIS (*gets up*) : My mother!

LINDKVIST (*takes up another, but blue, document and puts it on the table*) : Look, I'll put this document here, and it really is blue . . . though it doesn't have stamps on it yet!

ELIS: Good God! My mother! Everything repeats itself!

LINDKVIST: Yes, young lover of justice, everything repeats itself, everything! . . . That's how it can be! . . . If I were to put this question to myself: You, Anders Johan Lindkvist, born in poverty and brought up in privation and work, do you have the right in your old age to deprive yourself and your children—note *your* children, the support that you with industry, consideration, and self-denial—note self-denial—have saved cent by cent? What are you, Anders Johan Lindkvist, going to do if you want to be just? You didn't strip anyone, but if you think it was bad to be plundered, you can't live in a city any more, because no one wants to say hello to the merciless fellow who demanded what was his! Do you see there's a mercy that goes against justice, and above it? . . . That is mercy!

ELIS: You have the right; take everything! It belongs to you!

LINDKVIST: I have the right, but I don't dare use it!

ELIS: I'll think about your children and not complain!

LINDKVIST (*puts away the document*) : Good! Then we'll put away the blue document again! . . . Now we'll take one more step!

ELIS: Excuse me . . . do they really intend to prosecute my mother?

LINDKVIST: We'll take one more step first! . . . So you don't know the governor personally?

ELIS: No, and I don't want to know him!

LINDKVIST (*takes out the blue paper again and waves it*) : Don't say that, don't say that! . . . The governor, you see, was your father's friend when they were young, and he'd like to meet you! Everything repeats itself, everything! Won't you call on him?

ELIS: No!

LINDKVIST: The governor . . .

ELIS: May we change the topic?

LINDKVIST: You must be polite to me, for I'm defenseless . . . since you have public opinion on your side and I have only justice on mine. What do you have against the governor? He doesn't like bicycles and folk high schools—that's part of his peculiarities, but we can overlook them, overlook them and stick to essentials, human beings and their relations! And in the big crisis in life we have to take each other with weaknesses and flaws, swallow each other hide and hair . . . Go to the governor!

ELIS: No!

LINDKVIST: So that's the kind of man you are?

ELIS (*firmly*): Yes, that kind!

LINDKVIST (*gets up and begins to walk on the floor with his squeaking boots, waving the blue paper*): That is bad! That is bad! . . . Well, then I'll begin at another end . . . A vengeful person intends to accuse your mother. You can prevent that!

ELIS: How?

LINDKVIST: Go to the governor!

ELIS: No!

LINDKVIST (*goes up to* ELIS *and takes him by the shoulders*): Then you're the worst person I've run across in my life! . . . And now I'll go to your mother myself!

ELIS: Don't go!

LINDKVIST: Will you go to the governor then?

ELIS: Yes!

LINDKVIST: Say that once more, and louder!

ELIS: Yes!

LINDKVIST: Then *that's* clear! (*Gives* ELIS *the blue document*)
(ELIS *takes it without reading it.*)

LINDKVIST: Then there's number two, which is number one! . . . Shall we sit down? . . . (*They sit down as before.*) Look, if we can only meet halfway, it'll be shorter by half . . . Number two! . . . That's my claim on your household goods . . . Yes, no illusions, because I neither can nor want to give away my family's common property. I'm going to take what I have coming—to the last cent.

ELIS: I understand that!

LINDKVIST (*sharply*) : Oh, you do, do you?

ELIS: I didn't mean anything cutting . . .

LINDKVIST: No, I understand that. (*Lifts his glasses and stares intently at* ELIS) . . . The wolf! The mad wolf! Switch, switch! and the flesh-red carnelian: the giant of the Robber Mountains who doesn't eat children, just frightens them! I will frighten you so you'll lose your mind, I will. You'll pay every stick of furniture's full value, and if there's one scrap missing, you'll end up in prison where neither sun nor Cassiopeia will shine! Yes, I can eat children and widows when they irritate me . . . And public opinion? Bah, that . . . I'll just move to another town! (ELIS *silent*) You had a friend who's name is Peter, Peter Holmblad. He was a philologist and your pupil in languages. But you wanted to make him some kind of prophet . . . Oh, well, he was faithless. The cock crowed twice, didn't it? (ELIS *remains silent*.) Human nature is as unreliable as things and thoughts. Peter *was* faithless, I don't deny that, and I don't defend him. Not on that point. But the human heart is bottomless, and gold and dregs lie all mixed up! Peter was a faithless friend, but a friend all the same!

ELIS: A faithless . . .

LINDKVIST: Faithless, yes, but a friend all the same! Unknown to you, this faithless friend has done you a big personal favor!

ELIS: Even that!

LINDKVIST (*moves closer to* ELIS): Everything repeats itself, everything!

ELIS: Everything evil, yes! And good is rewarded with evil!

LINDKVIST: Not always: the good repeats itself, too! Believe me!

ELIS: I suppose I'll have to, or you'll torture my life out of me!

LINDKVIST: Not your life, but I'm going to squeeze pride and evil out of you!

ELIS: Continue!

LINDKVIST: Peter has done you a favor, I said.

ELIS: I don't want any favors from that man!

LINDKVIST: Are we there again? . . . Listen! Through your friend Peter's mediation, the governor was persuaded to go out of his way for your mother! That's why you're going to write a letter to Peter to thank him. Promise!

ELIS: No! Anybody else but not him!

LINDKVIST (*comes closer*): I suppose I'll have to squeeze you again, then . . . Listen: you have money on deposit in the bank.

ELIS: Well, does that concern you? Surely I'm not responsible for my father's debts?

LINDKVIST: Aren't you? Aren't you? Weren't you in on the eating and drinking when my children's money was spent in your house? Answer me!

ELIS: I can't deny that.

LINDKVIST: And since the furniture won't cover what I have coming, write a check for the rest right now—you know the amount.

ELIS (*crushed*): Even this?

LINDKVIST: Even this! Go ahead—make it out!

(ELIS *gets up, takes out his checkbook, and writes at the desk.*)

LINDKVIST: Make it to yourself or cash.

ELIS: It won't be enough, at that!

LINDKVIST: Then you'll have to borrow the rest! I'm going to have every cent!

ELIS (*gives the check to* LINDKVIST): Look, everything I have! It's my summer and my bride; I don't have any more to give you!

LINDKVIST: Then you'll have to borrow, I said!

ELIS: I can't!

LINDKVIST: Then you'll have to try to get security!

ELIS: There isn't anyone who will give security for a Heyst!

LINDKVIST: I give you two alternatives as an ultimatum: thank Peter or pay up the whole amount!

ELIS: I don't want to have anything to do with Peter.

LINDKVIST: Then you're the worst person I know! By means of a simple gesture of politeness you can save your mother's home and your fiancée's existence, and you won't do it! You must have reasons you don't want to admit! Why do you hate Peter?

ELIS: Kill me, but don't torture me any longer!

LINDKVIST: You're jealous of him! (ELIS *shrugs his shoulders.*) So that's it! (LINDKVIST *gets up and paces the floor. Pause*) Have you read the morning paper?

ELIS: Yes, unfortunately!

LINDKVIST: The whole paper?

ELIS: No, not all of it.

LINDKVIST: Really! . . . So-o? . . . You don't know Peter is engaged?

ELIS: No, I didn't!

LINDKVIST: And not to whom? Guess!

ELIS: How . . .

LINDKVIST: He's engaged to Miss Alice, and it was settled yesterday at a certain concert, where your fiancée served as go-between!

ELIS: Why should that be such a secret?

LINDKVIST: Haven't two young people the right to have their secrets from you?

ELIS: And I had to suffer this agony because of their happiness?

LINDKVIST: Yes! Think of the ones who have suffered to prepare your happiness!—Your mother, your father, your fiancée, your sister . . . Sit down; I'll tell you a story, a very short one. (ELIS *sits down unwillingly. It has begun to clear outside and continues to get clearer.*) It was about forty years ago. I came to Stockholm as a youngster, alone and unknown, to try to get a job. I had only a *daler,* and it was a dark evening. As I didn't know of any inexpensive hotel, I asked passers-by, but no one answered me. When I was giving up in despair, a man came up and asked me why I was crying.—I was crying, you see. I told him. Then he took me to a hotel, though it was out of his way, and comforted me with friendly words. When I went into the entrance, a glass door to a

shop opened and hit my elbow so that the glass was broken. The
furious shopkeeper grabbed me and demanded I pay for it or
he'd call the police. Imagine my despair with a night on the street
in prospect!—The kind stranger who had seen it all, stepped between us, went to the trouble of calling the police, and saved me!
—That man—was your father! . . . So everything repeats itself,
even what is good. And for your father's sake . . . I've crossed out
my claim! . . . So . . . take this paper, and keep this check! (*Gets
up*) Since you have a hard time saying thank you I'll go right
away, especially since I find it painful to be thanked! (*Approaches
the door at the back*) Go instead to your mother at once to free
her from her anxiety! (*Gestures to* ELIS *who wants to approach
him*) Go! (ELIS *hurries out to the right.*)

(*The doors at the back are opened.* ELEONORA *and* BENJAMIN
*come in, calm but serious; stop in terror when they see* LINDKVIST.)

LINDKVIST: Well, imps, come in—don't be afraid . . . Do you know
who I am? . . . (*With a disguised voice*) I'm the giant of the
Robber Mountains who frightens children! Muh! Muh! . . . But
I'm not so dangerous! . . . Come here, Eleonora. (*Takes her head
between his hands and looks into her eyes*) You have your father's
good eyes—and he was a good man—but weak! (*Kisses her forehead*) There!

ELEONORA: He's saying good things about Father! Can anyone think
good of him?

LINDKVIST: I can! Ask Elis!

ELEONORA: Then you can't want to do us any harm!

LINDKVIST: No, my dear child!

ELEONORA: Well, but help us, then!

LINDKVIST: Child, I can't help your father escape his punishment, nor
Benjamin get out of his Latin examination . . . but the rest has
already been helped. Life doesn't give one everything, and nothing
free of charge. So you're to help me. Do you want to?

ELEONORA: What can I, poor soul, do?

LINDKVIST: What day is it today? Take a look.

ELEONORA (*takes the calendar from the wall*): It's the sixteenth.

LINDKVIST: Good! Before the twentieth you're to see that your brother Elis has called on the governor and written a letter to Peter.

ELEONORA: Nothing else?

LINDKVIST: Oh, child! But if he doesn't, the giant will come and say "Muh"!

ELEONORA: *Why* is the giant coming to frighten children?

LINDKVIST: So the children will behave!

ELEONORA: That's true! The giant's right! (*Kisses* LINDKVIST *on the sleeve of his fur coat*) Thank you, good giant!

BENJAMIN: You should say Mr. Lindkvist, you know!

ELEONORA: No, that's so ordinary, that name . . .

LINDKVIST: Good-bye, children! Now you can throw the switch on the fire!

ELEONORA: No, it's to stay there, for the children are so forgetful!

LINDKVIST: How well you know children! (*Exits*)

ELEONORA: We'll get to go to the country, Benjamin! In two months! If they'd only go fast! (*Tears the sheets from the calendar and strews them in the sunshine streaming into the room*) See how the days go! April! May! June! And the sun is shining on all of them! See! . . . Now you're to thank God, who helped us to get to the country!

BENJAMIN (*shyly*): Mayn't I say it silently?

ELEONORA: Yes, you may say it silently! For now the clouds are gone, and it can be heard up there!

(KRISTINA *has come in from the left and stopped.* ELIS *and* MRS. HEYST *in from the right.* KRISTINA *and* ELIS *go toward each other with friendly looks, but the curtain falls before they reach each other.*)

[CURTAIN]

# Notes on 'Easter'

1. Maundy Thursday is the Thursday of Holy Week, the week before Easter Sunday. See John 13:5, 34: "After that he poureth water into a basin, and began to wash the disciples' feet, and to wipe them with the towel wherewith he was girded"; and, "A new commandment I give unto you, That ye love one another; as I have loved you, that ye also love one another." *Maundy* means "mandate" or "commandment."

2. *Die Sieben Worte des Erlösers am Kreuze (The Seven Last Words of Christ)* was composed in 1785 by Joseph Haydn (1732–1809) in four different versions (instrumental, string quartet, piano, and oratorio) for the cathedral of Cadiz. Strindberg's selection of the Haydn music for this play centering on one important church season was certainly highly appropriate. See the following biblical references: "Father, forgive them, for they know not what they do" (Luke 23:34); "Verily I say unto thee this day shalt thou be with me in Paradise" (Luke 23:43); "Woman, behold thy son, and thou, behold thy mother!" (John 19:26–27); "My God, my God, why hast thou forsaken me?" (Matthew 27:46); "I thirst." (John 19:31); and "Father, into thy hands I commend my spirit" (Luke 23:46). The music is available in various readings.

3. Genesis 8:11: "And the dove came in to him in the evening; and, lo, in her mouth was an olive leaf pluckt off: so Noah knew that the waters were abated from off the earth." The olive leaf symbolizes peace.

4. The words "here" and "this terrible town" refer to Lund, the university town at some distance from the sea in southwestern Sweden, while "there" refers to Strindberg's home city of Stockholm, farther north in a different kind of landscape. The steamboats and the shipyard Elis has in mind have to do with Stockholm waters and harbors.

5. See preceding note. Lake Mälare is one of Sweden's great lakes.

252

Stockholm, the city that Selma Lagerlöf said "floats on water," is on both the lake and the Baltic Sea.

6. Strindberg's sister Elisabeth, who died in 1904, was emotionally disturbed and was for some time confined in the asylum at Uppsala. See Martin Lamm's *August Strindberg,* translated by Harry G. Carlson (New York: Blom, 1971), pp. 367–372

7. In his post-Inferno years (1897–1912) particularly, Strindberg believed that the trials in life may be either tests or forms of punishment. See the Book of Job in the Old Testament for the account of the trials and tribulations one of Strindberg's favorite biblical characters had to endure. Elis is, of course, exposed to tests of a milder variety.

8. The Swedes make much more out of receiving the Ph.D. than most Americans do. Among the several expensive parts of defending a doctoral dissertation in Strindberg's day were the cost of printing several hundred copies well in advance of the defense and the elaborate and formal doctoral dinner after the successful defense. Formal dress was required at both the defense and the dinner.

9. Students held, and to a great extent still hold, a very special place in Swedish society. The white student cap set the student off from his contemporaries in what they must have regarded as an enviable way; the student song Elis quotes is only one of many that Swedes in general know, appreciate, and sing.

10. The town to which he has been exiled versus the city he loves. Deuteronomy 12:29 reads: "And it shall come to pass, when the Lord thy God hath brought thee in unto the land whither thou goest to possess it, that thou shalt put the blessing upon mount Gerizim and the curse upon mount Ebal." See also Joshua 8:30, 33. Ebal and Gerizim were, respectively, the Samarian mountains from which the curses and the blessings were pronounced.

11. See note 8, above.

12. In *Tjänstekvinnans son* (*The Son of a Servant*), Strindberg tells about various "gifts" his schoolmates sent unpopular teachers.

13. The old practice of punishing oneself, figuratively and literally, during the Lenten season, the penitential period from Ash Wednesday to Easter. See preceding note. The package Elis receives contains what for him is a form of punishment.

14. See Numbers 17:1–11; I Kings 8:9; and Hebrews 9:4 for an ex-

planation of the miraculous budding, blossoming, and bearing fruit of Aaron's rod. The coming of spring must seem like a series of miracles to a sensitive northerner like Elis.

15. LINDKVIST, liteally translated, means "linden branch." The name is typical of one common kind of Swedish family name. The basswood is a linden.

16. Elis probably both teaches and tutors.

17. The Swedish *påsklilja* (literally, "Easter lily") is the daffodil.

18. Eleonora's role as a Christ figure is clarified and emphasized in statements such as this. See John 10:30: "I and my Father are one." See Proverbs 15:10 for the immediately following quotation from the Bible.

19. See Genesis 35:18, 42:4; 43:14 ff. for an account of Jacob's youngest, gentlest, and most lovable son Benjamin.

20. The German philosophers Immanuel Kant (1724–1804) and Arthur Schopenhauer (1788–1860). See Psalm 34:21: "they that hate the righteous shall be desolate." "Desolate" here is equivalent to "forsaken."

21. Strindberg was well aware of the fact that Mr. Algren is merely mentioned; he considered loose threads quite typical of actual life.

22. The disciple who denied Christ three times and the disciple who betrayed Him. See, for example, Matthew 26:34–35 and 69–75 for Peter, the denier, and Matthew 26:46–49 for Judas, the betrayer. Apparently Peter Holmblad had not acknowledged his debt to Elis either in his preface or in a footnote.

23. Job 30:26.

24. See Luke 23:43 ("Father, forgive them; for they know not what they do.") *Largo* means "slow and dignified."

25. Gossip mirrors, which were so placed as to allow people to see what was going on outside without being seen from outside, were common in Strindberg's days.

26. In Strindberg's time Midsummer came on June 24; it has now been fixed by law on a week end. Strindberg dealt with this extremely popular Swedish holiday in many of his works, the best known of which is *Lady Julie*.

27. See note 22, above.

28. A vacation colony consisted of small plots of land in a suburb on which a city family could construct a small cottage and have a fairly good-sized garden.

29. Pontius Pilate was the Roman governor or procurator of Judea from A.D. 26 to 36 under whom Christ was tried, condemned, and crucified.

30. See Job 31:3.

31. See Psalm 22:1 and Mark 15:34: "My God, my God, why hast thou forsaken me?"

32. Since the matter of the blue paper becomes important later, it should be noted that the letters mentioned obviously refer to dunning, claims, and, in general, unpleasant reminders of an unhappy situation. As Lindkvist says later, such papers may have official stamps.

33. Luke 22:31.

34. See note 13, above. The Swedes decorate Easter eggs as many Americans do.

35. Elis is making a very personal attempt at reproducing the sound of boots in words.

36. See note 32, above. Apparently the white paper or documents have happier contents than the blue.

# Introduction to
# 'There Are Crimes
# and Crimes'

THIS PLAY HAS ENJOYED far greater success on the stage than *Advent*, which became its companion play under the title of *Before a Higher Court* (*Vid högre rätt*, 1899). The latter was originally designed for *There Are Crimes and Crimes* alone:

|  |  |
|:---:|:---:|
| *Vid högre rätt* | *Before a Higher Court* |
| eller | or |
| *Brott och brott* | *Crimes and Crimes* |

In a letter to Gustaf af Geijerstam, a fellow author, probably written in March, 1899, Strindberg had written: "Well, as far as the title goes! I'm not sure but think a covering title would be good! So why not: *Before a Higher Court* and then *Advent* and *Crimes and Crimes*. (The latter title would then be considered an ellipsis of the sentence: There are crimes and crimes, of course.)"

Another title that Strindberg had toyed with for the second play was *Intoxication* (*Rus*). Fortunately, he decided on *There Are Crimes and Crimes* stressing the idea that in addition to the crimes and sins, both detected and undetected, of breaking the law of the land and the moral law, there are crimes and sins whose commission is a matter of wish and thought, whether spoken or not.

Strindberg himself made this idea clear in another letter to af Geijerstam on February 24, 1900: "I've now wanted to deal with the problem of the Evil Will (*Den Onda Viljan*) and the responsibility for evil thoughts and the individual's court of self-punishment." If one equates the individual's court of punishment (*individens självbestraffningsrätt*) with the individual's conscience, and

257

recalls that the judge and his wife in *Advent* have actually not broken the letter of the law, the covering title for the two plays is seen to be highly appropriate. The human conscience, whether awakened from within or without, can indeed serve, Strindberg thought, as a higher court and mete out both sentence and punishment.

But Strindberg was as usual acutely aware of the fact that nothing in life is simple. As he says in the letter of January 7: "But wouldn't it be wiser to let the threads [the binding elements] go and let the play stand for what it is: a happening that isn't the work of human beings?" It is significant, too, that he adds in his letter of March 22: "The last act is Swedenborgian with hell already here on earth, and the hero, the Intriguer in the play, is the Invisible One (*den osyn-lige*)." It is a highly interesting comment about the implications of human thoughts and desires. Moral or ethical problems are, of course, rarely separate or simple but rather complex and interwoven. An examination of some preparatory material and a closer look at the content of the play may help to make all this clear.

A preliminary sketch in the Strindberg collection at the Royal Library in Stockholm suggests that Strindberg had thought of a third title—*Damné* (*Damned*). On the page labeled "Sketches for *Crimes and Crimes*," he included two very illuminating notes:

(a) He is at liberty to be observed and to be proved guilty. Appearance against him. [Had] half jokingly suggested killing mothers-in-law, etc.

(b) Damnation: nothing tastes right: everything is transformed; everything is ugly; everything is bad; that is cold; that is too warm; one's clothes don't fit; the soap is green; the matches red; love feels like hate; he believes he is hated by all, but is liked. The curtains white; the last cigars in the box. *Envoutement* (the casting of the spell): when the candle burns down, and he wastes away dead.

While *Damned* would hardly have been a typically accurate Strindberg title, the notes do throw light on what he had in mind when he was about to create the play: the danger of saying or doing anything that can be misinterpreted by others or by oneself, and the danger of slipping into the state of finding everything in life damnably wrong. Appearance versus reality, suspicion versus fact, and hate versus love are all implied.

Strindberg's essay, "Den kommande religionen" (the coming religion; that is, the religion of the future), includes a great deal about the ideas dealt with in the two plays. The following is translated from the manuscript in folder 6, carton 10, in the Strindberg collection of the Royal Library:

> "As a man sows, he must reap" expresses the principle of a Nemesis which would be the logical result of an evil act, the punishment meted out by the injured person. But since it most frequently happens that people do not exercise vengeance because of cowardice, laziness, or ignorance of the criminal's identity, and when they see an evil act get its punishment from a totally unexpected direction, they have to assume, I suppose, that the punishment was administered by an all-seeing unknown, who punishes even the most secret of evil intentions. . . . The logic of life, the interweaving of human destinies, is so infernally put together that every act, indifferent or good, causes disturbances painful for many. People themselves are demons and have the task of torturing each other. But even in the pangs of conscience an imminent means of punishment seems to have been found.

Thus, even when careless words, unwelcome desires, unexpected thoughts, and unapproved wishes represent no perceptible willing by the individual, sins or crimes of commission or omission have been committed, and punishment in one way or another will follow.

*There Are Crimes and Crime* may, then, be considered a study of guilt in dramatic form, for it deals with sins or—to use the Strindbergian term—crimes that are concealed and difficult if not impossible for the police and the courts to get at. The fact that they are on occasion not even clear to the individual who commits them adds to the complexity of the whole problem of crime and punishment.

Take, for example, Henriette's crime: helping a friend get rid of an unwelcome pregnancy. As Strindberg relates the incident, Henriette's intention was compassionate even though her "conditioning" through family, church, and community had labeled such an act of helpfulness a sin and a criminal act. The ironic paradox, the difficulty of unraveling the web of good and evil, and fear-ridden Henriette's vain attempt to escape from the implications of her act provide superb illustrations of Strindberg's use of the telling detail and the loaded suggestion. The reader or spectator is enabled to participate in the creativity of understanding and appreciation of one very important aspect of Strindberg's testimony about crime and punishment.

Strindberg has rarely created a more attractive protagonist than Maurice Gérard. Madame Cathérine, Jeanne, Adolphe, and even Émile testify that Maurice is an essentially fine and decent human being. They like him; he is a good father and has been a genuinely loyal mate and friend; he is dedicated and committed to his calling as a creative artist; he achieves success only to have it snatched away at the moment of triumph.

It is as if jealous powers intervene to punish the playwright who has suddenly committed such "crimes" as rejoicing over his triumph, yielding to the temptation to celebrate that triumph with a fair measure of pride and in the company of a demonic woman, and indulging in loose and careless thoughts and remarks that only in an artificial and superficial sense can be labeled dark sins or crimes.

In presenting the story, Strindberg presents testimony about how very puzzling and enigmatic life may be for human beings and how much in life is simply beyond human understanding. For sensitive observers such as Maurice and Adolphe, it is as if the whole human experience were a dream sequence ranging from the reasonable and logical to the irrational and absurd, or as if the drift of the imagination of a playful higher being caused puppetlike human beings to act in response to his whims whether they would or no. Certainly the sudden shifts from ecstasy to despair, from victory to defeat to victory again, would suggest that at times life may be as laughable as Madame Cathérine suggests. Even the unexpected "happy" ending can then be justified in terms of the strange reversals Strindberg believed he detected in human experience.

Strindberg's characters are, however, far more than puppets manipulated by a higher being. They are richly endowed with instincts and desires, never fully understood, ever ready to burst the bonds of self-control; with a mind not always under control; with a measure of freedom of will or choice; and, in the case of the Maurices and Adolphes, with an active conscience. For such beings, Strindbergian "characterless characters" in their complexity and dynamism, life is not easy, for the active conscience is poised ready to perform its role as both judge and disciplinarian:

> HENRIETTE (*after a silence*): Is conscience fear of punishment?
>
> ADOLPHE: No, it's our better self's contempt for the evil deeds of our worse self.

Strindberg makes it clear what he considers the basic dilemma, the source of confusion and much of human suffering:

> ADOLPHE: . . . There are things we can't explain, and that's why we haven't the right to judge. Besides: you saw how it all went. Maurice felt the danger in the air; I sensed it; I tried to prevent their meeting; Maurice wanted to flee, but nothing helped. It's as if some invisible person had woven an intrigue and deceitfully driven them into each other's arms. I could be challenged in this case, but I don't hesitate to pronounce the verdict: *Not guilty!*

As Maurice says: "Yes, yes, I'm guilty, and all the same absolutely innocent!"

The dilemma obviously involves guilt and innocence, crime and punishment, not only because of one's deliberate and intentional acts but also because of the loose flow of thoughts in one's mind, when one is awake or dreaming, and their expression in speech. Take the unfortunate talk between Maurice and Henriette, examples, if you will, of free association. Consider, moreover, the striking illustrations of the human tendencies to indulge in suspicions of other people's motivations and actions; in speculations even closer to downright evil; and, in certain states, in talking with complete lack of restraint.

The problem of the individual's responsibility for his thoughts is, Strindberg believed, a terrifying part of the whole matter of crime and punishment:

> MAURICE: If one were responsible for one's thoughts, who could go on living?
>
> HENRIETTE: So you, too, have evil thoughts?
>
> MAURICE: Yes, of course . . . just as I commit the most cruel acts in my dreams . . .

It is Maurice who makes crucial admissions about guilt:

> MAURICE: Have you ever been happy?
>
> HENRIETTE: Never!—What's it like?
>
> MAURICE: Well, what shall I say? I can't put it into words, but I'm thinking most of all of my enemies' disappointment . . . That's nasty, I know, but it's the truth!

And, in a moment of honest candor:

> MAURICE: Listen—we're sitting here washing ourselves white as angels; yet we're pretty much ready for any tidy little outrageous act if it's a question of honor, gold, or woman.

And:

> MAURICE: I wanted to run away from you, but someone hindered me, and tonight we were driven together like wild animals in a hunter's net. Who's to blame?
>
> HENRIETTE: And what is blame?

It is a remarkably interesting presentation of the nature of Maurice's crimes and sins and of his punishment for them that Strindberg has given us in *There Are Crimes and Crimes.* Even though arrest and other forms of public humiliation, such as the accounts in the newspapers and the canceling of the production of his play; his friends' apparent turning against him; and the development of his relationship with Henriette into a love-hate relationship not unlike that of Edgar and Alice in *The Dance of Death* are forms of punishment that Strindberg clearly demonstrates, punishments are meted out to him not least by Maurice's own sensitive and active conscience. It is, as the priest suggests, as if a very fine human being has been enticed into traps for disciplinary purposes, perhaps to prepare him for his particular mission.

For Strindberg such punishments had universal as well as personal implications:

> ADOLPHE: Have you never done anything bad?
>
> MADAME CATHÉRINE (*amazed*): Of course, since I'm a sinful human being. But the person who has gone through thin ice has the right and the duty to tell others: Don't go over there!

That is, in its way, a statement of Strindberg's conviction of the need of testimony.

*There Are Crimes and Crimes* has much to offer the theatergoer and the reader: interesting ideational content, effective structure, touches of irony, and a group of remarkable characterizations in keeping with what Strindberg wrote in the Preface to *Lady Julie* (1888). It is a play that bears seeing, hearing, and reading again and again.

There Are Crimes
and Crimes:
A Comedy

## Characters

MAURICE GÉRARD, *a dramatist*
JEANNE, *his mistress*
MARION, *their daughter, five years old*
ADOLPHE, *a painter, an artist*
HENRIETTE MAUCLERC, *his mistress*
EMILE, *a laborer, Jeanne's brother*
MADAME CATHÉRINE
THE PRIEST

## Settings

The cemetery
The café
Auberge des Adrets, an inn
The Bois de Boulogne
The café
Auberge des Adrets, an inn
The Luxembourg Gardens
The café

# ACT I

## Scene i

*The upper cypress walk in Montparmasse churchyard in Paris. One can see at the back burial chapels and stone crosses with the inscription, "O crux!* Ave spes unica!" *and the ivy-covered ruins of a mill.*

*A well-dressed woman in mourning is kneeling beside a flower-covered grave, softly saying her prayers.*

*JEANNE walks back and forth as if she were expecting someone.*
*MARION is playing with withered flowers, which she takes from a scrap heap on the walk.*
*PRIEST is walking farthest away on the walk reciting his breviary.*

POLICEMAN (*enters; goes up to* JEANNE): Listen, this isn't a playground.

JEANNE (*humbly*): I'm only waiting for someone who has to be here soon . . .

POLICEMAN: Maybe so, but no one may take any flowers . . .

JEANNE (*to* MARION): Put the flowers back, dear!

PRIEST (*comes up; the* POLICEMAN *greets him*): Mayn't the child play with the discarded flowers, officer?

POLICEMAN: The rules forbid touching even the discarded flowers since they think they carry contagion—if they really do, I don't know.

267

PRIEST (*to* MARION): In that case, all we can do is obey! What's your name, child?

MARION: Marion.

PRIEST: And who's your father?

MARION *does not answer; puts her finger in her mouth.*

PRIEST (*to* JEANNE): Forgive me for asking, madame; I meant no harm. I said it only to calm the little girl. (*The* POLICEMAN *has gone.*)

JEANNE: I know, Father, and I wish you'd say something to calm me, too—I'm very uneasy after waiting and waiting for two hours.

PRIEST: For two hours and for him! How people can torture each other! *O crux! Ave spes unica!*

JEANNE: Well, what does that mean? It's inscribed all over here!

PRIEST: It means, "Oh cross! Our only hope!"

JEANNE: Is it our only hope?

PRIEST: Our only sure hope!

JEANNE: I'll soon believe you're right, Father!

PRIEST: May I ask why?

JEANNE: You have already guessed. When he lets his woman and his child wait for two hours in a cemetery, the end isn't far off.

PRIEST: And when he deserts you, then . . .

JEANNE: Then we'll have to drown ourselves!

PRIEST: No, no!

JEANNE: Yes, indeed!

MARION: I want to go home, Mother.—I'm hungry!

JEANNE: A little more patience, dear—we'll soon be going.

PRIEST: Woe, woe unto those who call evil good and good evil!

JEANNE: What is that woman over there by the grave doing?

PRIEST: She seems to be talking to the dead!

JEANNE: One can't, can one?

PRIEST: She seems to be able to.

JEANNE: So the misery isn't over when we die?

PRIEST: You didn't know?

JEANNE: Where could I have learned that?

PRIEST: Hm! The next time you need enlightenment about that well-known fact, come to me in Saint-Germain's Chapel of Our Lady. —Isn't the man over there the one you've been waiting for?

JEANNE (*embarrassed*): It's not he, but I know the man who's coming . . .

PRIEST (*to* MARION): Good-bye, Marion dear! God protect you! (*Kisses the child; says [to* JEANNE] *as he goes*) In Saint-Germain-des-Prés!

EMILE (*enters*): Hello, Sister! What are you doing here?

JEANNE: I'm waiting for Maurice.

EMILE: Then you'll have to keep on waiting, I suspect.—I saw him an hour ago with breakfast companions on the boulevard.—Hi, Marion! (*Kisses the child.*)

JEANNE: Were there women along?

EMILE: Yes, of course; but we can't criticize him for that. Why, he's a playwright, and his new play's opening tonight. I imagine they were some of his actresses.

JEANNE: Did he recognize you?

EMILE: No; he doesn't know who I am, and that's not necessary, is it? I know my place as a working man, and I don't care for condescension from superiors.

JEANNE: But if he deserts us?

EMILE: Well, you see, when that time comes, I suppose I'll have to present myself. But you don't really expect that to happen, do you? He's really fond of you, and, above all, he's attached to Marion.

JEANNE: I don't know, but I have a feeling something terrible's going to happen to me . . .

EMILE: Has he promised to marry you?

JEANNE: No, he hasn't, but he gave me hopes.

EMILE: Hopes, yes! Do you remember what I told you at the start: don't hope, because people of higher rank don't marry beneath them!

JEANNE: But it has happened.

EMILE: Yes, it has, of course. But would you be happy in his circles?
I don't think so, for you wouldn't understand even what they say.
I sometimes eat—in the kitchen!—at his eating place, and I don't
understand a word of what they're talking about.

JEANNE: Oh, you do eat there?

EMILE: Yes, in the kitchen!

JEANNE: Imagine—he has never invited me to go there with him.

EMILE: You can't blame him for that—it really shows he respects his
Marion's mother, for it's a really queer crowd of women who eat
there.

JEANNE: Really?!

EMILE: But Maurice never bothers about those women; no, there's
something *decent* about that fellow.

JEANNE: I think so, too, but when a woman shows up, a man goes
crazy, of course.

EMILE (*smiles*): What's that?—But listen. Do you need money?

JEANNE: No, not money.

EMILE: Then it will still go.—Look! Look down the walk! He's
coming. So I'll leave. Good-bye, children.

JEANNE: He's coming? Yes, it's he!

EMILE: Don't drive him crazy—with your jealousy, Jeanne! (*Leaves*)

JEANNE: Of course not!

MARION (*runs up to him; he picks her up*): Daddy! Daddy!

MAURICE: Hello, darling! (*Then greets* JEANNE) Jeanne! Can you
forgive me for making you wait like this? Can you?

JEANNE: Of course I can!

MAURICE: But say it so I can hear you forgive me.

JEANNE: Come here—I'll whisper it to you.

MAURICE (*approaches her. She kisses him on the cheek*): I didn't
hear that. (JEANNE *kisses him on the mouth.*) Now I heard you.—
Well!—You know my fate's to be decided today; my play's to be
given and has all the prospects of succeeding . . . or failing . . .

JEANNE: I'll pray for you; then it'll be a success.

MAURICE: Thanks. Even if it doesn't help, it can't hurt.—Down there in the valley in the haze is Paris! [1] Today Paris doesn't know who Maurice is, but in twenty-four hours it will know. The cloud of smoke that has concealed me for thirty years will be dispersed when I blow on it, and I'll be seen, I'll take form and begin to be somebody. My enemies—that's to say, all those who want to do what I've done, will turn and twist in agony, which will be my joy, for they're going to suffer as I've suffered.

JEANNE: Don't say that! Don't!

MAURICE: Yes, because that's how it is.

JEANNE: Yes, but don't say it!—And afterward?

MAURICE: Afterward we'll have a roof over our heads, and you and Marion will bear the name I've made famous.

JEANNE: So you do love me?

MAURICE: I love you both, just as much, Marion perhaps more . . .

JEANNE: I'm glad—you can get tired of me, but not of her!

MAURICE: Don't you trust my feelings for you?

JEANNE: I don't know—I fear something, fear something dreadfully . . .

MAURICE: You're tired and exhausted from waiting so long.—Do forgive me! But what is there for you to fear?

JEANNE: What I can't foresee, what I can sense, without definite reasons . . .

MAURICE: But I sense only success—for definite reasons: the sure instinct of the theater people and their experience with the public, not to mention their personal knowledge of the critics. So, do calm yourself . . .

JEANNE: I can't, I can't! You know, there was a priest here a while ago who talked nicely to us. My faith, which you haven't wiped out but which you've crossed over in much the same way one whitens windows, wasn't there ready to use, but the old man brushed the whitening with his hand, the sunlight poured in, and it's clear my faith's alive.—I'll pray for you tonight in Saint-Germain!

MAURICE: Now I'm afraid!

JEANNE: The fear of God is the beginning of wisdom.

MAURICE: God? What's that? Who's He?

JEANNE: He's the one who gave joy to your youth and strength to your manhood! And He's the one who'll support us in the terrible time that lies ahead.

MAURICE: What lies ahead of us? What do you really know? Where did you find it out? What I don't know?

JEANNE: I can't say; I haven't dreamt anything, not seen it, not heard it, but during these two dreadful hours I've lived through so infinitely much suffering I'm prepared for the worst.

MARION: I want to go home, Mother; I'm hungry.

MAURICE: You shall, darling! (*Picks her up in his arms*)

MARION (*plaintively*): You're hurting me, Daddy.

JEANNE: We have to go home for dinner. So good-bye, Maurice. And good luck!

MAURICE (*to* MARION): Where did I hurt you? You surely know I wouldn't want to harm you!

MARION: Come with us home, then!

MAURICE (*to* JEANNE): Imagine—when I hear her say that, it's as if I ought to obey her; but then come common sense and duty . . . Good-bye, dear. (*Kisses his child, who puts her arms about his neck*)

JEANNE: When will we see you again?

MAURICE: Tomorrow, dear. And then never to be parted again.

JEANNE (*embraces him*): Never, never to be parted again. (*She makes the sign of the cross on his forehead.*) God protect you!

MAURICE (*touched against his will*): Dear, precious Jeanne!

(JEANNE *and* MARION *go toward the right;* MAURICE *to the left. Then they turn at the same time and throw kisses to each other.*)

MAURICE (*hastens over to them*): Jeanne! I'm ashamed! I'm always forgetting you, and you're the last person to remind me of it! Why, here's your ticket for tonight!

JEANNE: Thank you, dear, but—you're to be at your post alone; and I'm to be at mine—with Marion.

MAURICE: Your common sense is as great as the goodness of your heart; I swear no other woman would have sacrificed a pleasure to do her man a favor . . . I need to move freely tonight, and one doesn't take women and children out on the battlefield—you understood that!

JEANNE: Maurice! Don't think too highly of an insignificant woman like me—if you don't, you'll save your illusions!—But I'm just as forgetful as you!—Why, here's the tie and a pair of gloves I thought you might wear in my honor on your big day . . .

MAURICE (*kisses her hand*): Thank you, dear.

JEANNE: And, Maurice, don't forget—as you do so often—to go to the barber—I want you to be handsome, so that others, too, will like you . . .

MAURICE: You aren't jealous!

JEANNE: Don't say that word—it arouses evil thoughts.

MAURICE: You know, right now I could forego tonight's victory.— Yes, I shall have a victory!

JEANNE: Sh-h! [*Prolonged*]

MAURICE: And go home with you!

JEANNE: But you're not going to!—Go! Your destiny's awaiting you!

MAURICE: Good-bye, then! And let what's to be, be!

JEANNE (*alone with* MARION): *O crux! Ave spes unica!*

[CURTAIN]

## SCENE 2

*The café. To the right a buffet with an aquarium with goldfish, vegetables, fruit, preserves, etc. Farther away the entrance. At the back: a door to the kitchen, where laborers hang out; the kitchen exit to the garden can be seen. To the left, a counter and shelves with all sorts of bottles. To the right a long table with a marble top along the wall; another parallel to this toward the center of the stage; cane chairs by the tables. The walls are covered with paintings.*

MME CATHÉRINE *is sitting at the counter.* MAURICE *stands leaning on the counter, his hat on his head, smoking a cigarette.*

MME CATHÉRINE: So tonight's *the* night for you, Mr. Maurice?

MAURICE: Yes, tonight's it!

MME CATHÉRINE: Are you nervous?

MAURICE: Absolutely calm!

MME CATHÉRINE: Good luck in any case, and you deserve it, Mr. Maurice, after having struggled with hardships such as yours.

MAURICE: Thank you. You've been very good to me—if it hadn't been for your help, I'd have gone under by this time.

MME CATHÉRINE: We won't talk about that now—I help where I see work and willingness, but I don't like to be taken advantage of.— Can we count of your coming back here after the theater's closed so we can drink a glass with you?

MAURICE: You can count on that; naturally, since I promised you first.

(HENRIETTE *enters from the right.* MAURICE *turns, raises his hat, stares at* HENRIETTE, *who observes him carefully.*)

HENRIETTE (*to* MME CATHÉRINE): Mr. Adolphe hasn't come?

MME CATHÉRINE: No, ma'am. But he'll soon be here. Do be seated.

HENRIETTE: Thank you. But I'd rather wait for him outside. (*Goes out*)

MAURICE: Who . . . is . . . that?

MME CATHÉRINE: Why, it's Mr. Adolphe's friend!

MAURICE: Is . . . that . . . she?

MME CATHÉRINE: Haven't you seen her before?

MAURICE: No! Why, he has kept her out of my sight just as if he were afraid I'd take her away from him.

MME CATHÉRINE (*laughs; then*): What did you think of her looks?

MAURICE: Her looks? Let me see—I can't say.—I didn't see her—it was as if she flew into my arms at once, came so close to me I couldn't see her. And she left her mark in the air—why, I still see her as if she were standing there. (*He goes toward the door and*

*makes a gesture as if he were putting his arm about someone.*)
Ouch! (*Makes a gesture as if he has pricked his finger*) Why, she
has pins in her blouse. She's one of those who sting!

MME CATHÉRINE (*smiles*): You and your women!

MAURICE: Yes, it's crazy . . . crazy! But do you know what? I'll
leave before she comes in again, because otherwise, otherwise . . .
she's a terrible woman!

MME CATHÉRINE: You're afraid?

MAURICE: Yes, I'm afraid of myself, and afraid for some others . . .

MME CATHÉRINE: Well, leave then!

MAURICE: Imagine—when she sucked herself out through that door
she caused a little whirlwind that drew me along . . . go ahead,
laugh . . . but you can see how the palm over on the buffet is
still moving! She's a devil of a woman!

MME CATHÉRINE: But leave then, man, before you go absolutely
crazy!

MAURICE: I want to leave, but I can't . . . Do you believe in fate,
Mme Cathérine?

MME CATHÉRINE: No, I believe in the good God who helps us against
evil powers, if we ask Him nicely.

MAURICE: So—evil powers at any rate!—Aren't they the ones I hear
in the entrance?

MME CATHÉRINE: Of course, why it rustles about her as when the
linen draper tears cloth. Go! Quickly! Through the kitchen!

(MAURICE *rushes toward the kitchen door but bumps into*
EMILE.)

EMILE: I'm terribly sorry (*Draws back*)

ADOLPHE (*enters; then* HENRIETTE): Well . . . Maurice! How are
you? May I present my friend Miss Henriette to my best and old-
est friend, Mr. Maurice?

MAURICE (*greets her stiffly*): A very great pleasure.

HENRIETTE: We have seen each other before.

ADOLPHE: Really? When—if I may ask?

MAURICE: Just now. In here.

ADOLPHE: Oh!—Well, you can't go until we've had a chance to talk a little.

MAURICE (*after* MME CATHÉRINE *has signaled to him*): If I only had time!

ADOLPHE: Take time! We won't stay long.

HENRIETTE: I won't disturb you if you men have financial matters to talk about.

MAURICE: Our finances are in the sad state one doesn't talk about.

HENRIETTE: Then we'll talk about something else! (*Takes his hat and hangs it up*) There, behave yourself so I can get acquainted with the great writer!

    (MME CATHÉRINE *signals to* MAURICE, *but he does not notice.*)

ADOLPHE: That's right, Henriette! You catch him! (*They sit down at a table.*)

HENRIETTE (*to* MAURICE): You do have a good friend in Adolphe, Mr. Maurice; he never talks about anything but you . . . and so I often feel neglected . . .

ADOLPHE: Well-l! Henriette for her part never leaves me in peace because of you, Maurice. She has read what you've written and wants to know where you've got everything from; she has asked me what you look like, how old you are, what you like best—in a word: I've had you for morning, noon, and night—it's as if we three have lived together.

MAURICE (*to* HENRIETTE): Good heavens, why didn't you come over here to take a look at the wonder so your curiosity would have been satisfied in a hurry?

HENRIETTE: Adolphe didn't want to! (ADOLPHE *looks embarrassed.*) Not that he was jealous . . .

MAURICE: Why should he be, when he knew I loved someone else . . .

HENRIETTE: He must have been not sure your feelings were lasting.

MAURICE: I can't understand that; I'm well known for the constancy of my feelings . . .

ADOLPHE: That wasn't it either . . .

HENRIETTE (*interrupts him*): Probably because you hadn't been tested by fire . . .

ADOLPHE: Oh, then you know . . .

HENRIETTE (*interrupts*): . . . The world has never yet seen a faithful man.

MAURICE: Then it's going to see one!

HENRIETTE: Where?

MAURICE: Here.

(HENRIETTE *laughs*.)

ADOLPHE: Well, that sounds . . .

HENRIETTE (*interrupts him; still turned toward and addressing* MAURICE): Do you think I rely on Adolphe longer than a quarter of a year?

MAURICE: I have no grounds for challenging your lack of faith, but I'd vouch for Adolphe's loyalty.

HENRIETTE: You don't need to . . . I'm just talking, and I take it back . . . not because I feel inferior to you but because it's so . . . It's a bad habit I have of seeing only wickedness, and I keep it up even though I know better. But if I were to keep company with the two of you for some time, I'd become good again. Forgive me, Adolphe! (*She puts her hand on his cheek.*)

ADOLPHE: You're always talking wickedly but do the right thing; what you think—I don't know.

HENRIETTE: Who does?

MAURICE: If one were responsible for his thoughts, who could go on living?

HENRIETTE: So you, too, have evil thoughts?

MAURICE: Yes, of course . . . just as I commit the most cruel acts— in my dreams . . .

HENRIETTE: In your dreams, yes! Imagine: I . . . no, I'm ashamed to say it . . .

MAURICE: Go on! Go on!

HENRIETTE: Last night I dreamed that I quite calmly cut up

Adolphe's chest muscles—I'm a sculptor, you see—and he, who's always kind, didn't resist but helped me with what was difficult, for he knows more anatomy than I.

MAURICE: Was it as if he were dead?

HENRIETTE: No, he was alive.

MAURICE: That was nasty. Didn't you suffer because of it?

HENRIETTE: Not at all, and that's just what amazes me—I'm quite sensitive to other people's suffering. Isn't that right, Adolphe?

ADOLPHE: Absolutely . . . unusually so, not least when it's an animal.

MAURICE: On the other hand I'm relatively insensitive to both my own and other people's suffering . . .

ADOLPHE: Now he's lying about himself! Mme Cathérine, isn't that so?

MME CATHÉRINE: Mr. Maurice is the kindest fellow I know. Can you imagine—he was going to get the police because I didn't change water for the goldfish . . . the ones on the table over there . . . Look . . . look, it's as if they heard what I said . . .

MAURICE: Listen—we're sitting here washing ourselves white as angels; yet we're pretty much ready for any tidy little outrageous act if it's a question of honor, gold, or woman.—So you're a sculptor?

HENRIETTE: Somewhat.—Enough of a sculptor to do a bust—and I'm fully capable of doing a bust of you.—I've dreamed of doing that for a long time.

MAURICE: Go ahead. At least that dream can be fulfilled in a hurry.

HENRIETTE: But I want to begin seeing you after tonight's success when you'll first be the one you should be.

MAURICE: How sure you are it'll be a victory.

HENRIETTE: Yes! It's written in your face that you'll succeed at this, and you must feel it yourself.

MAURICE: Why?

HENRIETTE: Since I feel it! You know, I was sick this morning, and I'm well now.

(ADOLPHE *begins to be depressed.*)

MAURICE (*embarrassed*): Listen—I have one theater ticket left—just one. I'll hand it to Adolphe.

ADOLPHE: Thank you, but I'll hand it over to Henriette.

HENRIETTE: Fine, but is that all right?

ADOLPHE: Why not?—Besides I never go to the theater since I can't stand the heat.

HENRIETTE: Will you at least come and get me when the show's over?

ADOLPHE: If you really insist. But Maurice will be coming here, where we'll be waiting for him.

MAURICE: There's no reason why you can't go to the trouble of coming; I ask you to; I beg . . . and if you don't want to meet us outside the theater, wait for us at the Auberge des Adrets . . . Agreed?

ADOLPHE: Wait a minute: you can settle questions to your advantage before I've had time to think it over.

MAURICE: What's there to think over? If you're going to fetch your girl friend or not!

ADOLPHE: You don't know what that insignificant act can signify, but I sense it.

HENRIETTE: Sh-h! Don't be superstitious while the sun's shining. Let him come or not—we'll always find our way back!

ADOLPHE (*has risen*): Now I have to go in any case—my model's due. Good-bye.—Good luck, Maurice! Tomorrow you're on the other side! Good-bye, Henriette.

HENRIETTE: Are you really leaving?

ADOLPHE: Have to!

MAURICE: Good-bye, then. (ADOLPHE *goes, saying good-bye to* MME CATHÉRINE.)

HENRIETTE: Imagine—we finally got to meet each other!

MAURICE: Is that so wonderful?

HENRIETTE: It looks as if it had to happen since Adolphe did everything to prevent it!

MAURICE: Did he?

HENRIETTE: You've certainly noticed that!

MAURICE: I've noticed it, but why did you have to say it?

HENRIETTE: I had to!

MAURICE: I don't have to tell you I intended to run out through the kitchen to avoid meeting you, but I was hindered by a customer, who shut the door.

HENRIETTE: Why did you have to tell me that?

MAURICE: Don't know!

(MME CATHÉRINE *knocks over glasses and bottles.*)

MAURICE: Take it easy, Mme Cathérine; there's no danger.

HENRIETTE: Was that a signal or a warning?

MAURICE: Most likely both!

HENRIETTE: Am I like a locomotive since I'm to have guards . . .

MAURICE: And a switch engine! Switching tracks is the most dangerous!

HENRIETTE: How cruel you can be!

MME CATHÉRINE: Mr. Maurice isn't at all cruel; up to now he has been the kindest and most faithful person toward his people and the ones he has ties with . . .

MAURICE: Sh-h-h!

HENRIETTE (*to* MAURICE): The old woman's insolent!

MAURICE: We can walk down to the boulevard if you wish.

HENRIETTE: Fine! This isn't my place.—I can feel hate tearing at me . . . (*Leaves*)

MAURICE (*follows her*): Good-bye, Mme Cathérine.

MME CATHÉRINE: Just a second! May I say something, Mr. Maurice?

MAURICE (*stops unwillingly*): What?

MME CATHÉRINE: Don't do it! Don't do it!

MAURICE: What?

MME CATHÉRINE: Don't do it!

MAURICE: Don't be afraid! That woman's not my kind. But she interests me. Hardly that.

MME CATHÉRINE: Don't rely on yourself!

MAURICE: Well, I do rely on myself. Good-bye! (*Goes*)

[CURTAIN]

# ACT II

## SCENE I

*Auberge des Adrets. A café in theatrical seventeenth-century style. Tables and easy chairs here and there in corners and narrow passages. The walls are decorated with weapons and armor; the panels with glasses and tankards, etc.*

*MAURICE in tails and HENRIETTE in evening gown at one table with a champagne bottle and three filled glasses. They sit directly opposite each other. The third glass is standing on the fourth side of the table away from the audience. There a third easy chair is waiting for the absent "third man."*

MAURICE (*puts his watch on the table*): If he isn't here in five minutes, he won't come.—So shouldn't we drink with his ghost while we're waiting? (*Touches his glass to the unused third glass*)

HENRIETTE (*does the same*): Skål, Adolphe!

MAURICE: He won't come!

HENRIETTE: He will!

MAURICE: Won't!

HENRIETTE: Will!

MAURICE: What a night! What a wonderful day! I can't grasp that a new life has begun! Imagine: the director thinks I'm sure to make a hundred thousand francs . . . I'll buy a villa beyond the

city limits for twenty thousand; then I'll have eighty thousand
left! I won't understand this until tomorrow—I'm tired, tired,
tired. (*Sinks down in his chair*) Have you ever been happy?

HENRIETTE: Never!—What's it like?

MAURICE: Well, what shall I say? I can't put it into words, but I'm
thinking most of all of my enemies' disappointment . . . That's
nasty, I know, but it's the truth!

HENRIETTE: Is thinking about enemies happiness?

MAURICE: Whoever wins does count the dead and the wounded so
he'll have some idea of his victory.

HENRIETTE: Are you that bloodthirsty?

MAURICE: Actually, no; but when you've felt other people's heels
tramping on you for years, it's nice to throw off the enemy and
breathe again!

HENRIETTE: Don't you think it's strange you're sitting here alone
with me, an unknown unimportant girl, on an evening like this
when you must have had a need of showing yourself in your triumph before all the people, on the boulevards, in the big restaurants . . .

MAURICE: Yes, it is a little strange, but I like it, and your company's
all right.

HENRIETTE: You're not happy?

MAURICE: No, sad rather—I feel like weeping.

HENRIETTE: Why?

MAURICE: It's good fortune, which knows it is nothing or awaits misfortune.

HENRIETTE: Sad! What's wrong?

MAURICE: I lack the only thing that can make life worthwhile . . .

HENRIETTE: So you don't love her any more?

MAURICE: Not in the way I understand love. Do you think she has
read my play or wants to see it? She's very good, very self-sacri-
ficing, and sensitive, but going out with me to celebrate an occasion like this, she'd think sinful! I offered her champagne once;
instead of being pleased she picked up the wine list and figured

out how much it cost. And when she saw the price, she cried! She cried because Marion needed new stockings!

That's nice, of course, if you wish; it's touching; but I can't get any pleasure out of it! And I want pleasure before life is over! Up to now I've gone without, but now, now . . . life's beginning for me! (*The clock strikes twelve.*) Now a new day's beginning, a new time!

HENRIETTE: Adolphe isn't coming!

MAURICE: No, he won't come now! And now it's too late to go to Mme Cathérine's.

HENRIETTE: But they're expecting you.

MAURICE: Let them wait! They made me promise to come, and I take it back—Are you anxious to go there?

HENRIETTE: No, not in the least!

MAURICE: Do you want to give me your company?

HENRIETTE: Gladly! If you'll put up with mine!

MAURICE: But I've asked for it!—Imagine, the victory wreath is worthless if one can't place it at the feet of a woman: imagine, everything's worthless if one doesn't have a woman . . .

HENRIETTE: Do you need to be without a woman? You?

MAURICE: That's a question!

HENRIETTE: Don't you know that in the moment of success and fame a man is irresistible?

MAURICE: I don't know that, for I've never experienced it.

HENRIETTE: You're a strange person; at this moment the most envied man in Paris, you're sitting here worrying, probably have a bad conscience for neglecting the invitation to drink chicory coffee with an old woman at the café . . .

MAURICE: Yes, my conscience's torturing me because of that, and I can feel their disapproval, their hurt feelings, their justified anger all the way here. My comrades in bad times had the right to insist on my coming this evening; good Mme Cathérine has the first claim on my success, which would throw a glow of hope over the poor souls who haven't succeeded yet . . . And I've robbed them of their good faith in me. I hear them swear: "Maurice is coming, for he's a good man; he doesn't despise us; and he won't fail to keep his word!" Now they've foresworn themselves! (*During this speech someone in the next room has begun to play Beethoven's D-minor Sonata op. 31 No. 2, the Finale. The allegro is at first piano, then a steadily increasing forte, passionate, stirred up, finally wild.*) Who's playing here tonight?

HENRIETTE: Probably some night owls like us.—But listen! Your statement of the case isn't accurate. Remember that Adolphe promised to fetch us; we waited, and he broke his promise. So you're innocent.

MAURICE: Really? I believe you when you're talking, but when you stop, my conscience gets going again. What do you have in that package?

HENRIETTE: Oh, it's only a laurel wreath[2] I wanted to send up on stage, but I didn't get the chance. Let me give it to you now; it'll probably cool a hot forehead. (*She gets up, puts the wreath on his head, and kisses him on his forehead.*) Hail, conqueror!

MAURICE: No, not that!

HENRIETTE (*on her knees*): Hail, king!

MAURICE (*gets up*): No! I'm getting afraid!

HENRIETTE: You . . . afraid? You . . . timid, who fears even good fortune. Who took your self-confidence and made you a dwarf?

MAURICE: A dwarf? Yes, you're right; I don't work like the giant in the clouds with thunder and noise, but I shape my swords down in the quiet depths of the mountains! Do you think I'm afraid of the wreath of victory? No, but I despise it, because it's too small for me. Do you think I'm afraid of that ghost that sits with the green eyes of jealousy and keeps watch over my feelings, the strength of which you haven't the slightest idea.—Get thee gone, ghost! (*He brushes the third and untouched champagne glass off the table.*) Away, superfluous third man, you who have lost your right through absence if you ever had any! You stayed away from the battlefield because you felt yourself already defeated! As I crush this glass under my feet, I'll crush the image you've raised in a little temple that's not going to be yours any more!

HENRIETTE: Wonderful! That's the way! Wonderful, my hero!

MAURICE: Now I've sacrificed my best friend, my most faithful helper on your altar, Astarte! Are you satisfied?

HENRIETTE: Astarte! [3] What a beautiful name! I'll keep it.—You must love me, Maurice!

MAURICE: Of course!—Woman of misfortune, who awakens a man's courage and smells blood, where do you come from and where do you want to take me? I loved you before I saw you; when they talked about you, I shivered, and when I saw you in the doorway, your soul flew into mine; when you left, I still had you in my arms. I wanted to run away from you, but someone hindered me, and tonight we were driven together like wild animals in a hunter's net. Who's to blame? Your friend who served as pander!

HENRIETTE: Blame or not! What does that have to do with this? And what is blame?—Adolphe's to be blamed for not bringing us together before; he has committed the crime of robbing us of two weeks of bliss, two weeks he had no right to; I'm jealous of him for your sake; I hate him because he has deceived you by keeping me from you. I'd like to erase him from the list of the living and from memory, wipe him out of the past, make him uncreated, unborn!

MAURICE: Oh well, we'll bury him in our memories, we'll put branches over him in the wild forest and heap stones on his mound so that he can never look up any more! (*Raises his glass*) Our fate is sealed! Woe unto us! What's going to happen?

HENRIETTE: A new era!—What do you have in that package?

MAURICE: I don't remember!

HENRIETTE (*opens the package and takes out a tie and a pair of gloves*): What a horrible tie! I suppose it cost fifty sous!

MAURICE (*snatches the two objects*): Don't touch them!

HENRIETTE: They're from her?

MAURICE: Yes, they are.

HENRIETTE: Give them to me!

MAURICE: No, she's better than we are, than all others!

HENRIETTE: I don't think so—she's merely more simpleminded and stingier! One who cries because you're drinking champagne . . .

MAURICE: When our child doesn't have stockings. Yes, she's a good human being!

HENRIETTE: Middle class! You'll never be an artist! But I'm an artist, and I'll make your bust with a storekeeper's imprint . . . instead of a laurel wreath.—Her name is Jeanne?

MAURICE: Yes, how did you know?

HENRIETTE: Why, that's the name of all housekeepers!

MAURICE: Henriette!

(HENRIETTE *takes the gloves and the tie and throws them into the fire.*)

MAURICE (*listlessly*): Astarte! Now you want a woman as sacrifice! You'll get her, but if you want an innocent child, you may go!

HENRIETTE: Can you tell me what binds you to me?

MAURICE: If I knew that, I'd tear myself free! But I think it's the evil qualities you have and that I lack. I think it's the evil in you that draws me with the attraction of the irresistibility of what's new . . .

HENRIETTE: Haven't you ever committed a crime?

MAURICE: No, not a real one. Have you?

HENRIETTE: Yes.

MAURICE: Well! How did it feel?

HENRIETTE: Greater than doing a good deed, for that makes us other people's equal; it was greater than an achievement, for that places us above others and is rewarded. The crime put me outside, on the other side of life, the community, and my fellow human beings. Since that moment I've had only a half life, a dream life, and that's why reality never takes hold of me.

MAURICE: What did you do?

HENRIETTE: I don't want to tell you, for you'd get frightened again!

MAURICE: Can't you ever be found out?

HENRIETTE: Never! But that doesn't keep me from quite often seeing the five stones at Roquette Place, where they put up the guillotine, and that's why I never dare touch cards, for, if I do, the five of diamonds turns up . . .

MAURICE: Was it that kind of crime?

HENRIETTE: Yes, it was!

MAURICE: Why, that's terrible, but it's interesting! Don't you ever have pangs of conscience?

HENRIETTE: Never! But can't we please talk about something else?

MAURICE: Shall we talk about—love?

HENRIETTE: One doesn't talk about that before it's over!

MAURICE: Have you loved Adolphe?

HENRIETTE: I don't know! His natural goodness attracted me like a beautiful childhood memory. But there was so much about him that offended me, I needed a long time to erase, change, add, subtract about him to make him an acceptable figure. When he talked, I could tell he had learned from you and had often badly understood and awkwardly applied. Imagine how pitiful the copy seemed when I got to see the original.—That's why he was afraid to have the two of us meet; and when we had, he understood immediately his time was over.

MAURICE: Poor Adolphe!

HENRIETTE: I'm sorry for him, too, for he's suffering terribly . . .

MAURICE: Sh-h! Someone's coming!

HENRIETTE: Imagine if it were he!

MAURICE: That would be unbearable!

HENRIETTE: It isn't he, but if it had been, how would you imagine it would have gone?

MAURICE: First he would have been a little annoyed with you, because he had been wrong about the café—had looked for us in the wrong places—but his annoyance would quickly have become pleasure over seeing us; seeing *we* hadn't fooled him. And in his pleasure over having been unjust to us in his thoughts he would

love both of us, and then he'd have become delighted over our
being such good friends. That had always been his dream—hm!
he's giving a speech now!—his dream that we three would make
a triumvirate to show the world the great example of a friendship that demands nothing—"Yes, I rely on you, Maurice, partly
because you're my friend, partly because you have ties elsewhere!"

HENRIETTE: Bravo! Have you been in a situation like that? You *did*
hit it on the head exactly. You know Adolphe's the sort of third
man who can never enjoy anything with his mistress unless a
friend's along!

MAURICE: That's why I was to be called in to amuse you!—Sh-h!
There is someone out there!—It's he!

HENRIETTE: No! The ghostly hours have come, you know, and then
one hears so much, and sees—sometimes. To be awake when one
ought to be asleep has the same charm for me as crime—one has
placed himself above and outside the law of nature . . .

MAURICE: But the punishment is ghastly . . . I'm freezing or shiv-
ering, one or the other.

HENRIETTE (*takes her theater shawl and puts it about his shoulders*):
Let me put this on you; it will warm you.

MAURICE: Nice! It's as if I were in your skin, as if my awakened
body were being molded in your form; I feel how I'm being re-
shaped; but I even get a new soul, new thoughts, and here, where
your breast has made its imprint, it begins to rise. (*The pianist
in the next room has during this scene played pianissimo sometimes, furiously fortissimo occasionally, practiced the D-minor
sonata; at times silence; sometimes have been heard measures
96–107 of the Finale alone.*) What a monster to be sitting prac-
ticing on the piano at night! I'll get sick from this! You know
what? Let's ride out to the Bois de Boulogne and have breakfast
in the pavilion to see the sun rise above the lakes.

HENRIETTE: Fine!

MAURICE: But first I'll send a message home and have my mail and

the morning papers sent out to the place where we'll have breakfast. Listen, Henriette: shall we invite Adolphe?

HENRIETTE: Yes, that's too crazy, but do it! The ass is to be hitched
to the chariot of triumph! Let him come! (*They get up.*)

MAURICE (*takes off the shawl*): Then I'll call him!

HENRIETTE: Wait a minute! (*She rushes into his arms.*)

[CURTAIN]

SCENE 2

*A large, splendid restaurant room in the Bois de Boulogne; car-
pets, mirrors, chaise longues, divans. The back has glass doors and
windows facing the lakes. In front a table set with flower vases,
fruit bowls, wine decanters, oyster plates, many sorts of wine-
glasses, and two lighted candelabra. To the right a divan table
with newspapers and telegrams.*

MAURICE *and* HENRIETTE *are sitting across from each other at this
table.*

*The sun is rising.*

MAURICE: There's no doubt any more: the newspapers have said it's
so, and the telegrams have congratulated me on my success. It's a
new life that's beginning, and my fate linked with yours through
this night when you alone shared my hopes and my triumph. I
got the laurel wreath from you, and it seems to me I got everything from you!

HENRIETTE: What a wonderful night! Have we dreamed this or have
we lived it?

MAURICE (*gets up*): And what a morning after this night! It seems
to me it's the first day in the world which the sun shines on; earth
has just been created and torn itself free of the white mists, which
are floating away; there lies Eden in the rosy light of dawn; and
we are the first human beings . . . You know I'm so happy I'd

like to weep because the rest of humanity isn't as happy as I . . .
Can you hear the distant sound as if waves were pounding a stony
shore, like the wind in the forest? Do you know what that is? It's
Paris, which is whispering my name! Do you see the pillars of
smoke rising to the sky by the thousands and the tens of thousands! Those are my altar fires, and if they aren't, they must be,
because I want it! All of Europe's telegraph keys are pounding
out my name right now; the Orient Express is bringing the newspaper to the far east, toward the sunrise, and the ocean liner is
carrying it to the farthest west!—The world is mine, and that's
why it's beautiful! I'd like to have wings for us two, rise from
here and fly far, far away, before people have awakened me from
my dream—because most likely it is a dream!

HENRIETTE (*gives him her hand*): Feel . . . you're not dreaming!

MAURICE: It's not a dream, but it has been! You know, when I was
a poor young man walking out here in this forest and looked up
at this pavilion it seemed like a fairy-tale castle, and I always
thought of being in this room with its balcony and its thick curtains as perfect happiness! To sit here with a woman I loved and
watch the sun rise while the candelabra were still burning; that
was the most daring dream of my youth. Now it has come true,
and now I haven't anything more to wish for in life!—Do you
want to die now—with me?

HENRIETTE: No, you crazy man, now I want to start living!

MAURICE (*gets up*): Living: that is suffering!—Now comes reality.
I can hear his steps on the stairs, he's puffing with anxiety, his
heart's pounding with anguish for having lost the most precious
thing of all. Just imagine—Adolphe's here. In a minute he'll be
standing right here.

HENRIETTE (*uneasy*): It was a foolish notion to invite him, and I already regret it.—We'll see if your analysis proves accurate, won't
we?

MAURICE: One can be wrong about other people's feelings!

(*The* HEADWAITER *enters; hands* MAURICE *a card.*)

MAURICE: Ask the gentleman to come in. (*To* HENRIETTE) We'll regret this, I think!

HENRIETTE: We've thought of that too late!—Sh-h!

(ADOLPHE *enters; extremely pale and hollow-eyed*)

MAURICE (*tries to talk without embarrassment*): There you are! Where were you last night?

ADOLPHE: I looked for you at the Hôtel des Arrêts and waited an hour . . .

MAURICE: The wrong place! We waited for you at Auberge des Adrets for a couple of hours and are still waiting as you see.

ADOLPHE (*relieved*): Oh, God!

HENRIETTE: Good morning, dear! You are a bird of misfortune who always has to torture yourself unnecessarily. I suppose you've imagined we wanted to avoid you, and although we've sent for you, you still believe you're superfluous.

ADOLPHE: Forgive me; I was wrong, but this night has been terrible. (*They sit down. Uncomfortable silence*)

HENRIETTE (*to* ADOLPHE): Well, aren't you going to congratulate Maurice on his great success?

ADOLPHE: Oh, yes!— You've had a solid success, which even envy itself can't deny. Everything bends before you, and I feel very small in your presence.

MAURICE: Nonsense!—Henriette, give Adolphe a glass of wine.

ADOLPHE: Thanks, nothing for me. Nothing!

HENRIETTE (*to* ADOLPHE): What's wrong with you? Are you sick?

ADOLPHE: No, but I'm going to be.

HENRIETTE: Your eyes . . .

ADOLPHE: What's that?

MAURICE: How was it at Mme Cathérine's last night? I suppose they're angry with me?

ADOLPHE: No one's angry with you, but your staying away made them depressed—I was sorry to see that. But no one was angry, believe me; understanding friends thought of you and your staying away with the greatest of sympathetic indulgence. Mme Cathérine herself defended you and proposed a toast for you. All of us rejoiced over your success as if it were our own.

HENRIETTE: Imagine, such kind people! Imagine, what good friends you have, Maurice!

MAURICE: Yes, better than I deserve!

HENRIETTE: No one has friends he doesn't deserve; and you're lucky in having many . . . Can't you feel how gentle the air about you is today because of genuinely kind thoughts and greetings which are sent to you from a thousand hearts . . .

(MAURICE *gets up to conceal that he is touched.*)

ADOLPHE: . . . from the thousand hearts you've released from the nightmare that has oppressed them for a generation. Mankind has been slandered . . . and you have raised it up again; so people are grateful to you. Today they raise their heads again and say: See, we are a bit better than our reputation, and that thought makes them better . . .

(HENRIETTE *tries to conceal that she is touched.*)

ADOLPHE: Am I disturbing you? Let me merely warm myself in your sunlight for a little while, Maurice, and I'll go.

MAURICE: Why should you go? You've just come!

ADOLPHE: Why? Because I've seen what I've never needed to see; because I know now my time is over. (*Silence*) Your sending for me I understand as a thoughtful gesture, an acknowledgment of what has taken place, a frankness that wounds less than deceit. You hear I speak kindly about human beings, Maurice—you have taught me that, Maurice! (*Silence*) But, my friend, I walked through the church of Saint-Germain a little while ago and I saw a woman and a child there. I don't wish you had seen them, because what has happened can't be changed, but if you gave them a thought and a word before you pushed them into the open sea of the large city, you'd be able to enjoy your success untroubled. And now I'll say good-bye.

HENRIETTE: Why should you go?

ADOLPHE: *You* ask that! Do you want me to say it?

HENRIETTE: No, I don't.

ADOLPHE: Good-bye, then. (*Goes*)

MAURICE: The fall of man: And lo, they became aware of their nakedness.

HENRIETTE: That scene didn't turn out the way we had thought it would!—He's better than we are!

MAURICE: Now I think all people are better than we are!

HENRIETTE: Did you notice that the sun has gone behind the clouds and the forest has lost its rosy glow?

MAURICE: Yes, and the blue lake is black. Let's flee down there where the sky is always blue and the trees are always green.

HENRIETTE: Yes, let's!—But without saying good-bye!

MAURICE: No, *with* saying good-bye!

HENRIETTE: We should flee. You offered your wings—but have lead about your feet.—I'm not jealous, but if you pay a farewell visit and get two pairs of arms about your neck, you won't be able to tear yourself free.

MAURICE: You're probably right, but only two small arms are needed to hold me.

HENRIETTE: So it's the child who binds you, not the woman.

MAURICE: It's the child!

HENRIETTE: The child! Another woman's child! And because of that I'm to suffer! Why should that child be in my way, where I was to go forward, and have to go?

MAURICE: Yes, why? Better it had never existed!

HENRIETTE (*stirred up, walks back and forth*): That's sure! But it does exist! Like a stone on the road, a firmly placed, immovable stone that will tip over the carriage!

MAURICE: The chariot of triumph!—The ass has been killed, but the stone remains! Damnation! (*Silence*)

HENRIETTE: This is hopeless!

MAURICE: No! We must get married, then *our* child will make us forget the other one.

HENRIETTE: The one shall kill the other!

MAURICE: Kill! What kind of word is that?

HENRIETTE (*changing her tone*): Your child will kill our love!

MAURICE: No, our love will kill everything that stands in its way, but it won't be killed!

HENRIETTE (*picks up a deck of cards which has lain on the stove*): Look! the five of diamonds! The guillotine!—Is it possible that one's fate has been determined ahead of time? That one's thoughts are led through channels to their destined place without one's being able to prevent it? No, I don't want that! I don't want that! Do you know I belong to the guillotine if my crime is discovered?

MAURICE: Tell me about your crime—this is the right time!

HENRIETTE: No, I'd have to regret it afterward, and you'd despise me!—No, no, no! Have you ever heard it said that one can hate a person to death?—Well, Mother and my brother and sisters came to hate my father, and he melted away like wax before the fire. No! no! Let's talk about something else!—And above all else let's go away! The air has been poisoned here, your laurel wreath will be withered tomorrow, your triumph forgotten, and in eight days some other victor will be the center of attention. Away from here to work for new victories! But first, Maurice, you're to go to embrace your child and take care of her immediate future. You don't need to see her mother.

MAURICE: Thank you! Your heart does you credit, and you're doubly dear to me when you show the goodness you otherwise conceal!

HENRIETTE: And then drop in at Mme Cathérine's café and say goodbye to the old woman and your friends. Don't leave any unsettled affairs behind you, or you'll feel low on the journey.

MAURICE: I'll clear up everything, and tonight we'll meet at the railroad station.

HENRIETTE: Agreed! So! Out from here and on the way down to the sea, the sun!

[CURTAIN]

# ACT III

## Scene I

MME CATHÉRINE's *café. The gaslights are on.* MME CATHÉRINE *is sitting by the buffet.* ADOLPHE *by the table.*

MME CATHÉRINE: Mr. Adolphe, life is like that, but you young people demand too much and then you sit there afterward whimpering.

ADOLPHE: No, it isn't like that: I don't blame anyone, and I like both of them just as much still. But there's something that makes me sick. You see, I liked Maurice so much more, so much I didn't begrudge him what could make him happy, but now I've lost him, and that hurts me more than losing her. I've lost both of them, so my loneliness is doubly painful. But there's something else, too, which I don't fully understand yet.

MME CATHÉRINE: Don't worry so much. Work and amuse yourself. Don't you ever go to church, for example?

ADOLPHE: What should I do there?

MME CATHÉRINE: Oh, there's a lot to look at, and there's music, too. At least it isn't commonplace there!

ADOLPHE: Perhaps. But I probably don't belong in that sheepfold, for I don't have any reverence for it. And you see, faith is a gift, they say, and I haven't been given that yet.

MME CATHÉRINE: Wait until you get it, then.—But what about the reports I've been hearing today? Is it true that you've sold your painting in London for a very high price and that you've got the gold medal?

ADOLPHE: Yes, that's true!

MME CATHÉRINE: But, good heavens, you didn't tell me?

ADOLPHE: I'm afraid of good fortune; besides, it's almost worthless to me just now; I'm afraid as if it were a ghost; one mustn't tell that one has seen it; if one does, things will go wrong.

MME CATHÉRINE: Well, you always were strange!

ADOLPHE: No, but I've seen too many misfortunes accompany fortune, and I've seen that in defeat and setbacks one always has
faithful friends, but in success only false ones. You asked me if I
went to church, and I avoided a direct answer. This morning I
went into the church of Saint-Germain without knowing why,
really. I thought I was looking for someone in there that I could
thank silently, but I didn't find anyone.—Then I put a gold coin
in the poor box. That was all I could get out of going to church,
and that was quite commonplace.

MME CATHÉRINE: But still it was something, and your thinking about
the poor when you had had a good day was nice.

ADOLPHE: It wasn't nice or anything—it was only something I did
because I couldn't do anything else. But something else happened
to me in church: I saw Maurice's Jeanne and his child. Driven
over, crushed by his chariot of triumph. They seemed to grasp the
whole extent of their misfortune.

MME CATHÉRINE: Well, I don't know what you men have on your
conscience. But that a good person, a conscientious, sensitive man
like Mr. Maurice, can in a flash desert his woman and his child—
explain that to me.

ADOLPHE: I can't explain it, and he doesn't seem to understand it
himself. I saw them this morning, and everything seemed so
natural, so right, they couldn't imagine anything else. It was as if
they were enjoying the satisfaction of doing a good deed or fulfilling a precious duty. Mme Cathérine, there are things we can't
explain, and that's why we haven't the right to judge. Besides:
you saw how it all went. Maurice felt the danger in the air; I
sensed it; I tried to prevent their meeting; Maurice wanted to flee,
but nothing helped. It's as if some invisible person has woven an
intrigue and deceitfully driven them into each other's arms. I
could be challenged in this case, but I don't hesitate to pronounce
the verdict: *Not guilty!*

MME CATHÉRINE: Yes, to be able to forgive as you do: that's religion!

ADOLPHE: What? Would I be religious without knowing it?

MME CATHÉRINE: But to *let* oneself be driven or enticed to evil, like Mr. Maurice, that's weakness or wickedness; and if a person feels his strength giving way, he prays for help, and gets it. But he didn't do that, because he was too proud!—Who's that coming?—Why, it's the priest, I think!

ADOLPHE: What does he want here?

PRIEST (*enters*): Good evening, madame! Good evening, sir!

MME CATHÉRINE: What may I do for you, Father?

PRIEST: Has Mr. Maurice, the writer, been here today?

MME CATHÉRINE: No, not today. He has his play on at the theater and is most likely busy up there.

PRIEST: I have—sad news to tell him—sad in several ways.

MME CATHÉRINE: May I ask you what kind . . .

PRIEST: Well-l, it's no secret. His daughter by his mistress Jeanne is dead.

MME CATHÉRINE: Dead!

ADOLPHE: Marion dead!

PRIEST: Yes, she died suddenly this morning without having been ill previously.

MME CATHÉRINE: Oh, God! Who understands Your ways?

PRIEST: The mother's despair calls for Mr. Maurice's presence, and we have to try to get hold of him!—One question in confidence: Do you know if Mr. Maurice loved his child or was indifferent to her?

MME CATHÉRINE: *If* he loved his Marion? Father, all of us who knew him know how much he loved her.

ADOLPHE: There's no doubt of that, Father.

PRIEST: I'm glad to hear it, and that clears up the matter for me.

MME CATHÉRINE: Was there any doubt?

PRIEST: Unfortunately, yes! There's even a rumor in the neighborhood that he has deserted the child and her mother to go away with an unknown woman. In a few hours this rumor has grown into definite accusation, and at the same time people have become so bitter about it that they threaten his life and call him a murderer.

MME CATHÉRINE: Oh, God, what's this? What is it?

PRIEST: Now I want to make my opinion that the man is innocent clear, and the child's mother is just as certain as I. But Mr. Maurice has appearances against him, and he'll probably have a hard time when the police come to question him.

ADOLPHE: Are the police involved?

PRIEST: Yes, the police had to interfere to protect him against the nasty rumors and the fury of the mob. The commissioner will most likely be here very soon.

MME CATHÉRINE (*to* ADOLPHE): You see how it goes when you can't tell good from bad, and when you toy with vice. God punishes!

ADOLPHE: Then He's more merciless than human beings.

PRIEST: What do you know about that?

ADOLPHE: Not very much, but I do see what happens . . .

PRIEST: And understand it, too?

ADOLPHE: Probably not yet.

PRIEST: Let's look a little more closely at the matter.—There's the commissioner!

COMMISSIONER (*enters*): Gentlemen, Mme Cathérine. I have to disturb you for a moment by asking some questions about Mr. Maurice, who, as you may know, is the object of an unpleasant rumor, which, parenthetically, I don't believe.

MME CATHÉRINE: None of us believe it either.

COMMISSIONER: That strengthens my conviction, but for his own sake I must give him the opportunity to defend himself.

PRIEST: That's fine, and he'll surely get justice though that will be difficult.

COMMISSIONER: Appearances are against him, but I've seen innocent people on the guillotine before their innocence was revealed. This is what speaks against him: the child Marion had been left alone by her mother; the child was visited secretly by the father, who seems to have spied out when she'd be alone. A quarter of an hour after his visit the mother came home, and then the child was dead! That's an embarrassing circumstance for the defendant. —The autopsy revealed no injuries and no traces of poison, but the doctors explain there are newly discovered poisons that leave no traces!—This seems a coincidence to me, and I'm used to them. But there are worse things.—Last night Mr. Maurice was seen at Auberge des Adrets with another woman. They talked, according to the waiter, about crimes. The words Roquette Place and the guillotine were mentioned. A strange topic of conversation between two lovers of good upbringing and high position!

That can still be explained—experience tells us that people after staying up all night drinking sort of dig up the worst from the bottoms of their souls. The headwaiter's testimony from the champagne breakfast in the Bois de Boulogne this morning is even worse. He reports he heard them wish a child were dead. The man supposedly said, "Better if it had never existed," and the woman answered, "Certainly! But it does exist." And later on these words were uttered, "The one is to kill the other," to which the answer was, "Kill! What word is that?" and "Our love will kill everything that stands in its way"! and then: "The five of diamonds, the guillotine, Roquette Place.!"—That's hard to get away from, as is the trip abroad, which served as a frame for their night! Those are difficult matters!

ADOLPHE: He is lost!

MME CATHÉRINE: That's a terrible story! What is a person to believe?

PRIEST: This isn't the work of human beings! God be merciful unto him!

ADOLPHE: He's caught in the net and will never escape!

MME CATHÉRINE: What did he have to do there?

ADOLPHE: Are you beginning to doubt him?

MME CATHÉRINE: Yes and no! I can't have a definite opinion about this!—Haven't we seen angels turn into devils in a flash and then become angels again?

COMMISSIONER: It does look strange. But we'll have to wait to hear his explanation. No one is to be judged unheard! Good evening, gentlemen and Mme Cathérine. [*Goes*]

PRIEST: This can't be the work of human beings!

ADOLPHE: It really looks like the efforts of demons to ruin human beings!

PRIEST: It's either punishment for unknown faults or it's a terrifying test.

JEANNE (*enters, dressed in mourning*): Good evening.—Forgive me for asking, but have you seen Mr. Maurice?

MME CATHÉRINE: No, madame, but he is expected at any moment . . . So you haven't seen him since . . .

JEANNE: Not since yesterday morning . . .

MME CATHÉRINE: Permit me to express my sympathy in your great sorrow . . .

JEANNE: Thank you, madame—(*To the* PRIEST)—You're here, Father!

PRIEST: Yes, my child; I thought I could be of use to you, and it was lucky I got to talk to the police commissioner here.

JEANNE: The commissioner! He surely doesn't suspect Maurice, he too?

PRIEST: No, he doesn't—none of us here does. But appearances are against him in a terrifying way.

JEANNE: You mean because of that talk the waiters heard . . . That doesn't mean anything—I've heard Maurice say things like that before when he's been drinking. Then he imagines things about crimes and punishment. Besides it seems to have been the woman with him who said the worst things, and I'd like to look that woman in the eye.

ADOLPHE: Jeanne, dear, no matter how much harm that woman seems to have done you, she didn't have any evil intention at all but just did what her heart told her to. I know her as a good soul who can bear being looked in the eye!

JEANNE: Your opinion in this matter means a lot to me, Adolphe, and I believe you. So I can't look for the blame for what has happened except in myself. Yes, it's my sinfulness that's now being punished. (*She weeps.*)

PRIEST: Don't accuse yourself unjustly! I know how seriously you took being a mother, and the fact that your calling didn't have time to be blessed by the church and civil law isn't your fault. No, this is something else!

ADOLPHE: What?

PRIEST: I don't know!

(HENRIETTE *enters, dressed for traveling.*)

ADOLPHE (*gets up determinedly and goes up to* HENRIETTE): You here?

HENRIETTE: Yes, where's Maurice?

ADOLPHE: Do you know . . . or don't you know?

HENRIETTE: I know everything! Excuse me, Mme Cathérine. But I was ready to leave and had to come in here a moment. (*To* ADOLPHE) Who is that lady?—Ah! (HENRIETTE *and* JEANNE *stare at each other.* EMILE *appears in the kitchen doorway.*)

HENRIETTE (*to* JEANNE): I was going to say something, but it doesn't matter, for whatever I could say would sound like an insult. But if I simply ask you to believe that I share your great sorrow as much as anyone closer to you could, you mustn't push me aside . . . you mustn't, for I deserve your sympathy if not your forgiveness. (*She holds out her hand.*)

JEANNE (*stares at her*): Now I believe you, but a minute from now I can't! (*Takes* HENRIETTE'S *hand*)

HENRIETTE (*kisses* JEANNE'S *hand*): Thank you!

JEANNE (*withdraws her hand*): No, don't! I don't deserve it! I don't deserve it!

PRIEST: Excuse me, but while we're all here and seem to be in agreement for the moment, shouldn't you, Miss Henriette, clear up the uncertainty and the darkness in the major point of the complaint? I beg you as among friends to tell us what you meant by your talk about killing, crime, and Roquette Place. That these words didn't have anything to do with the little child's death, we think we know, but it would comfort us to hear what that talk was about! Will you tell us?

HENRIETTE (*after a pause*): I can't tell you! I can't!

ADOLPHE: Henriette! Tell us, tell us what will free all of us!

HENRIETTE: I can't! Don't ask me to!

PRIEST: This is not the work of human beings!

HENRIETTE: Imagine that this moment should come! And then . . . then! (*To* JEANNE) I swear I'm not to blame for your child's death. Is that enough?

JEANNE: It's enough for us, but not for justice!

HENRIETTE: Justice! If you only knew how right you are!

PRIEST (*to* HENRIETTE): And if you understood what you just said!

HENRIETTE: Do you know that better than I?

PRIEST: Yes! (HENRIETTE *stares at him.*) Do not fear, for even if I guess your secret, I won't reveal it. Besides, human justice is not my concern. But rather divine mercy.

MAURICE (*enters hastily, dressed for traveling; does not look at the rest of the people who are in the foreground but goes directly up to the counter where* MME CATHÉRINE *is sitting*): Mme Cathérine, you're not angry with me because I stayed away! I'm here to ask you to forgive me before I go south this evening at eight o'clock!
      (MME CATHÉRINE *silent, amazed*)

MAURICE: You are angry with me! (*Looks about*) What's this?—Is it a dream, or not?—I see it's real, of course, but it looks as something seen through a panorama glass . . . There's Jeanne like a statue dressed in mourning . . . And Henriette looking like a corpse . . . What does this mean? (*Silence*) No one answers!—So it means something terrible! (*Silence*) But tell me!—Adolphe, my friend, what is this?—And—(*gesturing toward* EMILE)—there's a detective!

ADOLPHE (*comes forward*): You apparently don't know.

MAURICE: No. But I have to know!

ADOLPHE: Well, then. Marion is dead.

MAURICE: Marion . . . dead?

ADOLPHE: Yes, she died this morning.

MAURICE (*to* JEANNE): So that's why you're dressed in mourning! Jeanne, Jeanne, who has done this to us?

JEANNE: The one who has life and death in His hand.

MAURICE: But I saw her healthy and well this morning! How did it happen? Who did it? There's someone who has done this to us! (*Looks at* HENRIETTE)

ADOLPHE: Don't look for anyone to blame here, for there isn't anyone. Unfortunately the police have suspicions about someone who ought to be above them.

MAURICE: What's that?

ADOLPHE: Well, you have to know that your careless talk last night and this morning has put you in an unfavorable light.

MAURICE: Did they listen to us?—Let me think—What did we say? —That's true!—Yes, then I'm lost!

ADOLPHE: But explain your thoughtless words! And we'll believe you!

MAURICE: I can't! I don't want to! I'll go to prison, but that doesn't matter! Marion is dead! Dead! And I've killed her! (*General amazement*)

ADOLPHE: Consider what you say; choose your words! Do you know what you said?

MAURICE: What did I say?

ADOLPHE: You said you had killed Marion.

MAURICE: Is there any being who can believe that I am a murderer and that I could kill my own child? Mme Cathérine, you who know me, tell me, do you believe, do you believe . . .

MME CATHÉRINE: Now I don't know what to believe. The mouth speaks what fills the heart, and you've spoken wicked words . . .

MAURICE: She doesn't believe me!

ADOLPHE: Well, explain yourself; explain what you meant by "your love kills everything in your way"!

MAURICE: Oh, they know that, too!—Won't you explain it, Henriette?

HENRIETTE: I can't!

PRIEST: Well, there's something evil in all this, and you have lost my sympathy, my friends. I wanted to swear just now that you were innocent, but I don't want to any more!

MAURICE (*to* JEANNE): What you'll say means more to me than everything else.

JEANNE (*coldly*): Answer this question first: Over whom did you utter the word "damnation" at the orgy out in the woods?

MAURICE: Did I say that? Perhaps! Yes, yes, I'm guilty, and all the same absolutely innocent! Let me leave because I'm ashamed, and my crime is too great for me to forgive!

HENRIETTE (*to* ADOLPHE): Go with him, or he'll do himself harm!

ADOLPHE: I?

HENRIETTE: Who else?

ADOLPHE (*without bitterness*): You'd be the closest.—Sh-h! There's a carriage.

MME CATHÉRINE: It's the commissioner! I've seen a lot in life. But I'd never have believed success and fame were so perishable.

MAURICE (*to* HENRIETTE): From the chariot of triumph to the police wagon! . . .

JEANNE (*simply*): And the ass in front. Who was that?

ADOLPHE: That was I, I suppose!

COMMISSIONER (*enters, with a paper in his hand*): A summons for Mr. Maurice Gérard . . . and Miss Henriette Mauclerc . . . to appear at the police station immediately . . . Are they here?

MAURICE and HENRIETTE: Yes!

MAURICE: Is this an arrest?

COMMISSIONER: No, not yet. This is merely an inquiry.

MAURICE: And after that?

COMMISSIONER: I don't know. (MAURICE *and* HENRIETTE *go toward the door.*)

MAURICE: Good-bye! (*All, moved. The* COMMISSIONER, MAURICE, *and* HENRIETTE *go.*)

EMILE (*enters, goes up to* JEANNE): Now, Sister, I'll take you home!

JEANNE: Well, what do you think of all this?

EMILE: The man's innocent!

PRIEST: Yes, but from my point of view it is and will be a despicable act to break a promise, and an unforgivable one, when it concerns a woman and child.

EMILE: I'd probably feel like that since it concerns my sister, but unfortunately I can't cast stones since I've committed the same mistake myself.

PRIEST: Although I'm innocent on that point, I still won't cast any stone, but the act is its own judge and will punish itself through its consequences.

JEANNE: Pray for him! For them!

PRIEST: No, I won't, because it's arrogant to want to change God's judgment. And what has happened is surely not the work of human beings!

SCENE 2

*Auberge des Adrets.* ADOLPHE *and* HENRIETTE *sit at the same table where* MAURICE *and* HENRIETTE *were sitting during Act II.* ADOLPHE *has a cup of coffee in front of him;* HENRIETTE, *nothing.*

ADOLPHE: So you believe he'll come here?

HENRIETTE: Absolutely. They released him from jail because of lack of evidence this noon, but he doesn't want to be seen before dusk.

ADOLPHE: Poor man!—You know, life seems horrible to me since yesterday.

HENRIETTE: And for me, then? I'm afraid to live, dare hardly breathe, dare hardly think since I know someone's spying not only on my words but on my thoughts!

ADOLPHE: So it was here you sat at night when I couldn't find you!

HENRIETTE: Yes, but don't talk about it; I want to die from shame when I think about it. Adolphe, you're made of better stuff than I and he . . .

ADOLPHE: Sh-h! [*Prolonged*]

HENRIETTE: Oh, yes! And what made me stay? I was lazy, I was tired; his intoxication over his success fascinated me; I can't explain it. But if you had come, it would never have happened!— But today you are the great man, and he the little one, less than the least. Yesterday he had a hundred thousand, and today he doesn't have a sou, since his play has been canceled. He can never be washed clean in public opinion, because it judges him for his crime of unfaithfulness just as strictly as if he were the murderer, and the most sharp-witted of people believe that his child died from sorrow and that he caused her death.

ADOLPHE: Henriette, you know what I think about this, but I want both of you absolutely cleared. Will you tell me what your terrible words meant? It can't be chance that your talk during a festive mood dealt with the dead and the guillotine!

HENRIETTE: It was no chance: it was something that had to be said and something I can't tell, probably because I have no right to appear pure and innocent to you. I'm not!

ADOLPHE: I don't understand this!

HENRIETTE: Let's talk about something else.—Don't you think that among us unpunished criminals go about free and are our intimate friends?

ADOLPHE (*uneasy*): How do you mean?

HENRIETTE: Don't you think that sometime in his life every human being has committed one or another act which would have had legal consequences if it had been discovered?

ADOLPHE: Yes, I think so, but no evil act goes unpunished by one's conscience at least. (*Gets up; unbuttons his coat*) And . . . no one who has not sinned is a really good person. (*Breathes heavily*) For to be able to forgive, one has to have needed forgiveness one-self . . . I had a friend whom we called the ideal human being; he never used a harsh word about anybody, forgave everything and everybody, and received insults with a strange satisfaction that we couldn't explain. Finally, far along in life, he told me his secret in one word: I am a penitent! (*Sits down*)

(HENRIETTE *silent; observes him with wonder*)

ADOLPHE (*as if to himself*): There are crimes that aren't included in the law books, and they're the worst ones, for we must punish them ourselves; and no judge is as strict as we are.

HENRIETTE (*after a pause*): Well, did your friend find peace for himself?

ADOLPHE: After long periods of self-torture he came to a certain degree of calm, but life never had any joy for him, and he didn't dare to accept recognition of any kind, could never feel he deserved a good word or just praise. In a word, he could never forgive himself!

HENRIETTE: Never? What had he done?

ADOLPHE: He had wished his father would die; and when his father suddenly died, the son imagined he had murdered him. This notion was considered sickly, and the son was put into an institution from which he was released after a time fit and healthy—as they put it. But he still felt guilty, so he kept on punishing himself for his evil thoughts.

HENRIETTE: Are you sure that ill will cannot kill?

ADOLPHE: You mean in a mystic fashion?

HENRIETTE: As you will! Let's say, "mystic." In my family I'm sure Mother and my brothers and sisters hated my father to death. You see, he had the horrible idea of consistently opposing everything we liked and wished; and where there was a genuine calling he tried to tear it up by the roots. So he stirred up opposition, which collected as a battery of hate elements; and that finally became so strong he wasted away, was neutralized, lost his will, and finally wished he was dead.

ADOLPHE: And you never had pangs of conscience?

HENRIETTE: No! As far as that goes, I don't know what conscience is.

ADOLPHE: No? You'll soon find out! (*Silence*) How do you think Maurice will look when he comes in here? What do you think he's going to say?

HENRIETTE: You know what? Yesterday morning he and I tried to guess the same thing about you when you were expected.

ADOLPHE: Well-l?

HENRIETTE: Our guess was absolutely crazy.

ADOLPHE: Can you tell me why you sent for me?

HENRIETTE: Meanness, arrogance, pure cruelty!

ADOLPHE: Imagine: you admit your faults, but you don't regret them.

HENRIETTE: I suppose that's because I don't feel fully responsible for them. They're like the dirt on objects one picks up daily, that sticks, and that one has to wash off in the evening.—But tell me one thing: do you really have such a high opinion of human beings as you claim?

ADOLPHE: Yes, we're a little better than our reputation—and a little worse.

HENRIETTE: That wasn't a straight answer.

ADOLPHE: No, it wasn't—But do you want to answer me frankly when I ask: do you still love Maurice?

HENRIETTE: I won't know until I see him. But right now I don't feel any longing for him, and I feel I could live very nicely without him.

ADOLPHE: That's likely so. But you're probably bound to his destiny . . . Sh-h! He's coming.

HENRIETTE: To think that everything repeats itself. Exactly the same situation and the same words as yesterday when you were expected.—

MAURICE (*enters, pale as death, hollow-eyed, unshaven*): Here I am, good friends, if it is I, for a night in jail has made me into another person. (*Observes* HENRIETTE *and* ADOLPHE)

ADOLPHE: Sit down and pull yourself together! Then we can talk about what can be done.

MAURICE (*to* HENRIETTE): Perhaps I'm superfluous?

ADOLPHE: Don't be bitter toward us.

MAURICE: I've become evil the last twenty-four hours and so suspect

I suppose I'll be left absolutely alone. Besides, who wants to keep company with a murderer?

HENRIETTE: But you've been acquitted!

MAURICE (*picks up a paper*): By the police, yes, but not by public opinion. Here you see the murderer Maurice Gérard, formerly a dramatist, and his mistress Henriette Mauclerc . . .

HENRIETTE: Oh, my mother and my family! My mother! Lord Jesus, help us!

MAURICE: Can you see I look like a murderer, too? And they suggest I've stolen my play. So there isn't a bit left of the conqueror of yesterday! And in his place my enemy Octave is advertised! And he'll pull in my hundred thousand! Oh Solon, Solon![4] That is good fortune, and that is honor! You're lucky, Adolphe—you haven't succeeded yet.

HENRIETTE: So you don't know Adolphe has had a great success in London and has received the gold medal.

MAURICE (*dark*): No, I didn't know! Is it true, Adolphe?

ADOLPHE: It's true enough, but I've returned the medal.

HENRIETTE (*emphatically*): That I did not know! Are you prevented from accepting recognition as much as your friend is?

ADOLPHE: My friend? (*Embarrassed*) Oh, yes! Yes!

MAURICE: I'm happy about your success, but it will drive us apart.

ADOLPHE: I had expected that, and I'll probably have to be as alone with my success as you with your failure. Think of it! One hurts people by being fortunate. Life is horrible!

MAURICE: You say that? What should I say? It's as if a black veil had been placed over my eyes and changed the form and color of my whole life. This room is like the room from yesterday, but it's completely different! I certainly recognize both of you, but you have new faces; I sit searching for words for I don't know what I should say to you; I ought to defend myself, but I can't. And I almost miss jail—at least it protected me from these curious glances which go straight through me. The murderer Maurice and his mistress! You don't love me any more, Henriette, just as little as I care for you. You're ugly today, clumsy, empty, and repulsive!

(*Two men in civilian clothes have—without being noticed— sat down at a table in the back.*)

ADOLPHE: Take it easy and pull your thoughts together! The news of your being acquitted and freed of all suspicion must appear in some evening paper. Then the whole case against you will have disappeared; you play will have to be put on again, and at the worst you can write a new one. Leave Paris for a year and let the whole thing be forgotten. You who have rehabilitated humanity will be vindicated yourself!

MAURICE (*laughs harshly*): Humanity!—(*Laughs*)

ADOLPHE: You have lost your faith in what is good!

MAURICE: Yes, if I ever had it! It was probably only a feeling, a way of looking, a politeness toward the beasts. When I, who was considered one of the best, can be so thoroughly bad, how bad mustn't the rest be?—

ADOLPHE: Now I'm going out to buy all the evening papers; then we'll get a point of departure for new observations!

MAURICE (*turns to the back*): Two detectives!—That means I've been released under surveillance so I'll reveal my guilt through careless talk!

ADOLPHE: They aren't detectives. You're just imagining that. Why, I recognize them! (*Goes*)

MAURICE: Don't leave us alone, Adolphe; I'm afraid Henriette and I 'll get to talking frankly.

ADOLPHE: Be sensible, Maurice, and think of your future. Henriette, try to calm him. I'll be back right away. (*Goes out*)

HENRIETTE: Maurice, what do you think now of our guilt or innocence?

MAURICE: I haven't committed murder; I simply talked carelessly when I was drinking. But it's your crime that has come back, and you've grafted that onto me!

HENRIETTE: So that's your tone?—Weren't you the one who cursed your child, who wished her dead and wanted to leave Paris without saying good-bye? And wasn't it I who asked you to visit Marion and to show up at Mme Cathérine's?

MAURICE: You're right; forgive me! You were more human than I; and the blame is all mine. Forgive me! But just the same I'm not to blame! Who has woven this net, out of which I'll never escape? Guilty or not guilty; not guilty and guilty. I'll go crazy from this! —Look: now they're sitting listening, over there!—And no waiter bothers about serving us! I'll go out to order a cup of tea for myself. Would you like something?

HENRIETTE: Nothing! (MAURICE *goes out.*)

DETECTIVE I (*goes up to* HENRIETTE): May I see your papers?

HENRIETTE: My what? You ought to be ashamed!

DETECTIVE I: Ashamed! I'll teach you, slut!

HENRIETTE: What is this all about?

DETECTIVE I: My job's to keep an eye on loose women, and yesterday you were with one man, today with another; that's called loose conduct. And unescorted women aren't served here, so: out, and come with me.

HENRIETTE: My escort will be back right away . . .

DETECTIVE I: A nice escort who doesn't protect a lady!

HENRIETTE: Oh God! My mother, my family!—Don't you know I come from a good family?

DETECTIVE I: It must be good! Besides you're too well known through the evening papers. Come!

HENRIETTE: Where? Where are you taking me?

DETECTIVE I: To the station, naturally, to get a little card, a certificate that permits you to get free medical care!

HENRIETTE: Lord Jesus, this can't be!

DETECTIVE I (*takes* HENRIETTE *by the arm*): Can't it?

HENRIETTE (*on her knees*): Save me!—Maurice! Help!

DETECTIVE I: What the hell! Keep your trap shut!

(MAURICE enters, accompanied by the WAITER.)

WAITER: Men like that aren't served! Pay and leave! and take the slut with you.

MAURICE (*crushed, searches in his purse*): Henriette, Henriette, pay for me and let's go! I haven't a sou on me!

WAITER: So it's the lady who pays for her Alphonse! Alphonse! Do you know what that is?

HENRIETTE (*searches in her purse*): My God! I haven't any money either! Isn't Adolphe ever coming?

DETECTIVE 1: What damnable tramps! Get out but put up something for surety. Bitches like that generally have lots of rings on their fingers.

MAURICE: Can this be possible? Have we sunk so low?

HENRIETTE (*removes a ring and gives it to the* WAITER): The priest was right! This isn't the work of human beings!

MAURICE: It's the devil's!—But if we leave before Adolphe comes, he'll think we've deceived him and stolen away!

HENRIETTE: That would be in keeping with the rest!—Besides, we'll have to drown ourselves now, won't we?

MAURICE (*gives* HENRIETTE *his hand and they go out*): Into the river, yes!

[CURTAIN]

# ACT IV

## SCENE 1

*In the Luxembourg Gardens. By the statue of Adam and Eve.*[5] *The wind is blowing in the trees, and on the ground leaves, straw, and pieces of paper are whirling about.* MAURICE *and* HENRIETTE *are sitting on a bench.*

HENRIETTE: You don't want to die?

MAURICE: No, I don't dare to! I imagine I'll freeze down in the grave with only a sheet over me and some chips under me. Besides, it seems as if I have something to straighten out, but I don't know what it is.

HENRIETTE: I can guess what it is!

MAURICE: Tell me!

HENRIETTE: Revenge!—You as well as I suspect that Jeanne and Emile set the detectives on us yesterday! Only a woman could think of a revenge like that.

MAURICE: Exactly what I think! But you know my suspicions go still further, and it seems to me my suffering the last few days have made me more sharp-witted. For example: can you explain why the waiter at Auberge des Adrets and the head waiter at the pavilion weren't called as witnesses at the hearing?

HENRIETTE: I hadn't thought about that. Yes, I do know why!—They hadn't anything to testify because they had never listened!

MAURICE: But how could the commissioner know our words?

HENRIETTE: He didn't know them, but he figured them out; he guessed, and guessed right; he had probably had a similar case before!

MAURICE: Or like this: he saw on us what we had said! Why, there are people who can read other people's thoughts.—He found it absolutely natural that we had called the deceived Adolphe an ass along with the nuance that he used to be called the idiot; but since there was talk about the chariot, the chariot of triumph, ass was closer. It's so easy, of course, to hit on the fourth when one knows three factors.

HENRIETTE: Imagine! We've let ourselves be fooled completely!

MAURICE: That's because we believe good of people. This is what one gets for that! But you see, behind this commissioner, who, parenthetically, must be a damnable rascal, I sense someone else!

HENRIETTE: You mean the priest, who acts like a private detective.

MAURICE: Yes, I do! He gets to hear a lot of people's confessions, and notice this: Adolphe himself said he had been in the church of Saint-Germain in the morning. What was he doing there? He was confessing everything and pitying himself, so the priest put together some questions for the commissioner!

HENRIETTE: Tell me one thing: do you believe in Adolphe?

MAURICE: I don't believe in any human being any more!

HENRIETTE: Not even in Adolphe?

MAURICE: That fellow least of all! How can I rely on an enemy, whose mistress I've taken!

HENRIETTE: Since you said it first, I'll give you some details about our friend. You heard that he returned his gold medal to London. Can you think of any reason?

MAURICE: No.

HENRIETTE: Well, he feels unworthy, and he once gave a vow of penitence never to receive any forms of recognition.

MAURICE: Really! What did he do?

HENRIETTE: He has committed a crime that isn't punishable by law. He told me that indirectly.

MAURICE: He, too! He, the best man, the ideal human being who never says anything bad about anybody and always forgives!

HENRIETTE: Yes, there you see we're not worse than the rest; yet we're pursued by devils night and day.

MAURICE: Even he! Then humanity isn't slandered!—But if he has been in a state to commit *one* crime, we can believe him capable of everything! It was perhaps he who set the police on you yesterday. When I think of it, why, he was the one who stole away from us when he saw us in the paper and he lied when he said they weren't police. Then one can believe anything of a deceived lover!

HENRIETTE: Could he be that low? No, that's impossible! Impossible!

MAURICE: Why? When he's a scoundrel?—What were you talking about yesterday before I came?

HENRIETTE: He spoke only favorably about you

MAURICE: You're lying!

HENRIETTE (*collects herself; changes her tone*): Listen!—There's
still another person whom you haven't thrown suspicions on—
why, I don't know!—Haven't you thought of Mme Cathérine's
inconsistent role in this matter? Didn't she finally say bluntly
that she could believe you capable of anything?

MAURICE: Of course she said that, and that shows what kind of person she is. For the person who without any reason can think
others capable of wickedness must be a horrible scoundrel himself!

HENRIETTE (*Stares at him. Silence. Then*): The person who without
any reason can think others capable of wickedness must be a horrible scoundrel himself!

MAURICE: What do you mean?

HENRIETTE: What I said.

MAURICE: Do you mean that I . . . ?

HENRIETTE: Yes, now I do! Listen: did you meet anyone besides
Marion on your visit that morning?

MAURICE: Why do you ask?

HENRIETTE: Guess!

MAURICE: Since you seem to know: yes, I saw Jeanne, too.

HENRIETTE: Why did you lie to me?

MAURICE: I wanted to spare you.

HENRIETTE: And now you want me to believe a person who lied to
me! No, now I think you did commit murder!

MAURICE: Just a minute! Have we come to the point where my
thoughts wanted to steal in, but I resisted as long as possible?—It's
strange that what's closest at hand one sees last, and what one
doesn't *want* to believe, one doesn't believe.—Tell me one thing:
where were you yesterday morning after we parted in the Bois de
Boulogne?

HENRIETTE (*uneasy*): Why?

MAURICE: You were either with Adolphe, but you couldn't have been,
for he was giving a lesson, or you were with—Marion!

HENRIETTE: Now I'm absolutely convinced you are the murderer!

MAURICE: And I that you are! Because you were the only one to benefit from having the child put out of the way—getting the stone out of the road, as you so properly expressed yourself! . . .

HENRIETTE: But you said that!

MAURICE: And the one who could benefit committed the crime.

HENRIETTE: Maurice! Now we've gone the whole miserable round and scourged each other. Let's take it easy for a moment, or we'll go absolutely insane.

MAURICE: You already are!

HENRIETTE: Don't you think it's time to part before we drive each other crazy?

MAURICE: Yes, I do!

HENRIETTE (*gets up*): Good-bye, then! (*Two plainclothesmen appear at the back.* HENRIETTE *turns, goes back toward* MAURICE) They're back!

MAURICE: The black angels, who want to drive us out of Paradise.

HENRIETTE: And push us together as if we were to be forged into one.

MAURICE: Or as if we were condemned to be united for life. Shall we really get married, settle down in the same house, and be able to shut the door on the world, and perhaps finally get peace?

HENRIETTE: Shut ourselves in to torture each other to death; lock ourselves in with each one having his ghost as dowry; you torturing me with that memory of Adolphe, and I plaguing you with Jeanne—and Marion.

MAURICE: Don't mention Marion's name again. You know she's being buried today, perhaps at this very moment.

HENRIETTE: And you're not there? What does that mean?

MAURICE: It means that both Jeanne and the police have warned me about the fury of the mob.

HENRIETTE: You're cowardly, too?

MAURICE: I have all the sins! How could you love me?

HENRIETTE: Because the day before yesterday you were another person who was worth loving . . .

MAURICE: And now has sunk so low.

HENRIETTE: No! But you're beginning to boast of faults that aren't yours!

MAURICE: But yours?

HENRIETTE: Perhaps, for when you apparently get worse, I immediately feel myself a bit better.

MAURICE: It's like going about planting certain diseases.

HENRIETTE: And you've become coarse, too!

MAURICE: I'm aware of all that myself, and I can't recognize myself since that night in jail. They put in a human being and released somebody else through that door that separates us from the community. You know I feel I'm the enemy of humanity, and I'd like to set fire to the earth, drain the sea, for only through a world on fire can my dishonor be wiped out.

HENRIETTE: I got a letter from my mother today. She's a major's widow and has been well brought up, has old-fashioned ideas about honor and things like that. Do you want to read her letter? No, you don't, of course!—You know I'm an outcast! My respectable acquaintances don't want to admit they know me; and if I go about alone, the police arrest me! Do you understand we have to get married?

MAURICE: We despise each other, and we must still get married! Why, that's hell! But, Henriette, before we unite our destinies, you have to tell me your secret so we'll be even.

HENRIETTE: Oh, well, I'll tell you!—I had a friend who got into trouble—you understand. I wanted to help her, because her whole future was at stake, and since I was rather clumsy about it, she paid with her life.

MAURICE: That was thoughtless, but it was almost beautifully done!

HENRIETTE: That's what you say now, but the next time you get angry you'll accuse me.

MAURICE: No, I won't, but I can't deny I've lost some of my confidence in you, and I'm afraid of your presence. Tell me: her lover's alive and knows you caused her death.

HENRIETTE: He was my accomplice!

MAURICE: What if his conscience should awaken—that sort of thing often happens—and if he should feel he had to give himself up? Then you'd be lost.

HENRIETTE: I'm certainly aware of that, and this constant anxiety drives me to live as I do so I never get time to awaken to full awareness.

MAURICE: And now you want me to have my marital share of your anxiety. That's asking too much.

HENRIETTE: But when I shared the murderer Maurice's dishonor . . .

MAURICE: Let's quit . . .

HENRIETTE: No, it isn't over yet, and I won't let go until I have you persuaded. For you're not going to believe you're better than I!

MAURICE: So you want a set to with me? Fine, you'll get it!

HENRIETTE: To life and death! (*A roll of drums in the distance*)

MAURICE: They're closing the gardens!—"Cursed be the earth for your sake; she shall bear thorns and thistles."

HENRIETTE: "And the Lord said to the woman . . ."

GUARD (*in uniform; politely*): The garden's to be closed!

## SCENE 2

*Mme Cathérine's. She is by the counter writing in a book.* ADOLPHE *and* HENRIETTE *are seated at a table.*

ADOLPHE (*calmly, in a friendly way*): When I assure you for the last time I didn't steal away but on the contrary believed you had deserted me, you have to believe me.

HENRIETTE: But why did you fool us by saying they weren't policemen?

ADOLPHE: I didn't think they were, and I said it to calm you.

HENRIETTE: I believe you, but you must also believe me when I reveal my most secret thoughts.

ADOLPHE: Tell me!

HENRIETTE: But you mustn't say as you usually do that they're fantasies and figments of the imagination.

ADOLPHE: You seem to have reason for being afraid of something like that.

HENRIETTE: I'm not afraid, but I know you and your skepticism.— Oh, well, you mustn't tell it to anyone—promise me that!

ADOLPHE: I promise!

HENRIETTE: Yes, can you imagine—though it's terrible: I have half proof Maurice is guilty, or at least justified suspicions . . .

ADOLPHE: What's that?

HENRIETTE: Listen; judge for yourself.—When Maurice left me in the Bois de Boulogne, he told me he wanted to see Marion alone while her mother was out. Now I find he met the mother, too! So he lied to me!

ADOLPHE: That's possible, and his motive may have been a good one, but how can you conclude from that he committed the murder?

HENRIETTE: Don't you understand that?—Don't you understand?

ADOLPHE: Not in the least!

HENRIETTE: Because you don't want to!—Then the only thing left for me to do is to inform on him, then we'll see if he has an alibi.

ADOLPHE: Henriette! Let me tell you the whole miserable truth. You —like he—are on the verge of—insanity. You're in the grip of the demons suspicion and are wounding each other with your half-evil conscience . . . I wonder if I'm guessing correctly: he suspects you of having killed his child, doesn't he?

HENRIETTE: Yes, that's how crazy he is!

ADOLPHE: You call his suspicions crazy, but not your own.

HENRIETTE: Prove I'm crazy first, or that I'm unjustly suspicious of him.

ADOLPHE: Yes, that's easily done!—A second autopsy has shown Marion died of a known disease, the strange name of which I've forgotten.

HENRIETTE: Is that true?

ADOLPHE: The official report's printed in today's newspaper.

HENRIETTE: I don't believe it; it can be falsified.

ADOLPHE: Henriette! Watch out or, without knowing it, you'll have gone over the verge. Watch out above all from making accusations that can put you in prison! Watch out! (*Puts his hand on her head*) You hate Maurice?

HENRIETTE: Immeasurably.

ADOLPHE: When love turns to hate, then the love was already infected!

HENRIETTE (*more calmly*): What shall I do? Tell me—you're the only one who understands me!

ADOLPHE: But you don't want any sermons.

HENRIETTE: Haven't you anything else to offer?

ADOLPHE: Nothing else. But they have helped me.

HENRIETTE: Preach away, then!

ADOLPHE: Try to turn your hate against yourself. Put your knife into your own boil—that's where *your* evil is!

HENRIETTE: What do you mean?

ADOLPHE: First: stay away from Maurice so you won't have a chance to tear at each other's conscience together. Give up your career as an artist, which wasn't based on any calling but on getting out, as it's called, to freedom and the happy life—you see how happy it was. Go home to your mother . . .

HENRIETTE: Never!

ADOLPHE: Somewhere else, then!

HENRIETTE: Adolphe, I assume you know that I've guessed your secret and that I know why you didn't accept the honor.

ADOLPHE: I suppose you understood a half-told tale?

HENRIETTE: Well!—But what did you do to get peace?

ADOLPHE: As I've suggested: I became conscious of my guilt, became repentant, decided to improve, and arranged my life like that of a penitent.

HENRIETTE: How shall I become repentant when I haven't any conscience? Is repentance a gift one receives like faith?

ADOLPHE: Everything is grace, but you won't get it unless you seek it.—Seek! (HENRIETTE *remains silent*.) But don't let the time of seeking pass, for you can become hard and tumble down into helplessness.

HENRIETTE (*after a silence*): Is conscience fear of punishment?

ADOLPHE: No, it's our better self's contempt for the evil deeds of our worse self.

HENRIETTE: Then I surely have a conscience, too?

ADOLPHE: Of course you do, but . . .

HENRIETTE: Tell me, Adolphe, are you what they call religious?

ADOLPHE: Not in the least.

HENRIETTE: It's all so strange.—What is religion?

ADOLPHE: You see, I don't know! And I think no one can say. Sometimes it seems to me like a punishment, for no one gets religion who doesn't have a bad conscience . . .

HENRIETTE: Yes, it's a punishment . . . Now I know what I'm going to do. Good-bye, Adolphe!

ADOLPHE: You'll leave Paris?

HENRIETTE: Yes, I'll leave. Home to Mother, as you said—Good-bye, my friend! Good-bye, Mme Cathérine!

MME CATHÉRINE: So you're off in a hurry?

HENRIETTE: Yes.

ADOLPHE: Do you want me to go along?

HENRIETTE: No, we aren't going to do that! I want to go alone, alone as I came to Paris, one spring day, believing I belonged here, where I didn't belong, believing there's something called freedom, which doesn't exist! Good-bye! (*Goes*)

MME CATHÉRINE: I wish that woman would never come back, and that she had never come here!

ADOLPHE: Who knows if she hasn't had a mission here? And in any case she deserves sympathy, boundless sympathy!

MME CATHÉRINE: I don't deny that, for we all deserve that . . .

ADOLPHE: She has even done less evil than we . . .

MME CATHÉRINE: Possibly, but not likely!

ADOLPHE: You're always strict, Mme Cathérine; tell me one thing: have you never done anything bad?

MME CATHÉRINE (*amazed*): Of course, since I'm a sinful human being. But the person who has gone through thin ice has the right and the duty to tell others: Don't go over there! And without having to be considered strict or merciless. Didn't I tell Mr. Maurice at once when that woman came in: Watch out; don't go over there! Then he did, and there he was. It's like mischievous and conceited children, and the person who behaves like that should have a spanking like a disobedient boy!

ADOLPHE: Hasn't he got his spanking?

MME CATHÉRINE: Yes, but it doesn't seem enough, for he's still feeling sorry for himself.

ADOLPHE: That's a very popular interpretation of that complicated question.

MME CATHÉRINE: Nonsense, you people go about philosophizing about your wickedness, and while you're still at it the police have solved the riddle. Let me figure this up in peace!

ADOLPHE: There's Maurice!

MME CATHÉRINE: Yes, God bless him!

MAURICE (*enters, excited; sits down beside* ADOLPHE): Good evening!
        (MME CATHÉRINE *nods, and continues counting.*)

ADOLPHE: How are you?

MAURICE: Oh, things are beginning to straighten out.

ADOLPHE (*hands a newspaper to* MAURICE, *but he does not take it*): So you've read the paper?

MAURICE: No, I don't read newspapers any more; there are only infamous lies in them.

ADOLPHE: Fine, but read this one first, then . . .

MAURICE: No, I don't want to!—It's only lies. But here's a new suggestion.—Can you guess who committed the murder?

ADOLPHE: No one! No one!

MAURICE: Do you know where Henriette was the quarter of an hour

the child was alone?—Well, she was *there!* And she's the one who
did it!

ADOLPHE: You're crazy, man!

MAURICE: Not I, but Henriette is crazy since she suggests me, and
she has threatened to inform on me!

ADOLPHE: Henriette was just here and said the same words as you!
You're crazy, both of you, because a new medical examination has
shown the child died of a known disease, the name of which I've
forgotten.

MAURICE: That's not true!

ADOLPHE: That's what she said, too. But the official report is printed
in this paper.

MAURICE: The official report! Well, then it's falsified!

ADOLPHE: That's what she said, too!—You have the same mental
illness, both of you; but I got so far with her that she admitted
her condition.

MAURICE: Where did she go?

ADOLPHE: She went far away to begin a new life.

MAURICE: Hm, hm!—Were you at the funeral?

ADOLPHE: Yes, I was there.

MAURICE: Well-l?

ADOLPHE: Well, Jeanne was resigned and didn't have a harsh word
for you.

MAURICE: She's a good woman.

ADOLPHE: Why did you give her up, then?

MAURICE: I was crazy, arrogant particularly, and we were drinking
champagne . . .

ADOLPHE: Do you understand now why Jeanne cried when you were
drinking champagne?

MAURICE: Yes, now I do understand!—That's why I've already written to her asking for forgiveness.—Do you think she'll forgive me?

ADOLPHE: I think so—she can't hate.

MAURICE: Do you think she'll really forgive me so we can pick up
where we left off?

ADOLPHE: That I don't know. You've given her such proofs of your unfaithfulness that she'll have a hard time entrusting her future to you any more!

MAURICE: Yes, but I have a feeling she still likes me; I know she'll come back.

ADOLPHE: How do you know that? How can you believe it? Why, you suspected her and her decent brother of getting the police to make a prostitute out of Henriette for revenge.

MAURICE: But I don't believe that any more: that's to say, that Emile is probably quite a fellow.

MME CATHÉRINE: Listen: what's that you're saying about Mr. Emile? He's only a working man, of course, but if we were all only as decent as he is! There isn't a flaw, but he has common sense and tact! . . .

EMILE (*enters*): Mr. Gérard?

MAURICE: Yes?

EMILE: Excuse me, but I have something to say to you in private.

MAURICE: Please speak out; we're only friends here . . .

(*The* PRIEST *enters; sits down.*)

EMILE (*with a glance at the* PRIEST): Perhaps in any case . . .

MAURICE: Doesn't matter; that father is a friend, too, though we have different beliefs.

EMILE: You know who I am, Mr. Gérard; my sister has simply asked me to give you this package as an answer to your letter.

(MAURICE *takes the package and opens it.*)

EMILE: I just want to add, since I'm a sort of guardian for my sister, that on her and my own behalf you're free of all obligations since the natural bond no longer exists.

MAURICE: But you must have a grudge against me!

EMILE: Must I? No, that I don't see. On the contrary I'd appreciate your stating here in the presence of your friends that you believe neither me nor my sister guilty of being so low as to send the police after Miss Henriette.

MAURICE: I take that remark back, and ask for forgiveness if you'll accept it.

EMILE: It's accepted. And I wish all of you a good evening. (*Goes*)

ALL: Good evening.

MAURICE: The tie and the gloves which Jeanne gave me for the evening performance and which I let Henriette throw in the stove. Who can have snatched it up? Everything is dug up, everything repeats itself!—And when she gave them to me in the churchyard, she said I should be nice and handsome so that others, too, would like me.—She stayed at home herself.—This hurt her too deeply, and rightly so! I can't be in the company of decent people. Oh! Have I done this? Spit at a gift from a good heart, ridiculed an offering to my well being. I threw this away for—a laurel wreath, which is lying on a refuse heap, and a bust, which should have stood on a pillory!—Father, now I go over to you.

PRIEST: Welcome!

MAURICE: Give me the word I need.

PRIEST: If you mean that I'm to deny your self-reproaches and tell you you haven't done anything evil?

MAURICE: Say the right word!

PRIEST: With your permission I'll say that I've found your behavior just as repulsive as you have found it.

MAURICE: What shall I do, what shall I do to get out of this?

PRIEST: You know that just as well as I do.

MAURICE: No, I know only I'm lost, that my life has been ruined, my career closed, my reputation forever lost in this world.

PRIEST: So you're seeking a new life in another better world, which you're beginning to believe in?

MAURICE: That's how it is.

PRIEST: You've lived according to the flesh and now want to live according to the spirit.—Are you sure this world has no more attractions for you?

MAURICE: None! Honor is appearance; gold, dry leaves; women, intoxication—Let me hide behind your consecrated walls and forget this ghastly dream, which has lasted for two days and extended through two eternities.

PRIEST: Fine! But this isn't the place to go into more personal questions. Let's meet in the church of Saint Germain this evening at nine o'clock. I'm preaching to Saint-Lazare's penitents, and that can be your first step on the hard path of penance.

MAURICE: Penance?

PRIEST: Yes, you did wish . . . ?

MAURICE: Yes, yes!

PRIEST: Afterward there are vigils between twelve o'clock and two.

MAURICE: That will be wonderful!

PRIEST: Give me your hand, that you won't look back.

MAURICE (*gets up, gives the* PRIEST *his hand*): Here's my hand and all my mind!

MAID (*enters from the kitchen*): A telephone call for Mr. Maurice.

MAURICE: From whom?

MAID: From the theater.

  (MAURICE *wants to take his hand from the* PRIEST, *but the latter holds it firmly*)

PRIEST (*to the* MAID): Did you ask what it's about?

MAID: Yes, they asked if Mr. Maurice wasn't coming to the performance tonight.

PRIEST (*to* MAURICE, *who wants to tear himself away*): No, I won't let you go!

MAURICE: What kind of performance is it?

ADOLPHE: Why don't you want to read the paper?

MME CATHÉRINE and PRIEST: He hasn't read the paper!

MAURICE: It's only lies and slander. (*To the* MAID) Tell them I'm busy tonight: I'm going to church! (*The* MAID *goes out into the kitchen.*)

ADOLPHE: Since you don't want to read the paper, I'll tell you. The theater is putting your play on again now that you've been vindicated, and your literary friends have arranged a tribute to you on stage this evening, a tribute to your unquestionable talent!

MAURICE: It's not true.

ALL: It is true.

MAURICE (*after a silence*): That I don't deserve.

PRIEST: Fine.

ADOLPHE: So on, Maurice!

MAURICE (*his face in his hands*): On!

MME CATHÉRINE: A hundred thousand! You see, they came back! And the villa outside the city! Everything will come back except Miss Henriette!

PRIEST (*smiles*): You should take this a bit more seriously, Mme Cathérine!

MME CATHÉRINE: No, you know, I can't; I can't keep serious. (*Laughs uproariously into her handkerchief*)

ADOLPHE: Maurice, it's eight o'clock at the theater!

PRIEST: But it's nine o'clock in church!

ADOLPHE: Maurice!

MME CATHÉRINE: Mr. Maurice, may we hear the conclusion now?
   (MAURICE *puts his head in his arms down on the table.*)

ADOLPHE: Release him, Father!

PRIEST: No! I neither release nor bind; he must do that himself!

MAURICE (*gets up*): Well, then, I'll go with the priest.

PRIEST: No, my young friend! I have nothing to give you beyond the scruples you can give yourself. And you have obligations to yourself and your good name. That you've got out of this matter so quickly is, for me, a sign that you've suffered out your penance as intensively as if it had been eternities. And when Providence has given you absolution, I have nothing to add.

MAURICE: Why was I punished so severely when I was innocent?

PRIEST: Severely? Only two days! And you weren't innocent, for our thoughts, words, desires are also responsible, and you committed murder in your thoughts when you wished your child were dead.

MAURICE: You're right.—But my decision is firm: I'll meet you in church tonight to settle this with myself—but tomorrow I'll go to the theater.

MME CATHÉRINE: A nice solution, Mr. Maurice!

ADOLPHE: Yes, that's the solution! Yes!

PRIEST: Yes, it is!

[CURTAIN]

# Notes on 'There Are Crimes and Crimes'

1. See any good encyclopedia for information about Paris and a map showing the places Strindberg mentions. For those who read Swedish, Stellan Ahlström's excellent book *Strindbergs erövring av Paris* (Stockholm: Almqvist & Wiksell, 1956) should be consulted for background information on the special significance Paris had for Strindberg as it has for many other artists and intellectuals.

2. See note 1 on page 75.

3. Astarte was the Phoenician goddess of sexual love and fertility. Strindberg is obviously concerned with Henriette as a seductive sex figure and as a potential mother of a child by Maurice to replace Marion, who stands in the way of their "union."

4. Solon, the sixth-century Athenian legislator and lawgiver, here represents the wise man who would have answers to disturbing questions such as those posed by Maurice.

5. Note Strindberg's numerous direct quotations from the Bible and allusions to biblical passages and persons. The statue of Adam and Eve and the references to Eden and the expulsion from Paradise are important elements in Strindberg's presentation of the human dilemmas faced by Maurice and the others.